INTERACTIVE MARKETING

INTERACTIVE MARKETING

Dr. K. Rama Mohana Rao

M.Com., M.B.A., Ph.D.

Professor,
Department of Commerce and Management Studies,
Andhra University, Visakhapatnam.

Dr. S. Gangadhara Rama Rao

M.Com., M.B.A., M.Phil., Ph.D.

Associate Professor,
VS Lakshmi Institute of Computer Applications and
Management Studies for Women, Kakinada.

First Edition : 2011

Himalaya Publishing House

MUMBAI • NEW DELHI • NAGPUR • BENGALURU • HYDERABAD • CHENNAI • PUNE • LUCKNOW • AHMEDABAD • ERNAKULAM • BHUBANESWAR • INDORE • KOLKATA • GUWAHATI

First Edition : 2011

Published by	:	Mrs. Meena Pandey for **Himalaya Publishing House Pvt. Ltd.**, "Ramdoot", Dr. Bhalerao Marg, Girgaon, **Mumbai - 400 004.** Phone: 022-23860170/23863863, Fax: 022-23877178 **E-mail: himpub@vsnl.com; Website: www.himpub.com**
Branch Offices	:	
New Delhi	:	"Pooja Apartments", 4-B, Murari Lal Street, Ansari Road, Darya Ganj, New Delhi - 110 002. Phone: 011-23270392, 23278631; Fax: 011-23256286
Nagpur	:	Kundanlal Chandak Industrial Estate, Ghat Road, Nagpur - 440 018. Phone: 0712-2738731, 3296733; Telefax: 0712-2721215
Bengaluru	:	No. 16/1 (Old 12/1), 1st Floor, Next to Hotel Highlands, Madhava Nagar, Race Course Road, Bengaluru - 560 001. Phone: 080-32919385; Telefax: 080-22286611
Hyderabad	:	No. 3-4-184, Lingampally, Besides Raghavendra Swamy Matham, Kachiguda, Hyderabad - 500 027. Phone: 040-27560041, 27550139; Mobile: 09848130433
Chennai	:	No. 85/50, Bazullah Road, T. Nagar, Chennai - 600 017. Phone: 044-28144004/28144005
Pune	:	First Floor, "Laksha" Apartment, No. 527, Mehunpura, Shaniwarpeth (Near Prabhat Theatre), Pune - 411 030. Phone: 020-24496323/24496333
Lucknow	:	Jai Baba Bhavan, Church Road, Near Manas Complex and Dr. Awasthi Clinic, Aliganj, Lucknow - 226 024. Phone: 0522-2339329, 4068914; Mobile: 09305302158, 09415349385, 09389593752
Ahmedabad	:	114, "SHAIL", 1st Floor, Opp. Madhu Sudan House, C.G. Road, Navrang Pura, Ahmedabad - 380 009. Phone: 079-26560126; Mobile: 09327324149, 09377088847
Ernakulam	:	39/104 A, Lakshmi Apartment, Karikkamuri Cross Rd., Ernakulam, Cochin - 622011, Kerala. Phone: 0484-2378012, 2378016; Mobile: 09344199799
Bhubaneswar	:	5 Station Square, Bhubaneswar - 751 001 (Odisha). Phone: 0674-2532129, Mobile: 09861046007
Indore	:	Kesardeep Avenue Extension, 73, Narayan Bagh, Flat No. 302, IIIrd Floor, Near Humpty Dumpty School, Indore - 452 007 (M.P.). Mobile: 09301386468
Kolkata	:	108/4, Beliaghata Main Road, Near ID Hospital, Opp. SBI Bank, Kolkata - 700 010, Phone: 033-32449649, Mobile: 09910440956
Guwahati	:	House No. 15, Behind Pragjyotish College, Near Sharma Printing Press, P.O. Bharalumukh, Guwahati - 781009 (Assam). Mobile: 09883055590, 09883055536
DTP by	:	HPH, Editorial Office, Bhandup (Swapnali)
Printed at	:	**Sri Bala Offset Printers**, Hyderabad.

Dedicated to

Lord Sri Veera Venkata Satyanarayana Swamy

Annavaram

Preface

The customer is the king and he is always right, is the universally accepted truth. If a satisfied customer can add 100 new customers, the dissatisfied can deduct 1000 customers. Researches have shown that as many as 68 per cent of the dissatisfied customers are so because of ill treatment and lack of courtesy but not of delay in services. A satisfied customer is the best ambassador. Service makes all the difference than the quality of product or attractive physical facilities. Respect and courtesy are the two mantras of customer's delight. The word "sorry" has a magical effect.

Banking is a service industry and delivers its service across the counter to the ultimate customer. The activities of banking industry are all about relationship. Hence, human resource assumes a very important role in the banking industry for providing better services to the customer with a smile in order to cultivate and maintain long lasting relationship with their customers.

Interactive marketing theory suggests that satisfaction and positive outcomes are directly associated with the extent of customer interaction.The quality of the relationships between customers and front-line employees, which incorporates both a professional and a social dimension, can strongly contribute to the customer's overall perception of quality of the service provider. Customers are influenced by the service provider and the quality of the experience. Receiving service is both a personal and psychological experience. There is a psychological and physical closeness between employees and customers in the service encounter.

Services are delivered during the interaction between customers and customer-contact employees, and thus, employees' attitudes and behaviors towards customers determine customers' perceived service quality, satisfaction, and performance. Contact employees in services become involved in what is termed as **"Interactive Marketing".** It is essential that they are responsive to customers' needs.Not only do buyer-seller interactions have an impact on purchasing and repeat purchasing decisions but also, crucially, that buyer-seller interactions provide a marketing opportunity for the organization. The Internal marketing is to get motivated and customer conscious employees.

In the changing demographics, the challenge is to capture the new generation customers, those who are high on technology and short on time.These customers are required to be serviced beyond the traditional brick and mortar branches.They require access to multiple delivery channels as ATMs, Internet banking, Tele banking and e-banking.They require access to their accounts and the flexibility to operate their accounts from anywhere in the country. It is only through adopting state of the art technology that Banks can deliver such flexible distribution channels. Faced with global competition, the banks have to shore up the efficiency of their operations, which will be possible through the use of high end technology and process reengineering to increase the speed and efficiency and reduce transaction costs.

Interactive marketing, therefore, plays pivotal role in offering quality services to the customers. It requires a strong foundation of internal marketing and external marketing. The present study is an attempt to analyse the internal, external marketing operations as a support to interactive marketing.

This book on interactive marketing provides conceptual framework as well as a case study of State Bank of India. The book is presented in eleven chapters. The chapter one is on Interactive Marketing – The Conceptual Framework – discusses the concept, interactive marketing operations and the philosophies of interactive marketing. Chapter two presents the review of literature. The research methodology is presented in Chapter three. Chapters four to nine present the organizational system and marketing operations of State Bank of India with special reference to interactive marketing. The opinion of the employees' collected based on empirical research are shown in Chapter ten. The findings of the study of consumer opinion are shown in Chapter eleven.

The work of this magnitude cannot be done without the support of many resourceful personalities. We express our gratitude to all of them for the help and cooperation extended to us in bringing out this book.

– K. Rama Mohana Rao

– S. Gangadhara Rama Rao

Contents

Detailed Contents

LIST OF TABLES

LIST OF FIGURES

LIST OF EXHIBITS

LEGEND

AICTE	:	All India Council for Technical Education
ARCIL	:	Asset Reconstruction Company (India) Limited
BCSBI	:	Banking Codes and Standards Board of India
BKE	:	Bilateral Key Exchange
CA	:	Current Account
CAG	:	Corporate Accounts Group
CAIIB	:	Certified Associate of Indian Institute of Bankers
CBG	:	Corporate Banking Group
CBS	:	Core Banking Solution
CMC	:	Central Management Committee
CPC	:	Centralised Processing Centers
CPPCs	:	Centralised Pension Processing Centers
CPQ	:	Customer Perceived Quality
CRO	:	Customer Relation Officer
CSO	:	Credit Support Officer
DEA	:	Data Envelopment Analysis
DIR	:	Differential Interest Rates
DPG	:	Deferred Payment Guarantees
DRT	:	Debt Recovery Tribunals
ELEANOR	:	Electronic Nostro Account Reconciliation
FAST	:	Funds Available in Short Time
FCNR	:	Foreign Currency Non Residential Bank Account
FTC	:	Foreign Travel Card
GAD	:	Government Accounts Department
HRD	:	Human Resource Development
HRM	:	Human Resource Management
IBG	:	International Banking Group
INFINET	:	Indian Financial Network
IRDP	:	Integrated Rural Development Programme
IVR	:	Interactive Voice Response
KCC	:	Kisan Credit Card
LHO	:	Local Head Office
LTPLR	:	Long-term Prime Lending Rate
MCG	:	Mid Corporate Group
MIS	:	Management Information System
MISLA	:	Management Information System for Loans and Advances
MOD	:	Multi Option Deposit

MTPLR	:	Medium-term Prime Lending Rate
MUVs	:	Multi Utility Vehicles
NBG	:	National Banking Group
NEFTS	:	National Electronic Fund Transfer System
NPAs	:	Non Performing Assets
NRI	:	Non Resident of India
PLR	:	Prime Lending Rate
PMS	:	Portfolio Management Services
PSUs	:	Public Sector Units
RDBMS	:	Relational Data Base Management System
RMME	:	Relationship Manager for Medium Enterprise
RRBs	:	Regional Rural Banks
RTGS	:	Real Time Gross Settlement
SAMG	:	Stressed Assets Management Group
SB Account	:	Savings Bank Account
SBI	:	State Bank of India
SBIICM	:	State Bank Institute of Information and Communication Management
SBIRD	:	State Bank Institute of Rural Development
SBUs	:	Strategic Business Units
SHG	:	Self Help Group
SMEs	:	Small and Medium Enterprises
SOC	:	SWIFT Operation Centre
SSB	:	Sales and Services Branch
SSI	:	Small Scale Industries
STEPS	:	State Bank Electronic Payment Systems
STPLR	:	Short-term Prime Lending Rate
SWIFT	:	Society for Worldwide Interbank Financial Telecommunication
SWO	:	Single Window Operations
TAT	:	Turn Around Time
TMG	:	Treasury Management Group
TQS	:	Total Quality Service
UGC	:	University Grants Commission
VSAT	:	Very Small Aperture Terminal
WAN	:	Wide Area Network

Chapter 1

INTERACTIVE MARKETING – THE CONCEPTUAL FRAMEWORK

Services sector has occupied predominant position in all the developed countries and in the majority of developing countries. The growth of services sector became *sine quo non* for the growth and development of an economy. The liberalization policies pursued by many countries opened-up the once predominant public sector to private and public- private participation. Thus, a fresh breeze of competition entered into the services sector and marketing of services became challenging. The marketing models which are suitable to the manufacturing sector were found ineffective or less effective when applied to service sector. This problem has been recognized in late 70s by a few marketing practitioners and tried to develop new methodologies for the marketing of services. The fundamental base to look out for a new marketing model is the conspicuous distinctions between goods and services. A service is a process that leads to an outcome during partly simultaneous production and consumption processes.[1] Compared to the marketers of physical goods, who offer tangible products, service firms rely on a set of resources - employees, physical resources, technology and systems, and customers – and a governing system that puts these resources to use when the customer requests a service. The interactions between the customer and the quality-generating resources controlled by the service provider form the heart of service marketing.[2] By analyzing the distinctions that are having services marketing applications, the researchers have identified the following six characteristics of services.

Intangibility: Services are intangible. They cannot be seen, tasted, felt, heard or smelt before they are bought unlike physical products.[3] The intangibility creates a feeling of uncertainty about the outcome of a service.

Inseparability: As the production, delivery and consumption are the simultaneous processes, the consumers and the service providers can not be separated. The inseparability characteristic of the service creates marketing challenges for market expansion and standardization of service quality at various service outlets.

Variability: It is not possible to provide exactly the same service to two customers simultaneously. Though the service provider may not differentiate the service between the two customers, the differences in the ability of the customers in participating the service process and the ability to perceive the service quality makes the service output different to each customer. The variability characteristic of service limits the service organisation to go for total standardization of service and communicate the same to the customers. However, variability helps to introduce innovativeness in the service processes.

Perishability: Services are perishable and as such they cannot be stored. When the demand is stable, perishability cannot be a problem to the service organization. But service firms face many problems when demand fluctuates. The major challenge to these firms is to balance the supply-demand positions. Thus, demand management is one of the major tasks for the service firms.

Customer Participation: Customers are co-producers of service. The production quality of the service not only depends upon the ability, skill and performance of the service employee but also on the ability and performance of the customer. Service firms should communicate the customers the details of service processes and their expected performances and should take necessary steps to train customers, if necessary, to provide quality experience of the service. Customization is one of the key strategies the service firms adopt to ensure efficient and effective participation of customers.

No Ownership: Service consumers will have experiences but not ownership. Since the services are intangible and perishable, the question of ownership does not arise. But this characteristic will add to the problems of the service marketer. Convincing the customer with tangible goods on which he will have ownership through transfer of title is much easier than selling an experience where nothing remains after consumption, except the memory of it.

Service marketers need to develop strategies keeping in view the six characteristics of services. Thus, services marketing is more challenging than goods marketing. The conventional 4P's (Product, Price, Promotion and Place) marketing mix is found to be ineffective when applied to services. Many researchers and marketing analysts suggested an addition of three more P's making, the marketing mix as 7P's of marketing. The additional P's suggested are Physical evidence, People, and Process.

1.1 THE SERVICES MARKETING TRIANGLE

One of the popular models used to manage marketing operations of service companies is the service triangle. As shown in Figure 1.1, the service triangle identifies three important parties for the success of service marketing. They are (i) the company (top management), (ii) employees, and (iii) customers. The model suggests that the integration of these three groups are essential for the effective performance of marketing mix operations. In order to achieve marketing goals, according to the model, the strategy should focus upon three dimensions. They are:

- Internal marketing (marketing activities between company and employees)
- External marketing (marketing activities between company and customers)
- Interactive marketing (marketing activities between customers and employees)

Thus, the model identified interactive marketing as one of the three basic strategic dimensions of services marketing.

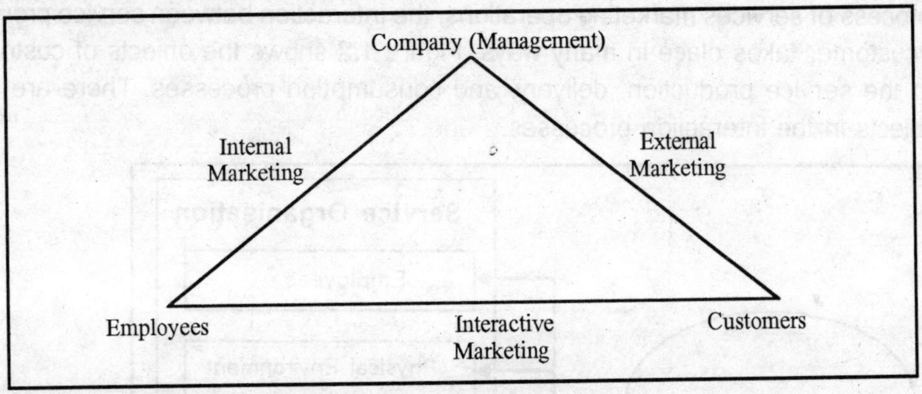

Fig 1.1: Service Triangle

What is Interactive Marketing?

Interactive marketing is "the managerial process through which a series of interactions between service provider and consumer are organised to facilitate efficient participation in service production and consumption that satisfies the needs and wants of the customer and creates positive customer-perceived quality."[4] The service production and consumption takes place only when the customers interact with the service organisation. "The interactive part of service production system consists of customers and the rest of the quality generating resources with which customers interact with directly. These are the direct buyer seller interactions where the moments of truth takes place. The quality generating resources in the interactive part are customer involvement process; contact persons, systems and operational routines, and physical resources and equipment."[5]

Interactive Marketing means that service quality depends heavily on the quality of the buyer-seller interaction during the service encounter.[6] Interactive Marketing involves the message that employees give to customers through such channels as personal selling, customer service interactions, service encounter interactions, and service scapes.[7] A closer relationship exists when there is face-to-face interaction between customers and representatives of the supplier (or "ear-to-ear" interaction by phone). Interactions may include negotiations and sharing of insights in both directions.[8] Buyer-seller communications in which the customer controls the amount and type of information received from a marketer, influence service quality significantly.[9]

Interactive marketing focuses on mutual exchanges between producers and consumers during the value creation process.These exchanges can be based on information, but monetary, physical and labor-based exchanges are also included. The fact that producers become dependent on consumer input in the value creation process is crucial in Interactive Marketing. In this sense consumers become co-producers.[10] It is necessary, therefore, to study the customer interaction objects and potential quality generating resources to develop effective interactive marketing strategies.

1.2 THE CUSTOMER INTERACTION OBJECTS

In the process of services marketing operations, the interaction between service provider and service customer takes place in many ways. Figure 1.2 shows the objects of customer interaction in the service production, delivery, and consumption processes. There are four nteraction objects in the interaction processes.

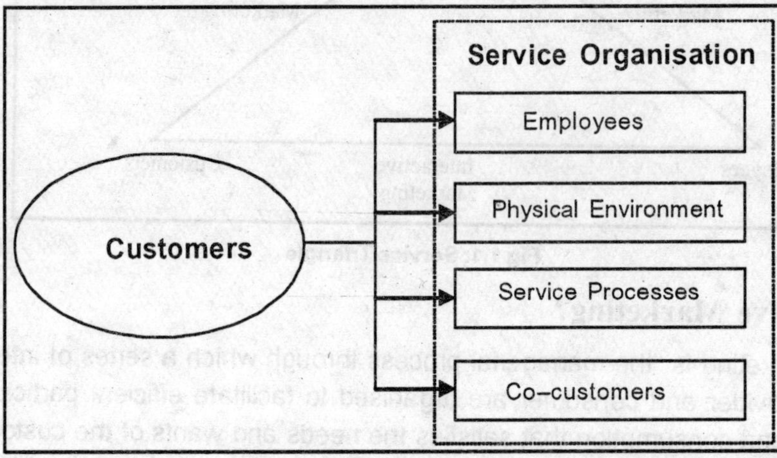

Fig 1.2: Objects of Customer Interaction

(a) Customer – Employee Interaction

The customer-employee interaction is crucial in quality management of service production. When the service customers and service employees interact for the service production and service delivery process, it is called '***service encounter***'. Because the delivery of service occurs during the interaction between contact employee and customers (the service encounter), the attitudes and behaviors of contact employees can influence customers' perceptions of the service.[11] Service firms must find ways to effectively manage their customer-contact employees to help ensure that their attitudes and behaviors are conducive to the delivery of quality service.[12]

The human element is critical in service interactions. Service organizations should recruit qualitative people for service positions. Besides, focusing on technical skills greater emphasis needs to be given for service inclination. Employees should be provided with special training on interactive skills. During employee-customer interaction, communication skills play a pivotal role. Each and every employee should be capable of understanding rightly the motives of consumers and be capable of empathizing customers.They should be trained to handle different situations that arise in communication process with different customers. Organizations must teach employees that they are all service providers, and emphasize their vital role in customer retention.[13] Every employee should realize that a customer has a right to be wrong and the employee doesn't have the right to be wrong. They should believe in the principle that 'customer is always right'. Even if the situation clearly establishes the fact that the customer is wrong, the employees should try to understand the reasons for such kind of disposition from the customer to solve such problems.

Work climate in service organizations plays a vital role in influencing the interaction. Work climate can be conceptualized from a social interactionist's perspective as evaluations of environmental attributes that have a social or situational construction component.[14] Service climate refers to the shared perception of employees concerning the practices, procedures, and kinds of behavior that get rewarded and supported in a particular setting.[15] The service climate is the message employees get about how important service is in their organisaton. Employees get this message from the experiences they have during their workday.[16] Employees of service organizations may experience at times some deficiencies in services production and delivery to the customers.Many of such deficiencies are forced rather than unforced. A sincere apology may do wonders with many customers. Employees some times do a little more to further please the customers.To face such situations the interactive employees should be equipped with service recovery skills. Unforced deficiencies are the deficiencies due to either erring employees or system defects and deficiencies. The top management of service organization needs to design control mechanism that eliminates or prevents unforced deficiencies in service interactions.

Employee empowerment is necessary because contact employees need the flexibility to make on-the-spot decisions to completely satisfying customers. Allowing contact employees to use their discretion in serving customers has many positive influences on their responses and the service encounter.[17] Face to face interaction is considered as the best form of interaction due to several reasons. It provides an opportunity to eliminate communication gaps between the individuals much better than any other interactive system. Frontline employees of the service organization interact with customers to know their problems to provide necessary services to the best satisfaction of the customers. Customers will have different sets of needs, wants, ego system, time pressure, situational pressures, adaptability, temperament, understanding, skill, knowledge and participative abilities. Similarly employees also are human beings with varied needs, wants, ego systems, situational pressures, temperaments, styles, abilities and involvement levels. Employee performance during a service encounter typically involves responding to customer needs, handling special requests, and performing under adverse circumstances.[18] When employee and customer are interacting, the best result will come out only when they are working positively with high level of understanding and involvement in service process. Contact employees who experience ambiguous or conflicting role expectations are likely to exhibit decreased job satisfaction and performance, which leads to a decrease in customers' perceived service quality.[19]

Many problems in the service organizations will be solved when the employees are good in customer interactions. Effective management of the service encounter involves understanding the often complex behaviors of employees that can distinguish a highly satisfactory service encounter from a dissatisfactory one, and then training, motivating, and rewarding employees to exhibit those behaviors.[20] The symbolic nature of interactions in the service encounter suggests that techniques such as personal interviewing and observation will be particularly useful for capturing the nuances of meaning in employee and customer interactions.[21] The ability of the employee to elicit information from the customer has been identified as a critical skill for developing credibility with the customer and enhancing dyad effectiveness.[22] Customer-provided cues or characteristics such as speech attributes, mannerisms, dress, and demographic variables such as age and gender that may play a meaningful role in the effectiveness of frontline customer segmentation.[23]

While responsiveness is a part of positive behavior, reactiveness is often considered as part of negative behavior. Service employees are supposed to be responsive but not reactive. They are required to control their emotional temperament in handling consumer problems. Communication bridges the gap between individuals and develops an effective way to solve the problems. When employees are bestowed with effective communication skills, the service organizations will be in a better position in achieving the objective of providing customer delight. On the other hand, a poor or ineffective communication skill of the employees leads to many unanticipated problems.

Service Culture: The culture of service organization represents traditions, values, ethics, interactions, perceptions and mutual respect within the group of employees. The design and promotion of right culture prevents many problems and provides ready solutions for the problems that arise between employees in either performance of the roles or perceptions of status. Service organizations should promote service culture within the organization among the employees. Motivation, morale and teamwork are the fruits of well defined, designed and promoted service culture.

Besides designing customer friendly systems and operational processes and providing quality physical resources and equipment with latest technological support, contact employees need to be motivated. Apart from technical expertise, the involvement of service employee with service inclination is likely to create greater quality perceptions to the consumers. Therefore, internal marketing should be managed effectively so that it stands as a foundation for interactive marketing.

Customer Participation: The customers have equally an important role to perform in the service production and consumption process, as customers are co-producers of service. The generated service quality also depends upon the customer's ability to participate in service process and also their ability to perceive the quality generated. Customers become attached to service providers for a number of positive reasons including faith in organizational competence, mutually aligned and congruent values, and to experience relational value that is obtained from the interpersonal dynamics of their service encounters.[24] Especially in high interaction service encounters, customer participation in service production is critically important in determining service quality and customer satisfaction.[25] Service customers need to be informed, educated or trained, if necessary, through external marketing efforts to make them able to perform their role in interactive marketing. Thus, the combined effort of internal marketing and external marketing provides a platform for interactive marketing.

Markets are no longer just transactional spaces or meeting places where buyers and sellers try to outwit each other and appropriate value from one another. From customer satisfaction we seem to have moved on to customer involvement, although it is not clear if this is just a passing fad or a major breakthrough in the way we do business. For example, an emerging trend in the more affluent economies has been labeled for some time now as the post-modern consumer. He/she is the consumer who can no longer be taken for granted, easily manipulated or managed and who, due the very success of marketing-led prosperity, has become more selective, skeptical and critical in accepting the persuasive messages. In other words, society having moved from an agrarian to an industrial to post-industrial or information/knowledge stage over the last three centuries, there is a corresponding transition if not transformation in the relationship of the buyer and user of goods and services to the providers thereof.[26] Customer participation was defined as the extent to which customers provide resources in the form of time and/or effort, information provision, and co-production during service production and delivery process.[27]

Service quality generates in the service providers and the customers interactions. The perception of the customer on quality is the ultimate measure of quality performance by any service company. In providing services to the customers' service organizations take care of quality standards. The customers, on the other hand, also set for themselves some critical quality checkpoints to ascertain the quality received. The customer assessment and analysis of quality factors are vital to any service organization. A study of customers' opinion on quality will be of immense help to the organization to realize their quality targets efficiently. The interactive process certainly is the most important quality generating opportunity for the service organization. An efficient interaction prevents many problems and cures some problems at the generation stage itself. On the other hand, a poor interactive process creates many problems, which ultimately affect the business of the organization.

(b) Customer – Physical Environment Interaction

Physical environment plays a vital role in influencing the behavior of customers as well as employees of any service organization including banking organization. In cultural encounters, it seems probable that both standards - desired and adequate service - are home-country based, which means that they are the results of customer experiences from their home countries. Foreign customers enter an inter-cultural encounter with their culturally-biased expectations. Consequently, an inter-cultural service provider performance gap occurs when the service performed by a company from one culture is seen as inadequate by a customer from another culture, due to expectations developed by each in their respective home cultures.[28]

The design of the service scape should facilitate comfortable and efficient participation of customers and employees in the service production and consumption process. The quality of the service will be influenced greatly in the way the process is facilitated. There are many dimensions, which can be exploited in the physical environment to create quality perceptions to the customers. The exterior, interior, ambience, signage, layout, equipment, facilities etc., are to be designed suitably, taking into consideration the production process requirements of the service and preferences of the target market. Of course, competition considerations cannot be overlooked in the design of physical environment. Whatever efforts the service provider makes in shaping the physical environment, it should suit the needs and desires of the target customers. They should remember that customer is the ultimate judge of the performance of the service provider. In fact service organization should focus on exploring new ways of presenting a service outlet by encouraging customers participation in introducing refinements and modifications in the physical environment. The beginning is definitely to know the opinion of the customers on the physical environment. The customer interaction with the physical environment is a vital input in shaping the first impression and also the quality perception of customers. The following are the critical factors of physical environment with which the service customer interacts.

Exterior of the service outlet influences the behavior of the consumer significantly. It is the first physical contact to the customer and therefore plays a vital role in shaping first impression on the service outlet.The exterior of the bank influences confidence level on service quality, status, and preference. Service organizations generally invest heavily on the design of the exterior in order to attract the customers and also generate pleasant feelings among them. An interior or a poor exterior of a service outlet generally keeps most of the customers away from the service outlet.

Ambience represents the surroundings of service outlet and an atmosphere in the service outlet that persuades the employees as well as customers to get involved pleasantly and comfortably in the service production and consumption process.This is the reason why ambience is considered as an important characteristic of a service scape.

Service environment is intended to fulfil the needs and wants of the customers. The layout of the service environment should facilitate functionality in a smooth and efficient manner. The layout in the service environment refers to the way in which machinery, equipment, furniture arranged, the size and shape of all those items and the relationships with one another.

Signs, symbols and artifacts, sign boards displayed on the exterior or interior provide explicit communication.These can be used to communicate rules, directions, cautions, processes, layout details and so on. Signs provide relief to such customers who are poor communicators or are not comfortable interacting with others. Signs can also be used to reduce perceived crowding. The quality of the materials used in the construction of physical structures at work, the presence of certificates and photographs, the floor coverings and architectural values communicate symbolic meanings and create an aesthetic impression.

(C) Customer – Service Process Interaction

The service interaction process can be broadly classified into three phases. Lehtinen (1983) named these phases as the joining phase, the intensive consumption phase and the detachment phase.

The Joining Phase: The joining phase is the first phase of the service consumption process. Some studies identified a pre-joining phase also wherein marketing personnel interact with the customers and persuade or sometimes sell the service. Anyhow, when services are provided at the service outlet, the customer begins with the joining phase. The two important activities in this phase are entry and registration.

The Intensive Consumption Phase: This is a critical phase wherein the service process aims at solving consumer problems.The first step in the process is the perfect diagnosis of the problem. Contact employees will discuss with the consumers and try to define the consumer's problem accurately by getting confirmation from the service consumer. The contact employee proposes the service process and also the cost involved in the service process. There are many factors that influence the effectiveness of the process at this stage. Documentation, queue system, time consumed, accuracy, transparency, customer approval, easy flow, equipment used, performance of the equipment, exclusivity (privacy), flexibility and exceptions are some of the factors that influence the quality.

Detachment Phase: There are two activities that generally take place during this phase. They are payment and registration for next visit. The payment system that is designed, whether cash, credit, installment, office billing, credit card and so on, is the factor that influences the customers. The registration system for the next visit, exit facilities and collection of feedback are the other aspects that need to be managed properly.

(d) Customer – Co-customer Interaction

Service customers quite often interact with co-customers present at the service outlet. The interactions may be more when waiting is longer. Service customers find in the co-customer a person with similar problems seeking solutions from the same service provider. The confusion in the mind of the customer due to intangibility characteristic of services, provokes him/her to interact with co-customers to either reassure their assessment or to broaden their understandings and expectations on the service provider. A very powerful word-of-mouth generates in the customer – co-customer interaction. The interaction of the accompaniers of the service customers further promotes the word-of-mouth communication. In order to achieve positive impact through customer – co-customer interactions, service organizations need to facilitate positive interactions among them. The issues that influence customer – co-customer interactions are:

1. Physical facility for customer socialization
2. Customer compatibility
3. Access to service information
4. Service process management and customer communication
5. Employee sensitivity to customer problems and
6. Empathy and courtesy followed.

Service companies should take care in designing the service layout in the elements of customer interaction with co-customers. Specifically allocated spaces with required furniture, facilities, ambience, and support service facilitate customer – co-customer interactions along with accompaniers. A right customer mix is an important dimension in managing customer – co-customer interactions. The combinations may be based on gender, social status, income, age, culture, ethnicity, religion, occupation, etc. The philosophy behind identifying customer-mix is to facilitate customer to feel comfortable and interact freely with others. Customer compatibility can be achieved by way of taking measures mentioned above.

Service organizations need to provide sufficient information to the customer either in the form of signage, leaflets, hoardings or information counters, within the service environment. The provision of such information will facilitate customers to find issues for interaction and also help them in developing quality perceptions.

Customer-co-customer interactions may take place at the joining phase or at the service production process phase or at the detachment phase or any two or in all phases. The facilitation of movement from one process to another and communication to the customer on the outcome on each process at the same process promotes positive interactions with co-customer as well as better quality perceptions.

The role of employees in promoting positive word-of-mouth among customers present at the service outlet is very significant. The sensitivity of the employee to the customer problems promotes positive word-of-mouth, while insensitivity to the customer problem triggers negative word-of-mouth.

The empathy towards customers and courtesy followed by the service organizations also play a vital role in influencing word-of-mouth between customers and co-customers. It is necessary therefore, to promote service culture in the organization.

Customer Perceived Quality (CPQ)

The key outcome of interactive marketing is customer perceived quality. The quality perceptions of the customer are greatly influenced by two important factors. They are (i) expected quality, and (ii) experienced quality.

(i) Expected Quality: Customers expect quality performance by the service organizations. The expectations of the customers will generally be based on the following factors.

- ***Marketing Communication:*** of the service provider which include service promises, and the way in which promises are facilitated for performance.
- ***Word-of-mouth Communication:*** Customers may interact often with customers of the same service provider or service consumers of similar companies or experts or well informed persons to broaden their understanding of the service and to develop realistic service expectations.
- ***Company Image:*** Company image also helps in formulating expectations. Customers expect perfection and high quality when the company enjoys an established positive image over the years.
- ***Situational factors*:** When things are normal the consumers develop rational expectations. When situation is unusual then the expectations of the consumers also change. In times of emergency, during natural calamities, social disturbances, pressure on service employees due to excessive demand, etc., service customers will try to modify their expectations considering the situational elements of pressure.

(ii) Experienced Quality: When consumers actually become the participants of service production process then they will have many experiences. There are basically two dimensions that influence consumer experience. They are :

(a) Technical Quality, and

(b) Functional Quality.

(a) ***Technical Quality***: This quality refers to design of the service product, its suitability and comprehensiveness. Any defect, short coming, omit or excesses in the design of service product are capable of providing differing experiences to the consumers. For example, the absence of reception counters in a hotel, cause experience of quality deficiency when people look for such part of the service. On the other hand, when customers find, three or four reception counters in the same hotel located in one hall, they may get confused or develop a feeling of excess in service provision. The consumers' experience is positive as well as negative in respect of the designed elements of the service provision.

(b) ***Functional Quality***: This quality refers to the way in which the designed service product elements are performed in the service production process. Employees are the key responsible group in providing functional quality experiences to the consumers. Besides the employee, the service environment, equipment and machinery, systems and maintenance of other physical infrastructure also influence the functional quality experiences of the consumers.

Consumers combine technical as well as functional factors in generating service quality experience in themselves. Consumers compare the experienced quality with expected quality to develop quality perceptions of service. The satisfaction of the customers depends upon the customer perceived quality of the service. When the experienced quality is better than expected quality, the customers generally will be highly satisfied or some times delighted. When the expected quality and experienced quality are at same level the customers are likely to be satisfied. When expected quality is more than the experienced quality then the service customers will be dissatisfied. In order to ensure customer satisfaction it is necessary to create better quality perceptions. Service companies should work continually for the enhancement of customer perceived quality. It is possible when service companies study and understand the ever changing consumer expectations to incorporate technical quality as well as functional quality to provide better quality experiences.

1.3 INTERACTIVE MARKETING STRATEGIES

Interactive marketing is critical for the success of service outlets. The service is actually produced, delivered and consumed in the interactive processes. Therefore, service companies should develop strategies to make interactive marketing effective and capable of enhancing customer perceived quality. As cited earlier in Figure 1.2, customers interact with many objects at the service environment. Each object has its own potential to generate quality experiences to the consumers. Service companies need to exploit the potentiality strategically by managing interactive marketing operations effectively. The interactive marketing strategies are shown in Figure 1.3. The key strategies followed by service companies for the effectiveness of interactive marketing are as follows.

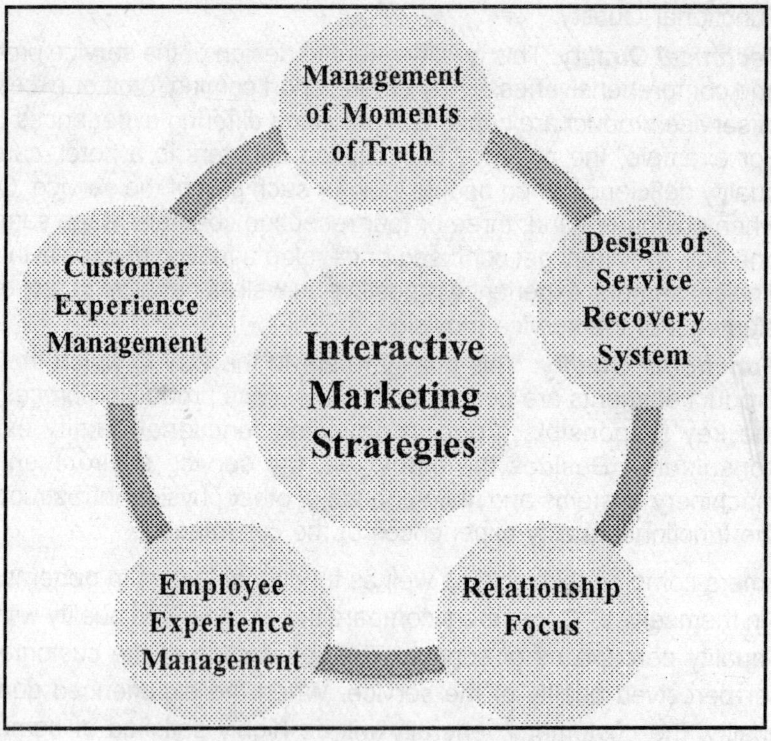

Fig.1.3: Interactive Marketing Strategies

1. Management of Moments of Truth

The service production and consumption process is a combination of several moments. A moment is an experience unit of customer interaction with any one of the interaction objects. The first sight of exterior of the service outlet is one moment or the close exposure to a part of the exterior may be another moment. Likewise every customer gets exposure to many moments at the service outlet while production and consumption processes are taken place. The concept of moments of truth is developed with an objective of directing attention and focus towards the management of moments. Every moment has some potentiality to create quality experiences to the consumers. A moment may influence directly or indirectly, individually or collectively the quality perceptions of consumers. The management of moments of truth involves the following.

1. Identification of moments
2. Defining each moment, its scope and potential to create experiences.
3. Classification of moments into major and minor – major moments are those that have higher potential to impact on customers and minor moments are those that have lower impact on customers.
4. Design each moment keeping in view the behavior of the customers to the social-cultural background and reaction tendencies.
5. Define the expected responses from the customers.
6. Group the moments in conference with service process design.

7. Assign a group of moments to each employee to monitor their functionality and effectiveness.
8. Develop appraisal system for the assessing the effectiveness of the management of moments of truth.
9. Continually improve the moments of truth based on feedback and creative thinking.

2. Design a Service Recovery System

Service recovery refers to responsiveness of the service organisation to the problems of the customers in the incidence of service failures either fully or partly. Service failures do occur in the service process due to many reasons that are beyond the control of the service organisation and some reasons due to inadequacy in service processes from the side of the service organisation.For example, power breakdown deficiencies in support service outsourced, negligence of an employee, delay in process to process connectivity due to technical problems, mall-functioning of support process equipment, etc. stand in the way of quality performance. Service failures in any form cause dissatisfactions among consumers. Service organizations can not afford to leave the situations as they happen in case of deficiencies either due to controllable or uncontrollable factors. It is true that the service companies need to take all possible measures to see that the service failures do not occur in any process at any time and to any customer. However, when failures occur in reality they should respond through a well designed recovery system that not only serves as a mechanism to heal customer problems but also make them happy. Zeithaml and Bitner[29] suggested six strategies for the effective service recovery.

(i) ***Perform the service right the first time itself:*** Consumers expect from service provider that everything should go right the first time itself. Any failure is a loss to the customer. Therefore, companies should focus on quality performances which ensure everything goes right the first time and all the time.

(ii) ***Welcome and encourage complaints:*** Customers have their own understanding, assessment against expectations and perceptions about the processes and the service outcome. The contact employee may not able to understand and assess what is going on in the mind of the customer about the quality of the outcome. The feedback from customers really helps to understand what has really happened from the customers' point of view and to initiate service recovery. Therefore, service companies are advised to welcome and encourage complaints from the customers.A complaint should be treated as opportunity to improve quality further.

(iii) **Act quickly:** Once it is observed that the deficiency in service occur either by observation or through service complaints, the service company should not loose time in initiating recovery process. The faster the recovery process the better would be the result out of it.

(iv) **Treat customers fairly:** Customers expect fair treatment in handling their complaints. They look for fairness in three dimensions; outcome fairness, Procedural fairness, and interaction fairness.

(v) **Learn from recovery experiences:** Recovery is a process initiative when failures occur. Service company should not make failures as a habit. They should learn from the experiences and institutionalize the correction process.

(vi) **Learn from lost customers:** When service organizations fail in taking-up recovery measures effectively they may loose customers.Sensible service organizations will try to learn the reasons for customer switchovers and take measures to see that all the customers are retained.

Service organizations are required to display their commitment in service recovery. They should formulate clear guidelines for effective service recovery. Employees play a key role in the service recovery process.Their behavior, interactions, and spontaneity in responding to the customer problems are critical when customers show their concern to the service failures. The service employees need to be given training to handle a customers with grievance and to make appropriate recovery decision. In the service recovery training there are at least five areas that must be specifically addressed. They are:

1. ***Information Processing***: Training may be given to employees to identify the information sources and the ways to which they can access the sources independently and without delay. The ability of the employees to process information as per the requirements of the problem helps to do the service right in the recovery process.
2. ***Emotional Response***: The service employees shall be given special training to handle the emotionally charged customers. If the employees are reactive to the emotional cues of the consumers, the problems may get multiplied.
3. ***Empowerment***: The recovery process requires spontaneous decisions by the front line employees and empowerment is the prerequisite for that.
4. ***Instilling Customer Confidence***: When a service failure transpires, the customer is most likely to be satisfied with the recovery initiative if he/she can be convinced the failure occurred due to a temporary cause rather than a stable one. Service companies through its contact employees should communicate to the customers that the failures will not be repeated and the recovery process initiative is the right one.
5. ***Service Recovery vs. Employee Satisfaction***: Employee satisfaction and the effectiveness of recovery efforts are correlated. The satisfied employees own the failures and sincerely put their efforts in initiating the effective recovery process.

3. Relationship Focus

Service companies realized the fact that relationship with customers beyond transactions will help not only in promoting long-term growth of the company but also in influencing positive mindset of the consumers in the service production and consumption process.The positive attitude of the consumers make job of the company easy to enhance customer perceived quality. The relationship bondage between the company and the customers helps in promoting mutual understanding, information sharing, and mutual benefits. The company's initiative to strengthen the customer relationship particularly facilitates effectiveness of interactive marketing due to the following reasons.

(a) The customers approach to the organisation with positive mind.
(b) Customer try to understand the service failures, if any, positively and try to recognize best performances.
(c) Customers leave a long rope before negatively confirming to the service quality.
(d) Customers respond positively to the recovery system.
(e) Customers play active role to reduce the tensions of new customers in case of service failures.
(f) They participate actively in the service production process and support the service employee to perform to the level of his/her potential.
(g) The mood and emotions of both employees and customers would be at the desired levels.
(h) The atmosphere of interactions will be positive and conducive for effective performances.
(i) The employees can better understand the consumers and accordingly customize the services.
(j) The sharing of processes, roles and responsibilities between employees and customers will be based on the ability, interest, and enthusiasm between the two parties.
(k) Customers and employees participate with confidence and mutual trust in the service process.

Taking into consideration the benefits of relationship focus to strengthen interactive marketing operations, the service companies need to focus upon building, maintaining, and enhancing customer relationships. They should develop a managerial framework to manage customer relations effectively. Research studies have shown that the ability of a company in resolving customer problems effectively has strong impact on customer satisfaction and customer loyalty. In other words, the customers who have experienced service failures and later satisfy based on the service recovery process of the service firm will be more loyal than those whose problems are not resolved.

4. Employee Experience Management

For the effective interactive marketing the involvement of employees is of vital importance. Service companies should take care of creating desired experiences to the employees in every perspective particularly in the service production processes. The service environment, the support services, the service culture, superior – subordinate relationships, socialization, empowerment, recognition and reward, and taking care of their personal goals and expectations are all the influencers of employee experiences. The continuously positive experiences of the employees promote employee motivation and morale. A study[30] on employee motivation and customer loyalty in retailing business revealed that committed employees build loyal customers. The strength of this relationship was surprising. A statistical analysis revealed that employee motivation explained as much as 40 per cent of customers' loyalty. This meant that a unit shift in employee motivation could bring about a shift of 0.4 in customer loyalty. Stores which had a higher employee motivation Index (more employees feeling strongly motivated towards the store) showed a significantly higher customer loyalty Index".

5. Customer Experience Management

Experiences are built around feelings, emotions, smells, colors, spaces, sounds, human contact, branding, and a thousand other factors, and time.[31] Great experience is created not only as a result of better product features and services, but also of their ability to make the customer feeling. In recent years competitive pressures are mounting around customer experiences that create ensuring memories and lasting relationships. In fact a new concept is gaining momentum in the name of customer experience, which is called as Customer Experience Management (CEM). CEM emphasizes a shift from technology driven relationships to human driven experiences. It believes that people create experiences. It concentrates on employee interactions with customers and management of moments of truth.

Customers gain experiences with every exposure in their interaction with various facets of the company. They consolidate all such experiences relating to particular activity or experiences relating to a series of activities with the company over a period of time to find out the benefits that they could able to make out.

1.4 PHILOSOPHIES OF INTERACTIVE MARKETING

Many researchers studied the impact of interactive marketing on the business proceedings of the service organizations. Based on their research and experiences they have identified certain philosophies followed by service companies for the successful implementation of interactive marketing operations. The following are some of the philosophies.

I. Management should have Service Orientation

One of the key support factors for effective interactive marketing is service orientation of the company management. This factor has been identified by Schneider[32] who distinguished service managers into two types; the service enthusiastic and service bureaucrats. *Service enthusiasts* are service managers who establish polices and procedures, and otherwise engage in behaviors that show concern for the organization's customers. *Service bureaucrats*, on the other hand, are interested in systems maintenance, routine, and adherence to uniform operating guidelines and procedures. The most important differences between these two orientations are the service enthusiast's emphasis on the importance of interpersonal relationships at work, concern for the customer, and a flexible application of rules. This orientation contrasts to the bureaucrat's avoidance of interpersonal issues and emphasis on formalized rules, formalized procedures, and systems maintenance. When managers are service oriented they guide front line employees in providing and improving quality. They influence work environment significantly.

II. Social Exchange Theory of Service Interactions

This theory identifies the exchange process as dynamic in service encounters, due to the evolving interaction between service providers and their customers. Service providers have an opportunity to offer something special that stands out in a customer's mind, thereby increasing the likelihood of that customer returning. Social relationships are a source of emotions, and attempts to characterize the distinct emotional effects of different exchange structures. The theory can be applied to a range of contexts including, for example, compliments from acquaintances, support among co-workers, information flows among firms, trading among nations, and relationships between firms and customers. The purpose of the affect theory of social exchange is to incorporate emotions as a core feature of social exchange processes, where a social exchange is conceptualized as a joint activity, with at least two parties, and each party has something the other values. In services, emotions influence how parties perceive and feel about their shared activity, their relationships, and their common group associations. According to the affect theory of social exchange, emotions are directed at the group context, and not limited to the service agent. In other words, the emotions resulting from social exchanges affect social relations, and a successful (unsuccessful) service encounter or relationship with a service employee will impact positively (negatively) a customer's view of the entire service firm. This is important, because if a customer has a positive experience at one service location, then he/she should develop positive feelings toward the same brand at different locations, producing increased loyalty to the service brand. Similarly, a bad experience at one service location should negatively affect loyalty to the service brand (at all locations).

Jeremy J. Sierra and Shaun McQuitty[33] who developed this theory proposed a conceptual model of social exchange theory of service loyalty which is shown in Figure 1.4.

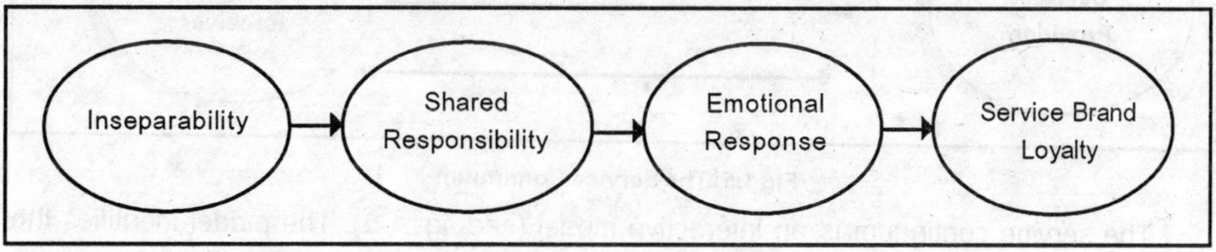

Fig.1.4: Conceptual model of social exchange and service loyalty

This study contributes to the services marketing literature by viewing inseparability as a potential source of service brand loyalty, developing original scales for measuring inseparability and shared responsibility in a services setting, and applying a previously untested theory to a marketing context. Employees play critical roles for a service firm's success, and they often are the only part of the firm that the customer sees. The inseparability between service employees and customers makes employees important for yet another reason, because they can also affect a customer's loyalty to the service firm. Consumers' perceptions of shared responsibility for service outcomes correspond with the extent to which consumers experience emotions in a service setting, which affects their willingness to purchase the service repeatedly. Thus, service employee training programs should emphasize the customer's role in the service experience to increase perceptions of shared responsibility and to create a positive emotional experience for customers.

III. Focus on Interactive Service Quality

Services are crucial issues in the strategic, tactical, and operative management of business operations in many organizations, although the actual performance of a service is taking place at an operative level in a service encounter. Goran Svensson[34] has developed a conceptual framework of interactive service quality. According to him, the service provider *per se* is encouraged and its performance enhanced if there is a continuous response of approval or satisfaction from the service receiver. A contradictory, unfavourable, or unpleasant response from the service receiver may cause malpractice, uncertainty and irregularities in the service provider's performance. This could initiate a vicious circle that harms the ultimate outcome of the service performance in a service encounter.

The framework of Interactive Service Quality in service encounters suggested by the researcher consists of the following three points. They are:

- The service continuum;
- The service cycles; and
- An interactivity model of service continuum and service cycles.

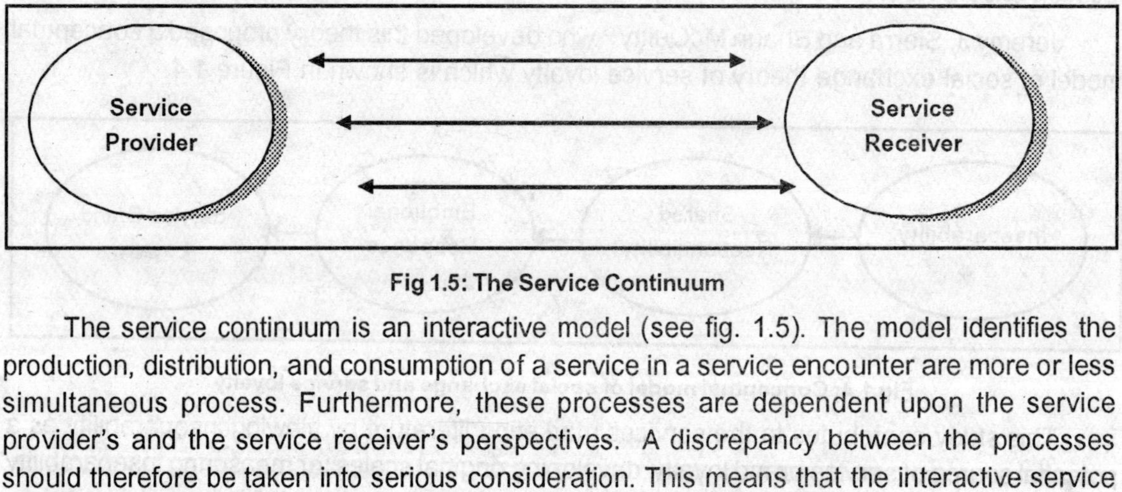

Fig 1.5: The Service Continuum

The service continuum is an interactive model (see fig. 1.5). The model identifies the production, distribution, and consumption of a service in a service encounter are more or less simultaneous process. Furthermore, these processes are dependent upon the service provider's and the service receiver's perspectives. A discrepancy between the processes should therefore be taken into serious consideration. This means that the interactive service quality is influenced by the impact that the production, the distribution, and the consumption of a service have on the service provider's and the service receiver's ultimate experience.

The service cycles of expectations vs. perceptions of the service provider and the service receiver significantly influence the service continuum. The construct of service quality is interactive in many ways. First, there is interactivity between the service provider and the service receiver in a service encounter. Second, the service provider's, as well as the service receiver's expectations of a service in a service encounter are mutually interdependent. Third, the service provider's and the service receiver's perceptions of a service in a service encounter are also mutually interdependent. Consequently, the service cycles of interactive service quality consist of four elements;

(1) The service provider's expectation;
(2) The service provider's perception;
(3) The service receiver's expectation; and
(4) The service receiver's perception.

These elements of the service cycles create four potential gaps of interest to be expected and described:

(1) The gap between the service provider's expectations and perception;
(2) The gap between the service receiver's expectations and perception;
(3) The gap between the service provider's and service receiver's expectations; and
(4) The gap between the service provider's and service receiver's perceptions.

The interactive service quality is satisfactory if there is overall congruence (i.e. no gaps) between the service provider's and the service receiver's service cycles in a service encounter.

The interactivity model of service continuum and service cycles exhibits the relationship between the two. It suggests that the ideal service continuum of production, distribution and consumption of service is possible when the service cycles of expectations vs. perceptions between service provider and service receiver reaches to the level of overall congruence.

IV. Focus on Customer to Customer Interactions

The majority of research concerning Customer to Customer Interactions (CCI) suggests that as one experiences a service, interpersonal encounters can add or detract from evaluations of the firm and influence patronage decisions.The existing literature has identified and categorized the form of the interaction, such as the number of persons spoken to during the service encounter, as well as qualitatively established that the interactions affect how one feels, inferring that CCI can influence common outcome measures of the service process such as satisfaction with the firm and purchasing decisions.CCI can be facilitated by the service environment and atmospherics. How customers perceive the atmospherics may assist in creating an overall feeling about the servicescape. Robert Moore, *et.al.*[35] have developed a theoretical model of service encounters incorporating customer to customer interactions. Figure 1.6 clearly exhibits the importance and role of customer to customer interactions and its final possible outcome.

In most service environments there is an interaction between customers. The interactions occur along a continuum from the mere observation of other customers in the service setting, to asking a fellow customer for an opinion concerning a potential purchase, to greeting and continuing a relationship formed primarily in the service setting. In any service experience a myriad of encounters can occur and each one has the potential of affecting one's satisfaction with the current service experience, future patronage decisions and WOM actions. This model suggests that positive perceptions of atmospherics will lead to positive CCI effects. If managers determine that they would like to enhance the quality of CCI, they should incorporate changes to the physical settings that enhance the type of interactions they desire. Managers should inform service contact staff about the importance of CCI and staff should be trained as to when they should intervene in customer interactions.

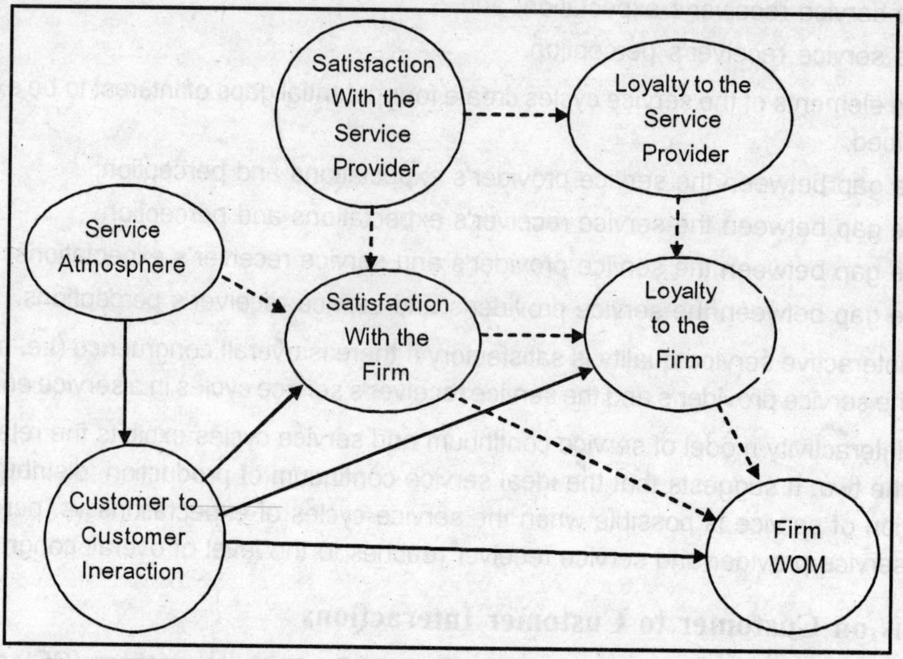

Fig 1.6: The incorporation of CCI in a theoretical model of service outcomes

V. Positive Service Encounter Behavior

One of the key issues identified as important for effective interactive marketing is the positive service encounter behaviour. Charles L. Martin and Steven Adams[36] developed the hierarchy of service encounter behaviors (see Figure 1.7). According to the researchers the omnipresence of interpersonal and routine transactional service behaviors casts them in roles as common denominators or foundational building blocks of more complex service encounters - although they have been found to be important elements of satisfying service encounters in and of themselves. A related appeal for the study of these basic service behaviors is their high degree of generalizability across most service encounters, regardless of industry, business, or other situational specifics. The same degree of generalizability does not exist among those service behaviors positioned higher in the hierarchy (e.g., problem solving) and more commonly associated with empowerment by design. Employees empowered by design or by default can be of great service to customers and employers alike. Knowing that it is not uncommon for customer-contact personnel to exercise behavioral discretion based on factors that have little or nothing to do with customers' service requirements, managers of service organizations can take several steps to curb the practice. Examples of such actions include:

- Reconsidering the extent to which frontline employees are – or should be – empowered;
- Careful screening prospective job applicants to prevent those with discriminatory tendencies from entering the organization;
- Thorough training to build interpersonal skills and address workers' prejudicial attitudes;
- Organizational development efforts to reevaluate and revise corporate practices that may have previously tolerated or encouraged service biases; and
- Montinuous monitoring of service encounters between employees and customers to detect service biases.

Strategic and tactical alternatives to these action steps include restructuring the service system to minimize the number of service encounters altogether, and/or granting customers a greater sense of control in their encounters with frontline personnel.

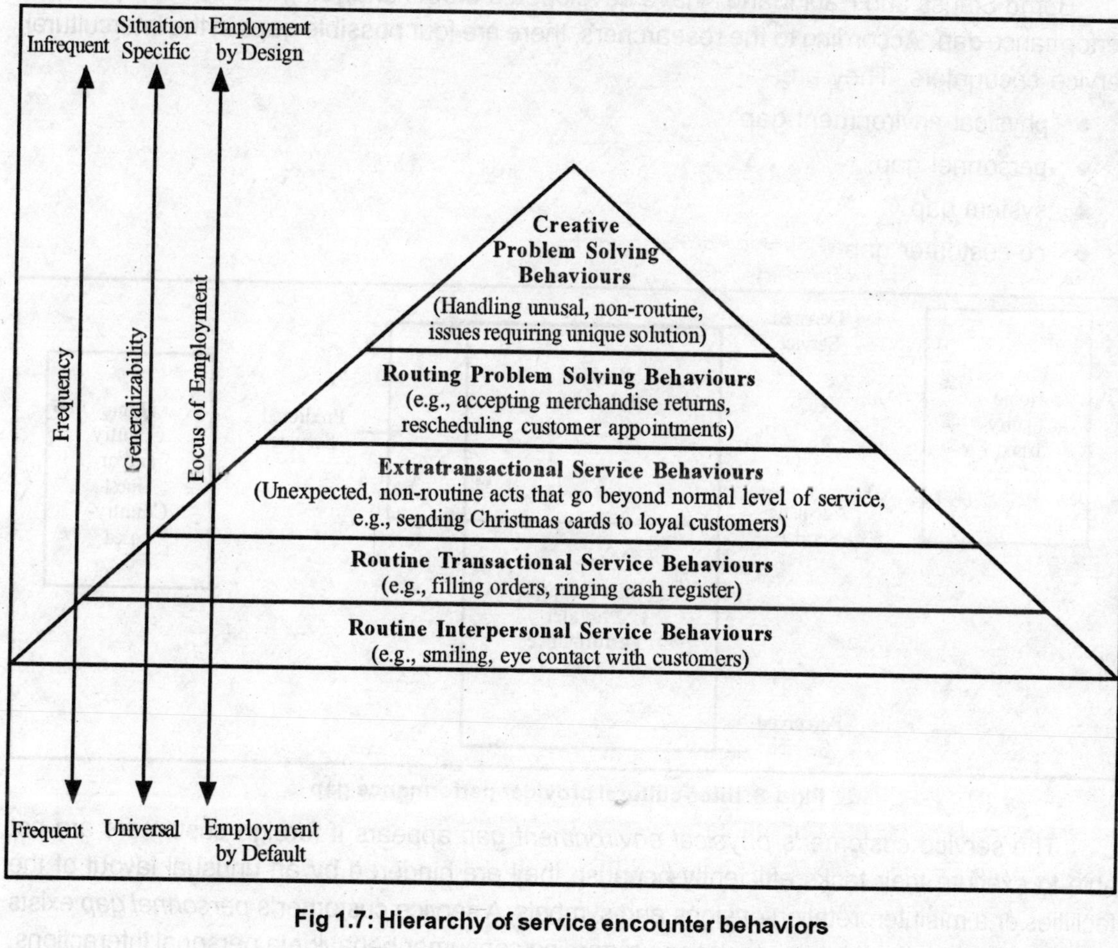

Fig 1.7: Hierarchy of service encounter behaviors

VI. Inter-culture Service Encounters

In cultural encounters, it seems probable that both standards – desired and adequate service – are home-country based, which means that they are the results of customer experiences from their home countries. Foreign customers enter an inter-cultural encounter with their culturally-biased expectations. Consequently, an inter-cultural service provider performance gap occurs when the service performed by a company from one culture is seen as inadequate by a customer from another culture, due to expectations developed by each in their respective home cultures. Problems in international service contacts also occur if customers do not perform their roles correctly and thus do not meet the culturally-determined expectations of service managers and employees. Customers have to execute certain functions within the service production process, e.g., providing information or handling machines. Service employees normally expect that customers have the knowledge and skills to perform these tasks.

Bernd Stauss and Paul Mang[37] have developed a model analyzing inter-culture provider performance gap. According to the researchers, there are four possible gaps in the intercultural service encounters. They are:

- physical environment gap
- personnel gap
- system gap
- co-customer gap

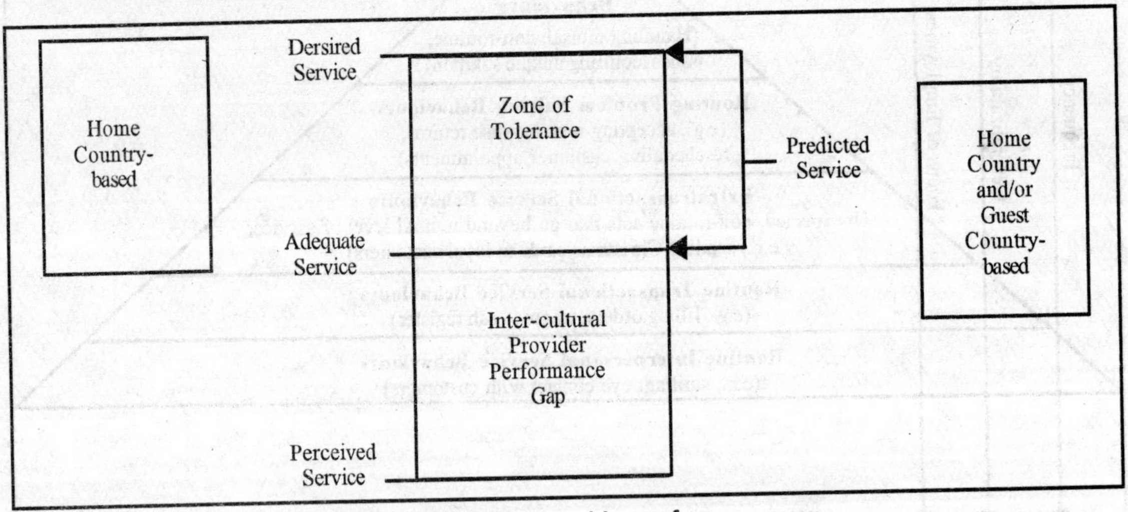

Fig 1.8: Inter-cultural provider performance gap

The service customer's *physical environment gap* appears if foreign customers are not able to execute their tasks efficiently because they are hindered by an unusual layout of the facilities or a misinterpretation of signs and symbols. A service customer's *personnel gap* exists if foreign customers violate expectations regarding consumer behavior in personal interactions, e.g., if they do not observe certain manners or rules. A service customer's *system gap* results when foreign customers are not familiar with the service systems of the service provider and, therefore, are not able to perform correctly from the service provider's point of view. This can be the case if they are confronted with appointment, reservation or queuing systems that deviate from those in their home countries. The *co-customer gap* of the foreign service customer manifests itself in a behavior that is perceived as disturbing and embarrassing by domestic customers, e.g., if foreign customers make loud music at a "wrong" place or time, or if they do not observe the company's rules for customers (e.g., smoking in non-smoking areas). This kind of behavior is perceived by domestic customers as an impairment of the service quality.

VII. Customer Competency in Interactive Marketing

Bonnie Farber Canziani[38] suggested customer competency as one of the key elements in interactive service process. Customer competency refers to the goodness of fit between customer inputs (skills, knowledge and motivation) and customers corresponding task roles in the service delivery system of the firm. These customer inputs (knowledge, skill and motivation) are aligned with three distinct categories of customer task roles: generic consumer, product core and firm specific as shown in Figure 1.9.

Service Process Task

CUSTOMER	GENERIC CONSUMER	PRODUCT CORE	FIRM SPECIFIC
Knowledge	1	2	3
Skill	4	5	6
Motivation	7	8	9

Fig 1.9: Visualization of customer competency

Job tasks assigned to or appropriated by customers can be detailed by answering the following questions:

- What does the customer do in the process?
- How does the customer do it (technical and functional quality)?
- When does the customer do it (with respect to real time or during the process sequence, i.e., pre-transaction/transaction/post-transaction)?
- How often does the customer do it (frequent repeated discrete cycles versus infrequent steps in a continuous service relationship)?
- With whom does the customer interface (employees, machines or self)?

It is argued that each of these elements within a customer role script can be assigned to customers in a very real sense – similar to employee job descriptions. The appropriate assignment of tasks to the best equipped or motivated person or machine becomes a factor in competitive advantage for firms that have substitution flexibility. Some tasks are strictly the domain of specialized employees, some tasks may be assigned to generic categories of people, some are best outsourced to highly skilled firms, some become the purview of intermediary establishments, and finally, other tasks are given to customers via transactional or self-service mechanisms.

VIII: Interactive Communication

The communication skills of employees and customers at the time of service encounter influence the outcome of the service significantly. It suggests that the service companies should focus upon developing communication skills of their employees which help them to understand the customers well and become understandable to the customers (see Figure 1.10).

Service Provider's Nonverbal Communication: Nonverbal communication (NVC) is usually understood as the process of communication through sending and receiving wordless messages. Such messages can be communicated through gesture; body language or posture; facial expression and eye contact; object communication such as clothing, hairstyles or even architecture; symbols and info graphics; prosodic features of speech such as intonation and stress and other paralinguistic features of speech such as voice quality, emotion and speaking style. Service employees should be given training on non-verbal communication particularly on the following key elements.

Paralanguage: Paralanguage (sometimes called vocalics) is the study of nonverbal cues of the voice. Various acoustic properties of speech such as tone, pitch, accent, etc., can provide nonverbal cues. Paralanguage can be used to modify meaning and convey emotion.

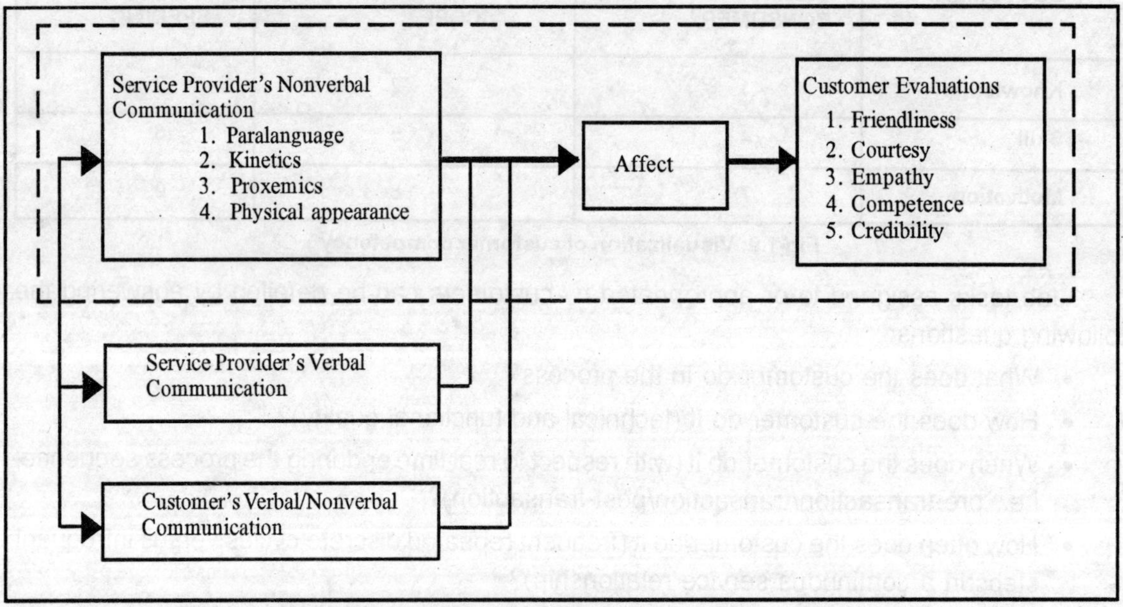

Fig 1.10: Nonverbal Communication Service Interactions

***Kinetics** (Body language):* Body language is articulation of the body, or movement resulting from muscular and skeletal shift. This includes all actions, physical or physiological, automatic reflexes, posture, facial expressions, gestures, and other body movements. The body communicates a lot about a person in many ways when interaction is taking place. Body movement can indicate attitudes and feelings while also acting as illustrators and regulators. Body movement includes head movement, eyes, shoulders, lips, eyebrows, neck, legs, arms, fingers, hands, and gestures. All these pieces can convey a person is comfortable, unhappy, friendly, anxious, or nervous. With so many parts conveying messages, one can see how easily things can get confused and how difficult it is to manipulate non-verbal communication. Body motions such as shrugs, foot tapping, drumming fingers, eye movements such as winking, facial expressions, and gestures communicate meanings to the service consumers.

Proxemics: Proxemics refers to how people use and interpret space. For most of us, someone standing very close makes feel uncomfortable. We feel that our personal space has been invaded. People seek to extend their territory in many ways to attain power and intimacy. Customers tend to mark their territory with permanent walls. Personal space is the space one places between self and others.

Appearance and Artifacts: Personal appearance is a major factor used to judge a person simply because the first impression of a person is based on appearance. People can change their appearance by changing their clothing styles, hairstyles, and other accessories or artifacts. Clothing and other artifacts are especially powerful signifiers and convey a great deal of detailed information about someone's job, personality, values, and lifestyle. For example, uniforms of one sort or another are a feature in many fields. Some uniforms are obvious like the army, the navy, or the air force, the police, hospitals, etc. Personal physical appearance usually provides the first available data about a stranger. To establish credibility, one should wear styles that fit the environment.

Service Provider's Verbal Communication: Verbal communication skills refer to words used in interactive communication – oral as well as written. The words used by contact employee to welcome, greet, request, suggest, direct, explain, take order, send off, empathise and so on influence the behavior of service consumers significantly. The excuses, sorry(s), thanks, etc. minimize or eliminate negative perceptions and many create positive dispositions. Successful service companies with high customer contact, standardize words, phrases, and sentences to minimize the risk of failure in verbal communication of their employees. The words are symbols of culture driven meanings. Therefore, word choice depends upon cultural background of the customers. Service companies when dealing with cross cultural customers should take into consideration the positive and negative meanings of different words, contextual meanings, liked and disliked words, word preferences and so on of the people of a culture.

Courtesy plays an important role in human interaction, particularly, in a country like India where culture is deep rooted. Recognition, a pleasing smile, a welcome note, thanks, sorry, respecting the ego, facilitating behavior, soft speech, concern, etc. will become part of courteous behavior.

Customers particularly from rural areas often will be under pressure in dealing with financial matters and also interacting with qualified persons. Such customers look for the service person who can understand the problem from their angle and suggest and provide the right kind of service effectively. To satisfy such customers, service employee need to be empathetic. They should try to understand the real problems of the customers by getting into the customers method of understanding and analysis. The employees should also try to understand the sensitivities, sentiments of the customers while designing the service package and in the production process.

Empathy is the right answer for the majority of consumer grievances. It can be used more effectively as prevention than a cure.

Competence is the ability to perform a specific task, action or function successfully.

Credibility refers to the objective and subjective components of the believability of a source or message.

Customer's Verbal/Nonverbal Communication: As like the employees' verbal and non-verbal communication skills, the ability of the consumers to communicate verbally and non-verbally influence the interactive marketing process significantly.

1.5 SUMMARY

Interactive marketing is one of the three basic strategic dimensions of services marketing. It is the managerial process through which a series of interactions between service provider and consumer are organised to facilitate efficient participation in service production and consumption that satisfies the needs and wants of the customer and creates positive customer-perceived quality. The service production and consumption takes place only when the customers interact with the service organisation. The interactive part of service production system consists of customers and the rest of the quality generating resources with which customers interact with directly. These are the direct buyer seller interactions where the moments of truth take place. The quality generating resources in the interactive part are customer involvement process; contact persons systems and operational routines and physical resources and equipment.

Customer Perceived Quality (CPQ) is the ultimate result of the service performance of any service organisation. The management of the movement of truth will greatly influence the customer perceived quality. Therefore, interactive marketing plays pivotal role in generating positive CPQ. For the purpose, besides designing customer friendly systems and operational processes and providing quality physical resources and equipment with latest technological support, contact employees need to be motivated. Apart from technical expertise, the involvement of service employee with service inclination is likely to create greater quality perceptions to the consumers. Therefore, internal marketing should be managed effectively so that it stands as a foundation for interactive marketing.

1.6 REFERENCES

1. Christian Gronroos, The perceived service quality concept – a mistake?, *Managing Service Quality,* Vol.11, No.3 (2001): 150.
2. Christian Gronroos, The perceived service quality concept – a mistake?, *Managing Service Quality,* Vol.11, No.3 (2001): 150.
3. K.Rama Mohana Rao, *'Services Marketing'*, Pearson Education, New Delhi, (2005): 8.
4. K.Rama Mohana Rao, *'Services Marketing'*, Pearson Education, New Delhi, (2005): 230.
5. Christian Gronroos, 'Services Management and Marketing', Maxwell Macmillan publishing, Singapore Pet. Ltd., Singapore, (1990): 209.

6. Philip Kotler and Gary Armstrong, *Principles of Marketing* 12/e, Prentice Hall of India, New Delhi, (2008): 242.
7. Zeithaml, V.A., Mary Jo Bitner, Gremler, D.D., and Ajay Pandit, *Services Marketing* 4/e, Tata McGraw-Hill Company Ltd., New Delhi, (2008): 449.
8. Christopher Lovelock, J. Writz., and J. Chatterjee, *Services Marketing* 4/e, Pearson Education, New Delhi, (2008): 337.
9. Kurtz, D.L., and Boone, L.E., *Principles of Marketing* 12/e, South-Western Cengage Learning, New Delhi, (2006): 23.
10. http://tobeinformed.com/marketing/interactive-marketing, dt. 1-4-2010.
11. Bowen D.E., and Schneider, B., Boundary-Spanning Role Employees and the Service Encounter: Some Guidelines for Management and Research, in *The Service Encounter: Managing Employee/Customer Interaction in Service Business,* John A. Czepiel, Michael R. Solomon, and Carol F. Surprenant, eds. (Lexington, MA: D.C.: Heath and Company, 1985): 127-47.
12. Michael D. Hartline and Ferrell, O.C., The Management of Customer-Contact Service Employees: An Empirical Investigation, *Journal of Marketing,* Vol.60 (October, 1996): 52.
13. Jennifer Potter-Brotman, The New Role of Service in Customer Retention, *Managing Service Quality,* Vol.4, No.4 (1994): 53.
14. Burke, M.J., *et al.*, Reconceptualizing psychological climate in a retail service environment: a multiple-stakeholder perspective, *Journal of Applied Psychology,* Vol.77, No.5 (1992): 717-29.
15. Schneider, B. *et al.*, Linking service climate and customer perceptions of service quality: test of a causal model, *Journal of Applied Psychology*, Vol.83, No.2 (1998): 150-63.
16. Schneider, B., and Bowen, D.E., *Winning the Service Game,* (Boston, MA: Harvard Business School Press, 1995).
17. Michael D. Hartline and Ferrell, O.C., The Management of Customer-Contact Service Employees: An Empirical Investigation, *Journal of Marketing,* Vol.60 (October, 1996): 52.
18. Bitner, M.J., *et al.*, The Service Encounter: Diagnosing Favorable and Unfavorable Incidents, *Journal of Marketing,* 54 (January, 1990): 71-84.
19. Schneider , B. The Service Organization: Climate Is Crucial, *Organizational Dynamics,* 9 (1980): 52-65..
20. Mary Jo Bitner, *et al.*, The Service Encounter: Diagnosing Favorable and Unfavorable Incidents, *Journal of Marketing,* Vol.54 (January 1990): 71.
21. McCracken, G., *The Long Interview,* (Newbury Park, CA.: Sage, 1988).
22. Mills, P.K., Chase, R.B. and Marguiles, N., Motivating the client/employee system as a service production strategy, *Academy of Management Review,* Vol.8, No.2 (1983): 301-10.
23. Lance A. Bettencourt and Kevin Gwinner, Customization of the service experience: the role of the frontline employee, *International Journal of Service Industry Management,* Vol.7, No.2 (1996): 7.
24. Abdullah Aldlaigan and Francis Buttle, Beyond satisfaction: customer attachment to retail banks, *International Journal of Bank Marketing,* Vol.23, No.4 (2005): 357.
25. Bateson, J.E.G., Perceived control and the service encounter, in Czepiel, J.A., Solomon, M.R. and Surprenant, C.F. (Eds), *The Service Encounter,*(Lexington, MA: Lexington Books, 1985): 67-82.
26. S.Ramachander, 'Interactive Marketing: Boon or Nightmare?', http://www.thehindubusinessline.com/catalyst/2004/04/08/stories/2004040800140400.htm, dt. 10-10-2010.

27. An-Tien Hsieh and Chang-Hua Yen, The Effect of Customer participation on Service Providers' Job Stress, *The Service Industries Journal,* Vol.25, No.7 (October 2005): 894.

28. Bernd Stauss and Paul Mang, "Culture Shocks" in inter-cultural service encounters?, *Journal of Services Marketing,* Vol.13, No.4/5, (1999): 333.

29. Zeithaml, A.V., and Bitner M.J, *Services Marketing*, Tata McGraw-Hill Publishing Co. Limited, New Delhi, (2003): 197.

30. Sanjay Badhe and Sridevi Rao, Increasing customer loyalty through employee focus, *Indian Management,* (March 2004): 49.

31. Alexandra Thusy and Langdon Morris, From CRM to experience management, *Indian Management,* (January-2005): 46.

32. Jean-Charles Chebat, Bary Babin, and Paul Kollias, What makes contact employees perform? Reactions to employee perceptions of managerial practices, *International Journal of Bank Marketing,* 20/7, (2002) 326.

33. Jeremy J. Sierra and Shaun McQuitty, Service providers and customers: social exchange theory and service loyalty, *Journal of Services Marketing,* 19/6, (2005): 392-400.

34. Goran Svensson, A generic conceptual framework of interactive service quality, *Managing Service Quality,* 13/4, (2003): 268.

35. Robert Moore, Melissa L. Moore and Michael Capella, The impact of customer-to-customer interactions in a high personal contact service setting, *Journal of Services Marketing,* 19/7, (2005) 482-491.

36. Charles L. Martin and Steven Adams, Behavioral biases in the service encounter: empowerment by default? , *Marketing Intelligence & Planning,* 17/4, (1999): 192-201.

37. Bernd Stauss and Paul Mang, "Culture Shocks" in inter-cultural service encounters? *Journal of Services Marketing,* Vol.13, No.4/5, (1999): 333.

38. Bonnie Farber Canziani, Leveraging customer competency in service firms, *International Journal of Service Industry Management,* Vol.8, No.1, (1997): 5-25.

Chapter 2 REVIEW OF LITERATURE

Banking sector, may be due to its omnipresence throughout the world and the role the sector plays in shaping economic progress, attracted the attention of many researchers around the globe.The research studies by and large focused on financial issues. A few researchers carried out research work on human resource management and customer relations. Interactive marketing is a new theme. Hence,the studies in this area are very limited.Therefore,the review of literature for the purpose of the study included some select studies on banking, customer-employee relationships, the philosophy and the application of interactive marketing in the banking sector.

2.1 STUDIES ON BANKING SERVICES

Block-Ernest[1] explained the prerequisites like attitudes and motives of the employees before introducing marketing strategies. Rashmi Arya[2] highlighted the rules for both male and female employees and the different status females have in society. Bhatt-Atul[3] highlighted bank marketing for efficient operations and market research for innovativeness in the Indian Banking system at large. Golan-Amos[4] has described production, pricing, and market structure of banks and other depository institutions and also on financial intermediation. Kulshreshtha K.[5] explained that the banking industry in the country has witnessed two phases of challenges during the last two and a half decades in the form of revolution in the functioning and shift in focus of bank lending. Sharma K. Ramakrishna[6] explained the developments in banking system, account of banking sector reforms, and the changing role of banks in the competitive environment. Bilgrami, S.A.R.[7] in his research work explained that nationalization of commercial banks brought about radical changes in the structure and policy objectives of the banking industry in India. Meir Kohn[8] in his study explained the structural changes in financial institutions and markets. He emphasized the change in role of financial institutions in view of changes in the financial markets across the nations, and he opined that financial institutions should gear up to the challenges ahead. Pepermans – Ronals, Verleye – Gino and Vaw Cappellen – Sarah Wall[9] conducted a study on attitudes towards wall banking, innovativeness and computer, attitudes and it also covers the factors which determine the choice of a bank, man-machine problems related to use of an ATM.

Shollapur M.R.[10] has made a comparative study about the performance appraisal of banks under service area approaches. Jain, Alok-Kumar[11] made an attempt to provide overview of the changing scenario of financial development, where bank marketing stands and what changes are needed for effective working. Rajesh[12] has highlighted the new face of retail banking in view of developments in retail marketing on account of liberalization policies.

V.A. Avadhani[13] in his study explained the various aspects of financial markets and financial services. He opined that developed financial markets are the need of the hour to provide better financial services as per changing expectations in view of developments in the financial markets all over the world. Bhole L.M.[14] in his study explained that Indian financial system has undergone revolutionary changes during the last decade and emphasized the need for changes in the structure and functioning of financial institutions in tune with the wide-ranging financial sector reforms and developments in the national and international financial markets. Chandra Sekhar, A.R.[15] in his research work titled 'market share of public sector banks in post-reforms period', enlightened the introduction of financial sector reforms and the measures initiated for making the banking system sound, vibrant and efficient. He opined that the entrance of new generation banks has affected the market share of public sector banks and induced competition in the banking sector.

Sharma R.D.[16] has made a thorough research and evaluation of inbuilt marketing orientation in Indian rural banking and focused on rural credit and economic development. Ganesan, G.[17] expressed opinions on the changing procedures and styles of functioning of commercial banks beyond 2000. Singh Rajender Kumar[18] highlighted cost control and cost reduction measures that banks have to pursue in a deregulated banking environment.

Barbara R. Lewis and Sotiris Spyrakopoulos[19] made an empirical investigation of service failures and service recovery in retail banking. Different types of failures and the recovery strategies used by Greek banks to respond to them were identified using the critical incident technique. According to their study, service failures were found to have varying importance and service recovery strategies are more effective for particular failures. Further, it was found that customers with long relationships or high deposits with their banks were more demanding with respect to service recovery.

Juan Carlos Fandos Roig, Javier Sanchez Garcia, Miguel Angel Moliner Tena, and Jaume Llorens Monzonis[20] in their research work, analyzed the dimensionality of the concept of perceived value in the banking sector, adapting the GLOBAL scale of measurement of perceived value to the banking services sector. A total of 200 customers of financial entities were surveyed and structural equation models were used to verify the reliability and validity of the scale of perceived value. Perceived value is found to be a multidimensional construct composed of six dimensions: functional value of the establishment; functional value of the personnel; functional value of the service; functional value of price; emotional value; and social value. This study proposes a scale of measurement of the value perceived by consumers in the banking sector which incorporates valuations of functional aspects and of affective aspects, thus obtaining an overall quantification of the value perceived by the customer of the purchase made.

Raphael K. Akamavi[21] examined a financial service innovation process, which is referred to as financial product innovation: improvements to existing services. This study conducted a critical analysis of the operational process of opening a Lloyds TSB Student Account at a local branch. The process of opening a student bank account is documented in a flowchart/flow network, which highlights operational steps and the visibility line between front-end and backroom staff. This study proposes a re-engineered process (i.e., e-process or virtual process), which removes these bottlenecks systematically. The results show the increased efficiency, productivity and customer satisfaction levels are the key factors for innovation process performance. The study concludes with evidence of non-financial performance results of this type of financial service innovation. It provides useful managerial recommendations for improving the process of opening a student account. This study provides a re-engineered process which is simpler, more economical and faster than the original process.It presents principles to diagnose appropriate service operation processes for re-engineering using action mapping programs and review their innovation performances. Managers will learn new frameworks, diagnostic tools and analysis techniques to better understand and improve their firm's service operations.

Babu P. George and Purva G. Hegde[22] in their study offered a fresh look at the paradigmatic shifts being experienced by the traditional, government supported banking establishments, especially those in the erstwhile socialist and mixed economies, in the newly embraced context of liberalization-privatization-globalization.

Avinandan Mukherjee, Prithwiraj Nath and Manabendra Nath Pal[23] in their study explored the linkage between performance benchmarking and strategic homogeneity of Indian commercial banks. They devised a method of benchmarking performance of Indian commercial banks using their published financial information.They also studied the ability of a bank to utilize its resources to generate business transactions and is measured by their ratio, which is then called the efficiency.The concept of efficiency is critical from a marketing perspective. Methodologically, in order to overcome some of the shortcomings of simple efficiencies obtained through self-appraisal of individual banks, a more "democratic" concept of cross-efficiency evaluated with the process of peer-appraisal has been brought in to benchmark the banks.

Philip Megicks, Atul Mishra and Jonathan Lean[24] in their research work aims to develop a conceptual understanding of the factors influencing market orientation in banking institutions, and to assess its impact on outreach performance. The attitudes and behaviours of managers, along with institutional characteristics, are identified as influences on market orientation, service innovation, customer satisfaction and outreach performance within RRBs.

G.S. Sureshchandar, Chandrasekharan Rajendran and R.N. Anantharaman[25] in their research study focused on the critical factors of customer perceived service quality in banks of a developing economy – India.The study compares and contrasts the three groups of banks in India with respect to the service quality factors from the perspective of the customers. It was found that there is a great amount of variation with respect to the level of service quality offered by the three groups of banks. The study identifies the factors that discriminate the three groups of banks. Customers in developing economies seem to keep the "technological factors" of services such as core service and systematization of the service delivery as the yardstick in differentiating good and bad service while the "human factors" seem to play a lesser role in discriminating the three groups of banks. The service quality indices with respect to the three groups and the Indian banking industry as whole, offer interesting information on the level of service quality delivered by banks in India.

Satyabhusan Dash, Ed Bruning, Kalyan Ku Guin[26] undertook cross-cultural study to examine the moderating effect of power distance on perceived interdependence and relationship quality in a bank-corporate client relationship. Results indicate that power distance moderates the interdependence and quality relationships.

Peter Jones[27] explains that while branch location is still seen as the most important single influence on a customer's choice of bank, the past decade has witnessed the widespread closure of branches.

Jamal, Ahmad[28] has investigated the effects of self-image congruence on satisfaction and brand preference. With the help of empirical research the author argues that while self-image congruence may be related to customer satisfaction in a normal context, it may not necessarily affect satisfaction levels when customers are using technology-based self-services. Furthermore, during encounters involving self-service technologies, customers might experience satisfying or dissatisfying incidents which may not be related to their overall satisfaction and brand preference levels. The study highlights the implications for brand managers in the retail banking sector.

Craig C. Julian, and B. Ramaseshan[29] conducted a study on 'The Role of Customer-contact Personnel in the Marketing of a Retail Bank's Service' and examined the effects of the customer-contact process on the retail bank's overall marketing effectiveness. The study concludes that service salespersons require considerable skill, especially in adapting the customized selling required by services. Because service selling requires considerable skill levels and extensive training of its personnel, the bank will need to place a high emphasis on teaching selling skills. One of the skills it will need to teach is how to best maximize the reputation of the organization. Second, the role of the customer-contact personnel in the marketing process of a retail bank is recognized as being important by the customer-contact personnel and the organization. However, the customer-contact personnel felt they were not well rewarded for their contribution to the retail bank's marketing effort, were not involved in an official training program, and a significant percentage felt they received greater blame, condemnation and threat of dismissal than did salespeople. The significance of these findings highlights the low self-esteem evident in the customer-contact personnel which could permeate itself within the organization. A result of this apparent low self-esteem could be poor customer service being provided by these customer-contact personnel to the bank's existing customers as these customer-contact employees may feel that it is satisfactory for them to treat the bank's customers the way the bank is treating them, i.e., without much respect. Third, the relationship between the salesperson and the customer is perceived as being of great importance in the marketing of the retail bank's financial services. Finally, in the marketing of the bank's financial services the service salesperson requires significant input from the customer if the service is to be successfully delivered.

Terrence Levesque, and Gordon H.G. McDougall[30] pointed out that customer satisfaction and retention are critical for retail banks, and investigated the major determinants of customer satisfaction and future intentions in the retail bank sector. The researchers identified the determinants which include service quality dimensions, service features, service problems, service recovery and products used. The study found that service problems and the bank's service recovery ability have a major impact on customer satisfaction and intentions to switch.

Abdullah Aldlaigan Saudi Arabia, and Francis Buttle[31] in their research work investigated different types of attachment that customers develop towards retail banks. The approach blends literature reviews, in addition to qualitative and quantitative methods. The primary research program analyses data from seven focus groups, 39 one-on-one interviews and 1,058 individual consumer questionnaires.The study identified three forms of positive attachments, based on three different foundations: the credibility of the organisation, compatibility between the values of the organisation and those of the consumer, and interpersonal or relational considerations. The study presents a statistically valid and reliable scale that can be used to measure these three forms of attachment. Also identifies other forms of customer-bank attachment grounded on less positive associations, including inertia and alienation.

Benjamin Schneider, John J. Parkington, and Virginia M. Buxton[32] used representative design for diagnosing effectiveness in retail service organizations for the study of employees' and customers' perceptions from twenty-three bank branches. The design builds on some boundary-spanning theory and on some practical realities which suggest that data should be collected from both employees and customers. Results of the study revealed some strong relationships between employee perceptions of branch practices and procedures in relation to service and customer perceptions of service practices and quality.

Yahya Melhem and Irbid, Jordan[33] in their research study found that trust, communication, knowledge, and skills of customer-contact employees may have a direct and strong impact on the empowerment of service employees. Empowerment antecedents (trust, incentives, communication, and knowledge) of customer-contact employees accounted for significant variation in the levels of empowerment among customer-contact employees in the banking industry.

Ding Hooi Ting[34] in his study focused on service quality and satisfaction judgments of customers in banking institutions throughout Malaysia. The study attempts to determine the relationship between service quality and satisfaction, where service quality is the independent variable and satisfaction is the dependent variable. The findings of the study provide a better understanding towards the behavior of customers as compared to the linear models.

G.S. Sureshchandra, Chandrasekharan Rajendran, R.N. Anantharaman, and T.J. Kamalanabhan[35] critically examined the banking industry in a developing nation – India, and focused on discrepancies among the various groups of banks in India with respect to the Total Quality Service (TQS) dimensions. The results of the study indicated that the three groups of banks in India such as public sector banks, private sector banks and foreign banks seem to vary significantly in TQS dimension. The study identified the dimensions that contribute most to discriminate between the groups. The researchers computed and analysed the total quality service indices with respect to 12 dimensions of quality for the three groups of banks and for the banking industry as a whole in order to ascertain the level of TQS implementation in the Indian banking scene. The study offers key insights on criticality of the different TQS dimensions with respect to the banking sector in developing economies.

Madhukar G. Angur, Rajan Nataraajan and John S. Jahera Jr.[36] examined the applicability of alternative measures of service quality in the developing economy of India and assesses related issues in that context. Based on data gathered from 143 customers of two major banks, overall results support a multidimensional construct of service quality and suggest that the SERVQUAL scale provides greater diagnostic information than the SERVPERF scale. However, the five-factor conceptualization of SERVQUAL does not seem to be totally applicable, and no significant difference was found in the predictive ability of the two measures. Further, although SERVQUAL and SERVPERF have identical convergent validity, SERVPERF appears to have higher discriminant validity than SERVQUAL.

Avinandan Mukherjee and Prithwiraj Nath[37] examined the role of trust encompasses the exchanges and interactions of a retail bank with its customers on various dimensions of online banking. The study specifically lays stress on the bank-to-customer exchanges taking place through the technological interface. It hypothesizes shared value, communication and opportunistic behaviour as antecedents to trust. Trust and commitment also have a causal relationship. The researchers observed that shared value is most critical to develop trust as well as relationship commitment. Communication has a moderate influence on trust, while opportunistic behaviour has significant negative effect. Also finds higher perceived trust to enhance significantly customers' commitment in online banking transaction. They concluded that the future commitment of the customers to online banking depends on perceived trust.

Mark Durkin, Barry Howcroft, Aodheen O'Donnell, and Danielle McCartan-Quinn[38] examined retail bank customer preferences in relation to personal and remote interactions. The empirical evidence suggests that despite of the increase in remote banking, retail bank customers still place significantly greater emphasis on face-to-face contact. The implications of this finding are that if banks want to encourage widespread customer adoption of remote banking they must better understand customer attitudes towards alternative delivery channels and use this information to educate their customers on the tangible service benefits which emanate from remote delivery.

Kaisa Snellman, and Tiina Vihtkari[39] examined complaining behaviour in traditional and technology-based service encounters. Drawing on 160 negative critical incidents within Finnish retail banking, the findings of the study shows that contradictory to common predictions, there are no significant differences in the complaining rates between the two types of service encounters. Complaints about technology-based service encounters have significantly higher response rates than complaints about traditional service encounters. In technology-based service encounters, customers who actually consider themselves guilty for the outcome were the most frequent complainers, while the ones attributing the outcome to technology failures or service process failures complain less often. These findings have interesting implications for designers of service recovery systems.

Abhiman Das and Saibal Ghosh[40] analysed the performance of Indian commercial banking sector during the post reform period 1992–2002. Several efficiency estimates of individual banks are evaluated using nonparametric Data Envelopment Analysis (DEA). Three different approaches, *viz.*, intermediation approach, value-added approach and operating approach have been employed to differentiate how efficiency scores vary with the changes in inputs and outputs. The analysis links the variation in calculated efficiencies to a set of variables, i.e., bank size, ownership, capital adequacy ratio, non-performing loans and management quality. The findings suggest that medium-sized public sector banks performed reasonably well and are more likely to operate at higher levels of technical efficiency. A close relationship is observed between efficiency and soundness as determined by bank's capital adequacy ratio. The empirical results also show that technically more efficient banks are those that have, on an average, less nonperforming loans.

Mohapatra[41] assessed the training needs of the employees of State Bank of India. He suggested that an employee has to get training at least once in every three years. Further, lateral changes require training once in every two years.

Merchant[42] has done a study on HRD plan for State Bank of India. The researcher in this study has mentioned the basic skills and competencies required for effective management of banking. People management skills are rated in this study as important for most of the key positions like Regional Managers, Branch Managers and Staff officers. The researcher revealed that HR is in important assets of an organization and human beings have tremendous potential to grow and just not motivated by monetary comforts. Investment in HR is necessary and the more an organization invests in its HR the more substantial will be the gain from the investment, says the researcher.

Neelu Rohmetra[43] studied 'Human Resource Development in Commercial Banks in India'. The author has made an attempt to investigate into the efforts made regarding the development of people in two commercial banks namely State Bank of India (SBI) and the Jammu and Kashmir Bank Ltd. (J&KB). She has presented a comparative study of prevailing development climate for facilitating Human Resource Development (HRD) in those two banks. She conducted the survey on attitudes of the employees towards prevailing HRD climate in both the banks. Only 12 per cent of the clerical group of employees has responded unfavorably. She concludes that any scenario of banking in the new millennium has to be necessarily based upon its manpower and what is more important, the development of their expertise to cope up with the increasing and changing demands on banking. As such, it has become imperative that the banking industry should concentrate seriously on establishing systems for development of human resources.

Chalam, G.V., and Srinivas, L.[44] studied the basic gender disagreement with respect to HRD Climate in the selected branches of the SBI. A sample of 200 employees from various levels was selected from the identified twenty branches of SBI in Andhra Pradesh by using the random sampling method. The study represents on cadre, service, and age levels. They suggested that the management is required to announce performance standards that arouse equal interest and competition among the male and female employees in the chosen bank. The management should find the reasons for such weak performance of the male employees and devise methods to overcome these deficiencies. Management should give priority to the women issues in order to obtain more assured results than that of the existing ones.

Kulwant Singh Pathania[45] studied 'HRD Program and Practice in Cooperative Banks'. In this study he suggested, a total revision of cooperatives HRD Policies and Practices with regard to manpower planning, selection, placement, wage and salary administration, training and development, transfer, promotion, performance appraisal etc.

Sambre Neena[46] in her study about alienation among bank employees has found dismal HRM practices and policies which she sums up as creativity in bank work is minimum. The work is too bureaucratic and individual has less option to decide and control his work. This resulted in loss of self-esteem. The relatively low work commitment may be due to this kind of work. There are no self-rewarding activities.

Rajendran[47] observed the role of HRD in banks and types of HRD practices as a system and values and cultures. He has suggested that the banks should promote quality consciousness culture, openness and transparency, trust, authenticity, collaboration and co-operation.

Shivaji[48] in his study focused on the issues relating to human resource development in co-operative banks, such as manpower planning, professionalization, technical staff, cost of effectiveness and productivity retirement, promotional avenues, incentives and suggested that, the training programs should include case study method, evolving of positive and dynamic policies etc.

Pathak[49] conducted a study of bank officers from four major public sector banks in India, and found that the bank officers, regardless of their job-involvement, wanted more decision-making authority, opportunity for personal growth and development and recognition for good work done. Recommendations of the study include adequate feedback and incentive for good work, widening the area of responsibility, larger delegation of authority, and tangible as well as symbolic modes of recognition for raising the level of need satisfaction and job involvement.

Swain and Srinivas[50] made an attempt to analyse the work motivation of branch managers of State Bank of India. Vijayakumar, V.S.R.[51] has made a study on job satisfaction of executives of private sector banks and their perceived management styles.

2.2 STUDIES ON INTERACTIVE MARKETING

Stephan H. Haeckel[52] in his book on "About the nature and future of interactive marketing" stated that the essence of interactivity is exchange. Degree of contingency and frequency are among the more important dimensions of marketing exchange. Technology enables and enhances these dimensions on a scale and scope unprecedented in human history. The author argues that information technology and the collaborative potential of the Internet may eventually change human cognitive processes as much or more than writing technology did. He offers anecdotal evidence that technology-assisted human collaboration can systematically lead to synergetic, "previously unthinkable," (and therefore unpredictable) breakthroughs. While it is therefore not reasonable to expect accurate predictions of what the breakthroughs in interactive marketing and "e-business" will be, it is possible to think about ways to discover them earlier. Two areas of research are suggested as being of special interest: whether or not the collaborative potential of technology is likely to transform business-as-games-against-competitors into business-as-games-with-customers?; and what are the necessary and sufficient conditions for interactive technology to lead to breakthrough creativity?

Ross D. Petty[53] in his work on "Interactive marketing and the law: The future rise of unfairness" argued that in the 20th century, the marketing law concept of deception evolved from the earlier legal concept of fraud. Stronger remedies also evolved to address the possibility of deception on a mass scale. In the 21st century, with the rise of interactive marketing, deception will continue as a primary concern, but additional emphasis will be placed on fairness to consumers. Practices that cause substantial unavoidable consumer injury without countervailing benefits will receive greater scrutiny in four areas: consumer control over advertising and the sales transaction, the targeting of vulnerable audiences and discrimination related to such targeting, the provision of information to consumers, and lastly, psychological pressure to buy, particularly as applied to targeted, vulnerable audiences.

Dawn Iacobucci[54] in his research work considers properties of interactive marketing and how network methods might be useful diagnostic tools for such interactive systems. Four content properties of interactive marketing are defined: technology, intrinsic motivation, the use of the resultant interactive marketing information, and the real-time aspect of the interaction. Four structural properties are also defined: customization, responsiveness, interactions among relevant groups, and a structure of networked networks - the meganet. Network methods are then integrated with the concerns of the interactive marketing manager.

Patrick Barwise and John U. Farley[55] conducted an empirical study of the state of interactive marketing (IM) in five large developed markets (United States, Japan, Germany, UK, and France) and two key emerging markets (China and Brazil). According to the study expenditure on IM is growing fast, already accounting for over 8% of total marketing spent. It is significantly higher in services versus products and B2B versus B2C markets but varies surprisingly little (as a percentage of marketing expenditure) between countries. It is growing especially fast in the United Kingdom, United States, and China, and more slowly in France and Japan. The fastest-growing IM activities are permission e-mail and online promotions/incentives. Other IM activities include web advertising and sponsorship, marketing Web sites and extranets, and new media such as wireless and iDTV.

Bezjian-Avery and Alexandra Miranda[56] in their work on cognitive processing of Interactive Marketing tested several aspects of the theoretic framework in an experiment investigating the role of interactivity, search goals and cognitive processing styles in the effectiveness of interactive systems. In this experiment, three factors were manipulated: the degree of control over the order of the information, the type of goal, and the stimulus characteristics. Cognitive processing style was a measured factor. Results of the experiment reveal that interactivity reduced the time spent on the advertisements for targeted products and the intention to purchase those targeted products. Interactivity appeared to limit visual processing of information. It was also found that an interactive system organized around a person's active goals resulted in lower affect for the system advertisements than a system organized around more general concepts.

John, Jeannie Denise[57] studied customer-employee interaction during service encounters, and the impact of the relationships between customer personality traits and quality of the employee's service delivery on the customer's participation, satisfaction, and repurchase intentions.

Peltier, James W., Schibrowsky, John A., Schultz, Don E., and Davis, John[58] studied the use of "interactive psychographics" to develop cross-selling strategies. The study concluded that interactive psychographics can provide a process for identifying psychographic-based segments, profiling the segments, matching individuals to the resulting segments, and developing actionable relationship strategies that best match the psychological and purchasing needs of each customer. Evans. Martin, Wedande, Gamini., Ralston, Lisa and van T. Hul. Selma[59] focused on the exploration of consumer experience and attitudes towards online interaction within virtual communities.

Christian Gronroos[60] compares traditional marketing models with that of service marketing models, stating that the most important characteristic of services is the fact that services are processes, not things. A service firm has no products, only interactive processes. Whereas the consumption of physical products can be described as 'outcome consumption', the consumption of services can be characterized as 'process consumption'.

Cathy Parker and Philippa Ward[61] focused on customer-to-customer interaction between strangers. It begins by reviewing the literature in the field and establishes a number of roles that customers may play while participating in this type of interaction.

Sally Kernbach and Nicola S. Schutte[62] in their study seek to examine whether higher emotional intelligence displayed by service providers leads to greater customer satisfaction. A community sample of 150 participants viewed video clips depicting a service provider displaying three different levels of emotional intelligence in high or low service difficulty transactions. Higher emotional intelligence displayed by the service provider led to greater reported satisfaction with the service transaction. Further, there was an interaction between emotional intelligence of the service provider and transaction difficulty. In the low transaction difficulty condition there was progressively more satisfaction at each higher level of emotional intelligence of the service provider. In the high transaction difficulty condition, there was low satisfaction in the low service provider emotional intelligence condition, but no significant difference in satisfaction between the high and medium levels of service provider emotional intelligence. A limitation of the research is that the study's experimental design sacrificed some external generalizability in order to maintain internal validity and obtain more definite information regarding the causal effects of service provider's emotional intelligence on customer satisfaction.

Mary Jo Bitner[63] in her work presented a typology of service organizations and a conceptual framework is advanced for exploring the impact of physical surroundings on the behaviors of both customers and employees. The ability of the physical surroundings to facilitate achievement of organizational as well as marketing goals is explored. By examining the multiple strategic roles that physical surroundings can exert in service organizations, the researcher highlights key managerial and research implications.

Joa˜o F. Proenc¸ and Luý´s M. de Castro[64] focused in their study on the interaction processes and short-term behaviours and motives in long-term relationships between banks and their corporate clients. The study highlighted the nature of business banking relationships, instability and stress therein, and suggests factors that can generate or intensify that instability. Short-term irregularities and stress are found to arise in the context of relationships' longer-term continuity and stability. The irregularities found were endogenous to the relationships and originated from one of the actors or from the transaction. Some instability was found associated with clients keeping a portfolio of banking relationships. The study provides a framework for corporate managers and bankers alike to better understand the process of banking relationships. It highlights some factors that should be monitored as they impact on buying behaviour and on the interplay between banks and firms. The study highlights some "stress" factors that can impact on buying behaviour and on the interplay between banks and firms, providing a new insight about the instability of business relationships in the banking business.

Peter Kangis and Vassilis Voukelatos[65] find that quality expectations and evaluation of services received were marginally higher in the private sector than in the public sector in most of the dimensions measured; the relative importance attached to each quality attribute was, however, of a similar profile for the two sectors. The perception of the profile of services received was, however, different between sectors, thus suggesting that they did deliver a different quality of service.

Mary Jo Bitner, Bernard H. Booms and Lois A. Mohr[66] identified that in service settings, customer satisfaction is often influenced by the quality of the interpersonal interaction between the customer and the contact employee. This study explores the sources in service encounters from the contact employee's point of view.

Charalambos Spathis, Eugenia Petridou, and Niki Glaveli[67] analysed the service quality of Greek banks on the basis of their customers' perceptions, and studied how gender differences affect customer's perceptions of service quality dimensions such as effectiveness and assurance, access, price, tangibles, service portfolio, and reliability. The results of an empirical study of 1,260 customers of Greek banks support the hypothesis that gender affects service quality perceptions and the relative importance attached to various banking service quality dimensions. This study provides important information for bank managers to use in developing operational, human resource, and marketing strategies, and in targeting those strategies in terms of the gender differences in quality perceptions among their customers.

2.3 STUDIES ON CUSTOMER-EMPLOYEE RELATIONSHIPS

Sunil Gupta, Donald R. Lehmann[68] in their work on "Consumers as assets" states that customers are important intangible assets of a firm that should be valued and managed. Edward C. Malthouse, Robert C. Blattberg[69] in their work on "Relationship Marketing" stated that relationship marketing assumes that firms can be more profitable if they identify the most profitable customers and invest disproportionate marketing resources in them. While intuitive, such strategies presume that a firm can accurately predict the future profitability of customers.

Jonathon R.B. Halbesleben, and M. Ronald Buckley[70] in their study on 'Managing Customers as Employees of the Firm: New Challenges for Human Resources Management', discussed the role customers play as human resources in service-based organizations. Dwayne D. Gremler, Mary Jo Bitner and Kenneth R. Evans[71] in their research work 'The Internal Service Encounter', found that the internal customer's (i.e., employee's) satisfaction with a service firm can be significantly influenced by service encounters experienced with internal service providers.

Lance A. Bettencourt and Kevin Gwinner[72] emphasized that customizing the delivery of service on the frontline is a key to customer satisfaction. The findings from an exploratory qualitative study provide illustrative support for the literature based propositions.

Mahn Hee Yoon, Jai Hyun Seo, and Tae Seog Yoon[73] in their study examined several sources of support for contact employees in service encounters. These sources of support, including organization support, supervisory support, and customer's participation, are proposed to affect the attitudes and behaviors of employees, and consequently affect customer's perceptions of employees' service quality. This study, which combines perceptions from customers and their contact employees, shows that these sources of support for employees contribute significantly to job satisfaction and employee service quality, while perceived organizational support and customer participation affect service effort. Also, the empirical results indicate that both employee service effort and job satisfaction play strong, central roles in determining customers' perceptions of employee service quality. They were found to be effective mediators linking employees' cognitive appraisal of various sources of support to service quality.

Karen Maru File, Judith L. Mack, and Russ Alan Prince[74] in their research study opined that the service providers worldwide are seeking competitive advantage through the creation of long-standing customer relationships. Current theory holds that interactive marketing contributes most to customer satisfaction which, in turn, provides customer motivation for long-term relationships. However, relatively little attention has been devoted to the specific provider and customer behaviors that constitute interactive marketing. The study explores the frequency and significance of 15 specific interactive marketing behaviors among 396 Chief Executive Officers (CEO) and clients of commercial loan services in five countries. Results of such study demonstrate that higher levels of interaction are associated with higher levels of satisfaction.

Karen Maru File, Ben B. Judd, and Russ Alan Prince[75] in their work, considered interactive marketing behaviours which result in the broadest word-of-mouth or the largest volume of new client referrals. The study concludes that the intensity and variety of client participation during the service delivery process is predictive of positive word-of-mouth and referrals.

Josée Bloemer and Gaby Odekerken-Schröder[76] in their study aims to investigate the impact of employee relationship proneness (RP) on the three different types of attitudinal loyalty (affective, calculative, and normative commitment (NC)) and relate these different types of attitudinal loyalty to employee loyalty behaviors in terms of word-of-mouth, intention to stay (ITS), benefit insensitivity (BI), and complaining (COM). An empirical research among 199 employees of a bank was conducted to test the hypothesized model. Structural equation modeling results reveal that employee RP is a strong antecedent of affective and NC. Affective commitment plays a pivotal role in creating all positive loyalty behaviours of employees, whereas NC only supports ITS and BI while it has a negative impact on COM. Calculative commitment has a negative impact on BI and COM. The main practical implication of the study is that banks should incorporate RP when assessing potential employees. These relationship prone employees are most likely to exhibit affective and NC, which can be considered as the foundation of employees' loyalty behaviours.

Jo Ann M. Duffy, John M. Miller and James B. Bexley[77] in their study, aims to examine the link between satisfaction and various recovery strategies. A total of 310 bank customers responded to a survey addressing customer demographics, levels of satisfaction, types of recovery strategies, and service recovery employees. The findings show no significant difference in recovery strategies or satisfaction by customer age, gender, or tenure with bank. However, the degree of customer satisfaction was strongly influenced by the type of recovery strategy used by the bank. The results indicate that recovery efforts are best directed toward empathic listening and fixing the problem rather than apologizing or making atonement.

Skaggs, Bruce C., and Huffman, Tammy Ross[78] in their study stated that the strategies of service firms affect the uncertainty they encounter in their dealings with customers. This strategically induced uncertainty then becomes the mechanism by which service firms organize their production processes. In a study of 234 service firms representing 96 different industries, the researchers found strong support for relationships between the organizations' strategies and the level of complexity in their production processes.

Van Dolen, Willemijn., De Ruyter, Ko and Lemmink, Jos[79] examined the effect of customer emotions and contact employee performance in creating encounter and relationship satisfaction. The performance of the contact employee has been analysed from an interactive perspective by specifying the employee performance into employee-specific and interaction-induced behaviors, using a multilevel approach.

McColl-Kennedy, Janet R., Daus, Catherine S. and Sparks, Beverley A.[80] in their study on role of gender in reaction to service failures and recovery found that male and female consumers place different emphasis on elements of the service recovery process. Perceptions were influenced by gender of the service provider and by a match of customer and service provider gender.

Bettencourt, Lance A., and Brown, Stephen W.[81] studied the positive relationships between contact employee fairness perceptions, their pro-social service behaviors (customer service behaviors and cooperation with fellow employees) and job satisfaction.

Jap, Sandy D., Manolis, Chris and Weitz, Barton A.[82] studied relationship marketing during interactions between buyers and sellers involved in ongoing relationships with varying degrees of relationship quality. Seven buyer-seller encounters (large US grocery chain) were observed and analyzed. Before this, in-depth interviews were conducted with the buyers to determine their perceived quality of the relationships. These interviews suggested that trust, affective and manifest conflict, disengagement, and expectations of continuity are the most often distinguished levels of relationship quality. Qualitative and empirically based evidence suggested that there were systematic behavioral differences across the interactions.

Christine Sanes[83] in their work on 'Employee impact on service delivery' stated that the customers expect suppliers to deliver a high standard of service before and after purchase, and in a competitive market this can mean the difference between success and failure. The study examines the role of employees in providing customer satisfaction, and ways in which management can support and motivate them. In conclusion, the researcher offers suggestions for improving quality in service delivery process.

Paolo Guenzi and Ottavia Pelloni[84] in their study on 'the impact of interpersonal relationships on customer satisfaction and loyalty to the service provider explores the impact of interpersonal relationships (both with a firm employee and with another customer) on customer satisfaction and loyalty towards the firm. Based on a review of different streams of research, the study develops and empirically tests an original multi-level and multi-subject model. The findings show that customer-to-employee and customer-to-customer relationships contribute differently to the development of customer loyalty

Ronald J. Burke, Jim Graham and Frank Smith[85] in their study, examined the correlations between measures of employee satisfaction and customer satisfaction before and after a major process reengineering initiative. Data were collected in 130 branches of a large financial services organization using employee and customer surveys. Scores on some employee satisfaction factors were predictive of customer satisfaction at both time periods. Other employee satisfaction factors were found to have a stronger relationship with customer satisfaction in one period but not both.

Lance A. Bettencourt and Kevin Gwinner[86] in their work on the 'Customization of the service experience: the role of the frontline employee' and discussed various interpersonal adaptive behavior approaches that may be used by frontline employees in customizing the service experience. This study has developed several propositions concerning employee customization in the service encounter. The study offers recommendations for managers interested in employee customization on the frontline.

Mahn Hee Yoon, Sharon E. Beatty and Jaebeom Suh[87] examined several work climate variables and their impact on service quality. While there exists a variety of work climates relevant to contact employees during service encounters, this study investigates two components for successful implementation of internal marketing, service climate and supportive management. Both climate variables are proposed to affect the attitudes and behaviors of employees, and consequently affect customers' perceptions of employees' service performance. This study, which combines perceptions from customers and their contact employees, shows that both climate variables contribute directly to job satisfaction and work effort, and indirectly impact on customers' perceptions of employee service quality. The empirical results indicate that in addition to job satisfaction, employees' work effort also plays a strong, central role in determining customers' perceptions of employee service quality.

Steve Sizoo, Richard Plank, Wilfried Iskat and Hendrick Serrie[88] in their study measured the effect of intercultural sensitivity on the cross–cultural performance of service employees. The results indicate that employees with high intercultural sensitivity scored significantly (p, 0:05) higher than employees with low intercultural sensitivity in terms of service attentiveness, revenue contribution, interpersonal skills, job satisfaction, and social satisfaction as they relate to cross-cultural encounters. There was no significant difference in scores for motivation-to-work and perceptions of primary rewards (compensation, recognition, etc.). Results suggest that service firms would benefit from testing for and provide training in intercultural sensitivity for employees involved in cross-cultural service encounters.

Neeru Malhotra and Avinandan Mukherjee[89] tested the relationships organizational commitment and job satisfaction have with service quality of customer-contact employees. A study comprising 342 employees was conducted in four telephone call centres of a major UK retail bank. The study further investigates on how different forms of organizational commitment and job satisfaction influence the service quality delivered by contact employees. Findings indicate that job satisfaction and organisational commitment of employees have a significant impact on service quality delivered. The affective component of commitment was found to be more important than job satisfaction in determining service quality of customer-contact employees.

Feremy F. Sierra and Shaun McQuitty[90] opined that the social exchanges can create a sense of shared responsibility to service settings, and predict that inseparability produces customer perceptions of shared responsibility for service outcomes, resulting in greater emotions. When emotions are positive, there should be increased loyalty to the service provider. A structural equation model evaluated the strength of relationships between these constructs. Support was found for the predicted relationships between inseparability and shared responsibility, shared responsibility and emotions, and emotions and service loyalty. They suggested that the service employee training programs should emphasize the customer's role in the service experience to increase perceptions of shared responsibility and to create a positive emotional experience for customers.

Michael D. Hartline, and O.C. Ferrell[91] have developed and tested a model of service employee management that examines constructs simultaneously across three interfaces of the service delivery process: manager-employee, employee-role, and employee-customer. The researchers examined the attitudinal and behavioural responses of customer-contact employees that can influence customers' perceptions of service quality, the relationships among these responses, and three formal managerial control mechanisms. The findings indicate that managers who are committed to service quality are more likely to empower their employees and use behavior-based evaluation. However, the use of empowerment has both positive and negative consequences in the management of contact employees. Some of the negative consequences are mitigated by the positive effects of behavior-based employee evaluation. To increase customers' perceptions of service quality, managers must increase employees' self-efficacy and job satisfaction, and reduce employees' role conflict and ambiguity. Implications for the management of customer-contact service employees and directions for further research are discussed.

Albert Caruana, and Peter Calleya[92] examined internal processes associated with delivering customer satisfaction focusing particularly on the relationship between the nature and extent of internal marketing and its outcome in terms of the level of organizational commitment on the part of employees. The findings of the study confirm a significant relationship between internal marketing and organizational commitment. The relationship of internal marketing is most significant with the effective dimension of organisational commitment.

G.S. Sureshchandar, Chandrasekharan Rajendran, and R.N. Anantharaman[93] studied the relationship between service quality and customer satisfaction. The study views customer satisfaction as a multi dimensional construct just as service quality and states that customer satisfaction should be operationalized. Based on this approach, the link between service quality and customer satisfaction has been investigated. About 150 customers were randomly selected and data was collected using the personal contact approach. The results have indicated that the two constructs are indeed independent but are closely related, implying that an increase in one is likely to lead to an increase in another.

Mary Jo Bitner, Bernard H. Booms, and Mary Stanfield Tetreault[94] in their research work collected 700 incidents from customers of airlines, hotels, and restaurants. The incidents were categorized to isolate the particular events and related behaviors of contact employees that cause customers to distinguish very satisfactory service encounters from very dissatisfactory ones. Key implications for managers and researchers are highlighted.

Beth G. Chung-Harrera, Nadav Goldschmidt, and K. Doug Hoffman[95] in their study examined perceptual similarities and differences between customers and employees in terms of critical service incidents. Specifically, the study explored the extent to which customers and employees were similar or different in summary perceptions of service failures and recovery, the attributions made by the two perspectives in terms of causes for failures and recovery efforts, and whether each perspective believed that age, gender or race contributed to service failures or recovery. The critical incidents technique was used to collect 1,512 customer-reported incidents and 390 employee-reported incidents. Results of the study revealed that customers and employees had both similar and different views depending on the ultimate outcome of the encounter. Overall, customers and employees were fairly similar in their perceptions regarding failures that ultimately resulted in a good recovery effort.

Christo Boshoff, and Janie Allen[96] are of the opinion that some organisational factors can have impact on a service firm's ability to return dissatisfied customers to a state of satisfaction through service recovery. The results of their study revealed that organisational commitment exerts a strong positive influence on the service recovery performance of frontline staff as does empowerment and rewarding them for service excellence. When frontline staff members are performing service recovery effectively, they are less likely to resign and report higher levels of job satisfaction.

2.4 SUMMARY

The review of literature on banking services, interactive marketing with special reference to banking sector and customer relationships management issues in banking sector reveals that there is a research gap in identifying issues, problems and methodologies related to interactive marketing of banking services. There is no comprehensive study covering all the details of services marketing particularly the interactive marketing. Considering the growing importance of interactive marketing in the banking sector to gain competitive advantage in serving the customers, there is a need to takeup a comprehensive study on interactive marketing.

2.5 REFERENCES

1. Bloch-Ernest, 'Research in Investment Banking: Some Prerequisites for Developing a Marketing Strategy', New York University, (1987): 16.
2. Rashmi Arya, *'Women in Public Sector Special Reference to Banking Industry'*, Manak Publications Pvt. Ltd., Delhi, (1990).
3. Bhatt-Atual, *'Bank Marketing', Market Research and Indian Banks,* Prajnan, (1991): 45.
4. Golan – Amos, 'A multivariate stochastic theory of size distribution of firms with empirical evidence', London, (1994): 46.
5. Kulshreshtha K., *'Emerging Scenario in Banking and Finance'*, R.B.S.A. Publishers, Jaipur, (1995).
6. Sharma K. Ramakrishna, *'Financial Sector Reforms in India'*, Abhigyan, (1996): 19-23.
7. Bilgrami S.A.R., *'Growth of Public Sector Banks'*, Deep and Deep Publications, New Delhi, (1996).
8. Meir Kohn, *'Financial Institutes of Markets'*, Tata McGraw-Hill, New Delhi, (1996).
9. Peperrmans –Ronals, Verleye – Gino, and Vaw Cappellen – Sarah Wall, 'Banking Innovativeness and Computer Attitudes – 25-40 year old ATM – Users on the spot', *Journal of Economic – Psychology*, (1996): 731-48.
10. Shollapur, M.R., 'Performance Appraisal of Banks under service area approach – A Comparative study', *Maharastra Co-operative Quarterly,* (1997): 34-39.
11. Jain – Alok-Kumar, 'Marketing Challenges for Commercial Banks in India', (1997).
12. Haldipur. Rajesh, 'The new face of retail banking', *Indian Management*, (1998): 19-2.
13. Avadhani, V.A., *'Marketing of Financial Services'*, Himalaya Publishing House, Mumbai, (1999).

14. Bhole, L.M., *'Financial Institutions and Markets'*, Tata McGraw-Hill, New Delhi, (1999).
15. Chandra Sekhar, A.R., 'Market share of Public Sector Banks in post reform period', *Indian Journal of Commerce*, New Delhi, (1999).
16. Sharma, R.D., 'Evaluation of Inbuilt Marketing Orientation in Indian Rural Banking', (2000): 33-38.
17. Ganesan G., 'Commercial Banking beyond 2000', *Kisan World*, (2000): 23-24.
18. Singh Rajender Kumar, 'Costing in a Designated Banking Environment', *The Management Accountant*, Kolkata, (2001): 352-56.
19. Barbara R. Lewis, and Sotiris Spyrakopoulos, 'Service Failures and Recovery in Retail Banking: The Customers' Perspective', *International Journal of Bank Marketing;* Vol.19, No.1, (2001).
20. Juan Carlos Fandos Roig, Javier Sanchez Garcia, Miguel Angel Moliner Tena and Jaume Llorens Monzonis, 'Customer Perceived Value in Banking Services', *Journal of Bank Marketing,* Vol.24, No.5, (2006): 283.
21. Raphaël K. Akamavi, 'Re-engineering Service Quality Process Mapping: e-Banking Process', *International Journal of Bank Marketing,* Vol.23, No.1, (2005): 53.
22. Babu P. George, and Purva G. Hegde, 'Employee Attitude towards Customers and Customer Care Challenges in Banks', *International Journal of Bank Marketing*, Vol.22, No.6, (2004): 406.
23. Avinandan Mukherjee, Prithwiraj Nath, and Manabendra Nath Pal, 'Performance Benchmarking and Strategic Homogeneity of Indian Banks', *International Journal of Bank Marketing,* Vol.20, No.3, (June 2002): 122 – 139.
24. Philip Megicks, Atul Mishra, and Jonathan Lean, 'Enhancing Microfinance Outreach through Market-Oriented New Service Development in Indian Regional Rural Banks', *International Journal of Bank Marketing,* Vol.23, No.1, (January 2005): 107 – 125.
25. G.S. Sureshchandar, Chandrasekharan Rajendran, and R.N. Anantharaman, 'Customer Perceptions of Service Quality in the Banking Sector of a Developing Economy: A Critical Analysis', *International Journal of Bank Marketing,* Vol.21, No.5, (October 2003): 233 – 242.
26. Satyabhusan Dash, Ed Bruning and Kalyan Ku Guin, 'The Moderating Effect of Power Distance on Perceived Interdependence and Relationship Quality in Commercial Banking: A Cross-Cultural Comparison', *International Journal of Bank Marketing,* Vol.24, No.5, (2006): 307 – 326.
27. Peter Jones, 'The Changing Use of Old Bank Premises', *Property Management*, Vol.14, No.3, (September 1996): 27 – 30.
28. Jamal, Ahmad, 'Retail Banking and Customer Behaviour: A Study of Self Concept, Satisfaction and Technology Usage', *The International Review of Retail, Distribution and Consumer Research,* Vol.14, No.3, (July 2004): 357-379.

29. Craig C. Julian and B. Ramaseshan, 'The Role of Customer-contact Personnel in the Marketing of a Retail Bank's Service', *International Journal of Retail & Distribution Management*, Vol.22, No.5, (1994): 29-34.

30. Terrence Levesque and Gordon H.G. McDougall, 'Determinants of customer satisfaction in retail banking', *International Journal of Bank Marketing*, Vol.14, No.7, (1996): 12-20.

31. Abdullah Aldlaigan Saudi Arabia, and Francis Buttle, 'Beyond satisfaction: customer attachment to retail banks', *International Journal of Bank Marketing*, Vol.23, No.4, (2005): 349-359.

32. Benjamin Schneider, John J. Parkington and Virginia M. Buxton, 'Employee and Customer Perceptions of Service in Banks', *Administrative Science Quarterly*, Vol.25, No.2, (1980): 252-267.

33. Yahya Melhem and Irbid, Jordan, 'The antecedents of customer-contact employees' empowerment', *Employee Relations*, Vol.26, No.1, (2004): 72-93.

34. Ding Hooi Ting, 'Service quality and satisfaction perceptions: curvilinear and interaction effect', *International Journal of Bank Marketing*, Vol.22, No.6, (2004): 407-420.

35. G.S. Sureshchandra, Chandrasekharan Rajendran, R.N. Anantharaman and T.J. Kamalanabhan, 'Management's perception of total quality service in the banking sector of developing economy – a critical analysis', *International Journal of Bank Marketing*, Vol.20, No.4, (2002): 181-196.

36. Madhukar G. Angur, Rajan Nataraajan and John S. Jahera Jr., 'Service quality in the banking industry: an assessment in a developing economy', *International Journal of Bank Marketing*, Vol.17, No.3, (1999): 116-123.

37. Avinandan Mukherjee and Prithwiraj Nath, 'A model of trust in online relationship banking', *International Journal of Bank Marketing*, Vol.21, No.1, (2003): 5-15.

38. Mark Durkin, Barry Howcroft, Aodheen O'Donnell and Danielle McCartan-Quinn, 'Retail bank customer preferences: personal and remote interactions', *International Journal of Retail & Distribution Management*, Vol.31, No.4, (2003): 177-189.

39. Kaisa Snellman and Tiina Vihtkari, 'Customer complaining behavior in technology-based service encounters', *International Journal of Service Industry Management*, Vol.14, No.2, (2003): 217-231.

40. Abhiman Das and Saibal Ghosh, 'Financial deregulation and efficiency: An empirical analysis of Indian Banks during the post reform period', *Review of Financial Economics*, Vol.15, (2006): 193-221.

41. Mohapatra, 'Training and Human Resource Development', *Journal of Management Development*, Vol.17, No.45, 46, 47 & 48, (Jan.-Dec. 1987):.61-69.

42. Merchant, R.Y., 'HRD Plan for State Bank of India', *National Institute of Bank Management*, Pune (1980):.2-3 and 23.

43. Neelu Rohmetra., 'Human Resource Development in Commercial Banks in India', *IJIR*, Vol.34, No.3, (January 1999): 380-382.

44. Chalam, G.V and Srinivas, L., 'Genderwise Perceptions and Attitudes on HRD Climate in Indian Banking Sector', *The Indian Journal of Commerce*, Vol.58, No.4, (Oct. – Dec. 2005): 62-71.

45. Kulwant Singh Pathania., 'HRD Programme and Practice in Cooperative Banks', *The Indian Journal of Commerce*, Vol.L, No.192, Part III, (September 1997): 8-13.

46. Sambre Neena., 'A Sociological Study of Alienation among Bank Employees', *SNDT University*, Mumbai, (1980): 415-416.

47. Rajendran, N., 'HRD Practices in Banking Industry', *Co-operative Perspectives*, Vol.38, (Oct.-Dec. 2003).

48. Shivaji, K., 'Human Resource Development in Co-operative Banks', *Indian Co-operative Review*, (April 1994): 333-334.

49. Pathak. R.D., 'Job involvement and need satisfaction of bank officers in India', *Vikalpa*, Vol.8, No.4, (1983).

50. Swain and Srinivas, 'A study on work motivation of branch managers in State Bank of India', Pune, *National Institute of Bank Management*, (1993).

51. Vijayakumar, V.S.R., 'Perceived management styles and job satisfaction of executives of private sectors banks', *Indian Journal of Applied Psychology*, Vol.33, No.2, (July 1996): 86-93.

52. Stephan H. Haeckel, 'About the Nature and Future of Interactive Marketing', *Journal of Interactive Marketing*, Vol.12, No.1, (1998): 63-71.

53. Ross D. Petty, 'Interactive Marketing and the Law: The Future Rise of Unfairness', *Journal of Interactive Marketing*, Vol.12, No.3, (1998): 21-31.

54. Dawn Lacobucci, "Interactive Marketing and the Meganet: Networks of Networks', http://www3.interscience.wiley.com/cgi-bin/, dt. 9-10-2009.

55. Patrick Barwise and John U. Farley , 'The State of Interactive Marketing in Seven Countries: Interactive Marketing Comes of Age', www3.interscience.wiley.com, dt. 10-10-2009.

56. Bezjian-Avery and Alexandra Miranda, 'Cognitive Processing of Interactive Marketing', Dissertation Abstracts International Section A: *Humanities & Social Sciences*, 58(4-A), (October 1997): 1370.

57. John, Jeannie Denise, 'The Effects of Employee Service Quality Provision and Customer Personality Traits on Customer Participation, Satisfaction, and Repurchase Intentions', Dissertation Abstracts International Section A: *Humanities & Social Sciences*, 65(7-A), (No Month Specified, 2005): 2684.

58. Peltier, James W., Schibrowsky, John A., Schultz, Don E. and Davis, John, 'Interactive Psychographics: Cross-Selling in the Banking Industry', *Journal of Advertising Research*, Vol.42, No.2, (Mar.-Apr. 2002): 7-22.

59. Evans, Martin; Wedande, Gamini; Ralston, Lisa; Van T Hul, Selma, 'Consumer Interaction in the Virtual Era: Some Qualitative Insights', *Qualitative Market Research: An International Journal*, 4(3), (2001): 150-159.

60. Christian Gronroos, 'The perceived service quality concept – a mistake?' *Managing Service Quality*, Vol.11, No.3, (2001): 150-152.

61. Cathy Parker and Philippa Ward, 'An analysis of role adoptions and scripts during customer-to-customer encounters', *European Journal of Marketing*, Vol.34, No.3/4, (2000): 341-358.

62. Sally Kernbach and Nicola S. Schutte, 'Impact of service provider emotional intelligence on customer satisfaction', *Journal of Services Marketing*, Vol.19, No.7, (2005): 438-444.

63. Mary Jo Bitner, 'Servicescapes: The Impact of Physical Surroundings on Customers and Employees', *Journal of Marketing*, Vol.56, (1992): 57-71.

64. Joa˜o F. Proenc¸a and Luý´s M. de Castro, '"Stress" in business relationships: a study on corporate bank services', *International Journal of Bank Marketing*, Vol.23, No.7, (2005): 527-541.

65. Peter Kangis and Vassilis Voukelatos, 'Private and public banks: a comparison of customer expectations and perceptions', *International Journal of Bank Marketing*, Vol.15, No.7, (1997): 279-287.

66. Mary Jo Bitner, Bernard H. Booms, & Lois A. Mohr, 'Critical Service encounters: The Employee's Viewpoint', *Journal of Marketing*, Vol.58, (1994): 95-106.

67. Charalambos Spathis, Eugenia Petridou and Niki Glaveli, 'Managing service quality in banks: customers' gender effects', *Managing Service Quality*, Vol.14, No.1, (2004): 90-102.

68. Sunil Gupta, Donald R. Lehmann, 'Consumers as assets', *Journal of Interactive Marketing*, Vol.17, No.1, (2003): 9-24.

69. Edward C. Malthouse , Robert C. Blattberg, 'Relationship Marketing', *Journal of Interactive Marketing*, Vol.19, No.1, (2005): 2-16.

70. Jonathon R.B. Halbesleben, M. Ronald Buckley, 'Managing Customers as Employees of the Firm: New Challenges for Human Resources Management', *Personnel Review*, Vol.33, No.3, (2004).

71. Dwayne D. Gremler, Mary Jo Bitner, and Kenneth R. Evans, 'The Internal Service Encounter', *International Journal of Service Industry Management*, Vol.5, No.2, (1994).

72. Lance A. Bettencourt, and Kevin Gwinner, 'Customization of the Service Experience: The Role of the Frontline Employee', *International Journal of Service Industry Management;* Vol.7, No.2, (1996).

73. Mahn Hee Yoon, Jai Hyun Seo and Tae Seog Yoon, 'Effects of Contact Employee Supports on Critical Employee Responses and Customer Service Evaluation', Journal of Services Marketing; Vol.18, No.5, (2004).

74. Karen Maru File, Judith L.Mack, and Russ Alan Prince, 'The Effect of Interactive Marketing on Commercial Customer Satisfaction in International Financial Markets', *Journal of Business & Industrial Marketing*, Vol.10, No.2, (May 1995), 69 – 75.

75. Karen Maru File, Ben B. Judd, Russ Alan Prince, 'Interactive Marketing: The Influence of Participation on Positive Word-of-Mouth and Referrals', *Journal of Services Marketing*, Vol.6, No.4, (1992).

76. Josée Bloemer, Gaby Odekerken-Schröder, 'The role of Employee Relationship Proneness in Creating Employee Loyalty', *International Journal of Bank Marketing*, Vol.24, No.4, (2006): 264.

77. Jo Ann M. Duffy, John M. Miller, and James B. Bexley, 'Banking Customers' Varied Reactions to Service Recovery Strategies', *Journal of Bank Marketing,* Vol.24, No.2, (2006): 132.

78. Skaggs, Bruce C. and Huffman, Tammy Ross, 'A Customer Interaction Approach to Strategy and Production Complexity Alignment in Service Firms', *Academy of Management Journal*, Vol.46, No.6, (December 2003): 775-786.

79. Van Dolen, Willemijn; de Ruyter, Ko and Lemmink, Jos, "An Empirical Assessment of the Influence of Customer Emotions and Contact Employee Performance on Encounter and Relationship Satisfaction", *Journal of Business Research*, Vol.57, No.4, (April 2004): 437-444.

80. McColl-Kennedy, Janet R., Daus, Catherine S., Sparks, Beverley A., 'The Role of Gender in Reactions to Service Failure and Recovery', *Journal of Service Research*, 6 (1), (August 2003): 66-82.

81. Bettencourt, Lance A.; Brown, Stephen W., 'Contact Employees: Relationships among workplace fairness, job satisfaction, and Pro-social service behaviors', *Journal of Retailing*, 73(1), (September 1997): 39-61.

82. Jap, Sandy D., Manolis, Chris., Weitz, Barton A., 'Relationship quality and buyer-seller interactions in channels of distribution', *Journal of Business Research*, 46(3), (November1999): 303-313.

83. Christine Sanes, 'Employee impact on service delivery', *Management Development Review*, Vol.9, No.2, (1996): 15-20.

84. Paolo Guenzi and Ottavia Pelloni, 'The impact of interpersonal relationships on customer satisfaction and loyalty to the service provider', *International Journal of Service Industry Management*, Vol.15, No.4, (2004): 365-384.

85. Ronald J. Burke, Jim Graham and Frank Smith, 'Effects of reengineering on the employee satisfaction-customer satisfaction relationship', *The TQM Magazine*, Vol.17, No.4, (2005): 358-363.

86. Lance A. Bettencourt and Kevin Gwinner, 'Customization of the service experience: the role of the frontline employee', *International Journal of Service Industry Management*, Vol.7, No.2, (1996): 3-20.

87. Mahn Hee Yoon, Sharon E. Beatty and Jaebeom Suh, 'The effect of work climate on critical employee and customer outcomes: An employee-level analysis', *International Journal of Service Industry Management*, Vol.12, No.5, (2001): 500-521.

88. Steve Sizoo, Richard Plank, Wilfried Iskat and Hendrick Serrie, 'The effect of intercultural sensitivity on employee performance in cross-cultural service encounters', *Journal of Services Marketing*, Vol.19, No.4, (2005): 245-255.
89. Neeru Malhotra and Avinandan Mukherjee, 'The relative influence of organizational commitment and job satisfaction on service quality of customer-contact employees in banking call centres', *Journal of Services Marketing*, Vol.18, No.3, (2004): 162-174.
90. Feremy F. Sierra and Shaun McQuitty, 'Service providers and customers: social exchange theory and service loyalty', *Journal of Services Marketing*, Vol.19, No.6, (2005): 392-400.
91. Michael D. Hartline and O.C. Ferrell, 'The Management of Customer-Contact Service Employees: An Empirical Investigation', *Journal of Marketing*, Vol.60, (1996): 52-70.
92. Albert Caruana and Peter Calleya, 'The effect of internal marketing on organizational commitment among retail bank mangers', *International Journal of Bank Marketing*, Vol.16, No.3, (1998): 108-116.
93. G.S. Sureshchandar, Chandrasekharan Rajendran and R.N. Anantharaman, 'The relationship between service quality and customer satisfaction – a factor specific approach', *Journal of Services Marketing*, Vol.16, No.4, (2002): 363-379.
94. Mary Jo Bitner, Bernard H. Booms, and Mary Stanfield Tetreault, 'The Service Encounter: diagnosing favorable and unfavorable incidents', *Journal of Marketing*, Vol.54, (1990): 71-84.
95. Beth G. Chung-Harrera, Nadav Goldschmidt and K. Doug Hoffman, 'Customer and employee views of critical service incidents', *Journal of Services Marketing*, Vol.18, No.4, (2004): 241-254.
96. Christo Boshoff and Janine Allen, 'The influence of selected antecedents on frontline staff's perceptions of service recovery performance', *International Journal of Service Industry Management*, Vol.11, No.1, (2000): 63-90.

Chapter 3 RESEARCH DESIGN

The banking scene in India changed completely after independence. The banking system in the country recorded rapid progress over the years. The change process began with the passing of the Banking Regulation Act in 1949. The Act is considered as a landmark in the history of commercial banking in India. It was passed with the object of consolidating and regulating the banking system in India. For the first time, the Act introduced a system of regulation for banks. It prohibited the opening of new branches with out the permission of the Reserve Bank of India. The major reasons for the progress of Indian banking sector are planned economic growth, increase in money supply, growth of banking habit, control and guidance by the Reserve Bank of India and the nationalization of banks. A variety of specialized institutions have been set up in the country to cater to the specific needs of industry, agriculture and foreign trade.

State Bank of India is the biggest Public Sector Bank in the country. The origins of the State Bank of India date back to 1806, when the Bank of Calcutta (Later called the Bank of Bengal) was established. In 1921, the Bank of Bengal and two other presidency banks (Bank of Madras and Bank of Bombay) were amalgamated to form the Imperial Bank of India. In 1955, the controlling interests of the Imperial Bank of India were acquired by the Reserve Bank of India and the State Bank was created by an Act of Parliament to succeed the Imperial Bank of India. Over the years, the bank has expanded rapidly and today commands one fifth of the Indian Banking business. Under the State Bank of India (subsidiary banks) Act 1959, the State Bank of India took over eight former state associated banks as its subsidiaries. As a result of merger of two of these subsidiaries got merged with each other and remaining seven banks remained subsidiaries of the State Bank of India. These are State Bank of Bikaner and Jaipur, State Bank of Indore, State Bank of Mysore, State Bank of Patiala, State Bank of Saurashtra, State Bank of Travancore and State Bank of Hyderabad. At present, the State Bank of Group comprising State Bank of India, seven associates, banking subsidiaries and eight non-banking subsidiaries have resulted in a super market. The SBI group has diversified their activities into insurance, credit cards, factoring leasing, mutual funds, merchant banking, home finance, securities trading, etc.

According to Business Today-KPMG Survey of Best Banks in the country 2009, State Bank of India occupies 11th position in the overall performance of the bank in the year 2009. A comparative analysis of the size of the bank among the top 10 rated banks in the survey reveals that the State Bank of India occupy 1st position in terms of Deposits, Operating Profit and the size of the balance sheet (Table 3.1). The gap between the first and the second ranked bank is significance in terms of Deposits, Operating Profits as well as the size of the Balance Sheet. In terms of growth of the banks, the position of State Bank of India is not very impressive when compared to the Top 10 ranked banks.

State Bank of India is the leading commercial bank in India. The bank is in the public sector carrying the responsibility of promoting the business in the interest and for well-being of the society. The changing competitive scenario, particularly after the liberalization policies initiated in the economy in 1991, forcing the public sector banks to reorient themselves towards providing satisfaction to the customers. Owing to the dominance in the market as the public sector bank, the State Bank of India over the years has not given enough focus to the customers of the bank. The business was seller-oriented owing to the absence of strong competition and the banks are of equal size in network. The situation is fast changing due to the rapid pace of change in technology and the entry and successful operations of private sector banks and foreign banks. The SBI has a need to face the challenges emerging in the environment with proper policy framework.

Table 3.1: Top 10 Best Banks in India (2009) and State Bank of India
(Balance Sheet size more than Rs.24,000 crore)

RANK	BANK	DEPOSITS (RS. CR.)	OPERATING PROFIT (RS. CR.)	BALANCE SHEET SIZE (RS. CR.)
1	Axis Bank	117374.11(10)	3724.88(11)	147722.05(10)
2	Bank of India	189708.48(5)	5456.80(4)	225501.76(5)
3	Punjab National Bank	209760.50(3)	5744.35(3)	246918.62(3)
4	Bank of Baroda	192396.95(4)	4305.01(7)	227406.73(4)
5	HDFC Bank	142811.58(7)	5178.96(6)	183270.77(7)
6	Indian Bank	72581.83(18)	2228.83(14)	84121.75(21)
7	Federal Bank	32198.19(34)	1259.77(24)	38850.87(33)
8	Corporation Bank	73983.91(17)	1796.61(16)	86905.81(20)
9	Union Bank of India	138702.83(8)	3082.00(12)	160975.51(9)
10	Citi Bank	51677.46(25)	5406.47(5)	105263.59(16)
11	State Bank of India	742073.13(1)	17915.22(1)	964432.09(1)

Source: India's Best Banks – The Business Today – KPMG Survey, Business Today, 13th December, 2009, Pp.88-89.

The competition in the banking sector is increasing day by day due to the aggressive business policies pursued by the private sector banks. Besides, mergers and acquisitions are taking place among various banks posing serious threat to the SBI. The Business Today and KPMG Survey of Indian Best Banks 2004 gave 36th Rank to State Bank of India indicating a steep fall from 19th position the bank enjoyed in the year 2003. In 2005, the bank has improved its position and secured 29th position. The position of the bank further improved in 2006 and the bank secured 17th rank. According to Business Today-KPMG Survey on India's Best Banks 2007, the bank fell back to 29th position. In 2009 the bank could reach to 11th position. These statistics show that the bank has not improved its position consistently. The State Bank of India though maintained its premier position in terms of deposits, profits and size of the balance sheet, it could not find any place in the top ten in terms of business growth, return on capital employed, net performing assets by net advances and capital adequacy. These indications are enough to establish the fact that serious problems are ahead for the bank unless it initiates reorganization process, to bring out high level of efficiency and customer centric focus.

The major differentiating parameter that distinguishes the new private sector banks in India from other banks in the system is the high level of service. Leveraging of their strengths and competencies – management, operational efficiency and flexibility superior product positioning and higher employee productivity skills – forms some of the key efficiency instruments of these new private sector banks. Such far-reaching changes are basically aimed at maintaining long-term profitability and strengthening the competitive edge of banks in conformity with transforming market realities. To survive and flourish in a global economy, business must respond to major trends reshaping markets. Hence, the dynamics of the underlying forces at work require a renewed thrust on Business Process Reengineering in banks to contribute to management and diversification of growth horizons by impacting on profitability and productivity.

3.1 NEED FOR THE STUDY

Interactive Marketing is the key element in the process of reengineering. Detailed study of the process factors is essential for redesigning. Besides incorporating state of art technologies that brings out drastic improvement of current performance in cost, service and speed, involvement of human resource for exploring new ways of creating value added interactions is of vital significance. The human factor is most critical in the management of interactive marketing. Very little focus has been given so far by the State Bank of India to this most important parameter of services marketing, may be due to the favorable market condition enjoyed hitherto. The need for a specialized focus on consumer sensitivity and the quality of interactions is increasing. Therefore, the need for the study of interactive marketing has been identified.

The findings of the study are helpful to the SBI to identify the defects and deficiencies in the interactive processes and to redesign the system that is capable of generating quality perceptions to the customers and providing competitive edge to the State Bank of India.

Hypothesis: The study presupposes that managerial problems in interactive marketing are one of the serious problems that stand in the way of progress of State Bank of India.

Objectives: The specific objectives of the study are;

- To study the organization system and developments of State Bank of India.
- To analyse the marketing operations including product, price, distribution, physical evidence, internal marketing, and external marketing.
- To study the interactive marketing management of the bank.
- To analyse interactive behavior of the employees and their opinion on interactions and interactive process.
- To study the opinion of the customers on their interaction to the bank.
- To identify problems and suggest measures for improvement wherever necessary.

3.2 METHODOLOGY

To pursue the above-mentioned objectives, data from secondary sources and primary sources are necessary. Besides literature survey, the secondary data was collected from the records of State Bank of India. For the collection of primary data the following methodology was adopted.

Objective 1: ***To study the organization system and developments of State Bank of India.***

In pursuance of this objective the data and information are collected from secondary as well as primary sources related to the organisation structure, roles and responsibilities of various managerial positions at central level, regional level, division level, and branch level. The development of State Bank of India is analysed by measuring historical background, nationalisation of the Imperial Bank, organisation structure and management, core operations like Corporate Banking Group, National Banking Group, International Banking Group, Associates and Subsidiaries, Business Process Reengineering and Progress of the Bank during 1999-00 to 2008-09. The progress of State Bank of India is analysed by using relevant statistical techniques.

Objective 2: ***To analyse the marketing operations including product, price, distribution, physical evidence, internal marketing and external marketing.***

In pursuance of this objective the data and information are collected from secondary as well as primary sources related to the product, price, distribution, physical evidence, internal marketing, and external marketing of the organization. The marketing operations of State Bank of India are studied by analyzing Product Mix, Product Lines, Pricing Policies and Strategies including the System of Administered Interest Rates, Reasons for Regulation, Deregulation of Interest Rates, Trends during 1990s and the Deregulation, and Prime Lending Rate. Distribution System includes Branch Network of State Bank of India, Branch Management, Branch Layout, Management Information System, Redesigning of Branches, Alternate Channels Design, Branch Image Building, Model Branch, Personalised Branch Net work, and Policy on Uneconomical Branches. Internal Marketing and External Marketing operations are also analysed.

The data related to marketing operations are analysed by using statistical techniques such as percentage, growth rates, and annual compound growth rates.

Objective 3: *To study the interactive marketing management of the bank.*

The interactive marketing operations are analysed based on secondary data and information, and personal interviews with the officers and other employees of the bank.

Objective 4: *To analyse interactive behavior of the employee and their opinion on interactions and interactive process.*

In pursuance of this objective the data and information are collected based on empirical study. The opinion on Recruitment, Selection and Training, Employee – Management Interactions', Interaction with Colleagues, Employee – customer interactions, etc. are elicited from the respondents and analysed by using appropriate statistical techniques.

Objective 5: *To study the opinion of the customers on their interaction to the bank.*

In pursuance of this objective the data and information are collected from primary sources. The respondents' opinion on relationship with bank, interactive opinion on physical environment and process, customer – employee interactions, service interaction process, and interactive abilities of State Bank of India vs. other banks.

Objective 6: *To identify problems and suggest measures for improvement where ever necessary.*

By way of reviewing the performance of the bank on various fronts and based on the findings of the empirical study, suggestions are made for further development of the bank particularly in interactive marketing.

Period of the study: The study covers the ten year period from 1999-2000 to 2008-2009. The primary data was collected from the respondents during 2007-08.

Area of the study: The opinion survey is confined to Andhra Pradesh State. The State Bank of India divided the state into five zones in Andhra Pradesh, *viz.*, Hyderabad, Secunderabad, Visakhapatnam, Vijayawada and Tirupati. Therefore, the five zones of the state are taken as the area of the study.

Sample selection: To collect primary data from the customers and employees of State Bank of India, a purposive sample of 300 SBI customers and 150 employees of SBI were selected. The sample of customers was equally divided among five groups of SBI customers namely Employees, Businessmen, Professional, Agriculturalists, and Housewives. The sample selected for the study is shown in the following Table 3.2.

Table 3.2: Sample of the study

STRATUM	SBI EMPLOYEES	CUSTOMERS
Hyderabad	30	60
Secunderabad	30	60
Visakhapatnam	30	60
Vijayawada	30	60
Tirupati	30	60
Total	150	300

Design of Questionnaires: Two separate questionnaires were designed – one for the employees and the other for the customers. To elicit information from the respondents open-ended questions, dichotomous questions, and multiple choice questions are used. For some questions scaling and ranking techniques are used. The questionnaires designed were pre-tested and required corrections were incorporated.

Survey: The respondents were contacted personally with the structured questionnaire at a time and place convenient to them.

Statistical Techniques: The data collected was tabulated and for the purpose of analysis and interpretation, statistical techniques such as Percentage, Averages, Standard Deviation, Scaling Techniques, ANOVA, etc., were used.

Likert Scale: Likert Scale is used on a five point scale varying from *very good* to *very poor* or *strongly agree* to *strongly disagree*. The scale is used against the following questions.

Questionnaire for employees:

1. Opinion on the emoluments being received
2. Opinion on upward communication system
3. Opinion on physical environment and systems
4. Interactions with colleagues
5. Agreement on the concept called "Customer is always right?"
6. Experience with the interaction of the customers
7. Opinion on customers
8. Opinion on the bank

Questionnaire for customers:

1. Opinion on banking interactive facilities
2. Opinion on employees behaviour
3. Opinion on physical facilities
4. Interactive abilities of employees compared to other bank employees.

Ranking Scale: Ranking scale is used to elicit information on the following issues.

Questionnaire for employees:

1. Motivational factors for joining the job
2. Problems encountered in interactions with colleagues
3. Types of customers preferred to interact
4. Handling reactive customers

Questionnaire for customers:

1. Motivating factors to establish relationship with the bank
2. Criteria for choosing a bank to open an account
3. Information sources
4. Reactive behaviour for service problems
5. Best things to value interactions

Conversion of Scale into Score: The opinion expressed by the respondents on Likert Scale was converted into score by assigning weightages in the following order for the opinions and accordingly the score was calculated.

OPINION	WEIGHTAGE
Strongly Agree/Very Good	5
Agree/Good	4
Neutral	3
Disagree/Poor	2
Strongly Disagree/Very Poor	1

Wherever ranking scale is used the first three ranks given by the respondents was taken into consideration. The ranks were given weightage in the following order to calculate score.

RANK	WEIGHTAGE
1	3
2	2
3	1

The scores obtained were converted into mean scores by using SPSS.

3.3 SUMMARY

State Bank of India is the leading commercial bank in India. The bank is in the public sector carrying the responsibility of promoting the business in the interest and for well being of the society. The changing competitive scenario, particularly after the liberalization policies initiated in the economy in 1991, forcing the public sector banks to reorient themselves towards providing satisfaction to the customers. Owing to the dominance in the market as the public sector bank, the State Bank of India over the years has not given enough focus to the customers of the bank. The business was seller-oriented owing to the absence of strong competition and the banks are of equal size in network. The situation is fast changing due to the rapid pace of change in technology and the entry and successful operations of private sector banks and foreign banks. The SBI has a need to face the challenges emerging in the environment with proper policy framework. The present study is designed to review comprehensively the progress of the bank, its marketing operations with specific focus on interactive marketing.

Chapter 4 STATE BANK OF INDIA – ORGANISATION SYSTEM AND OPERATIONS

State Bank of India came into existence on 5th July, 1955, as per the State Bank of India Act of 1955. The Bank was the outcome of the implementation of the recommendations of All India Rural Credit Survey Committee, which was appointed by the Reserve Bank of India in 1951.[1] The committee recommended the setting up of a State Bank as one strong integrated state partnered commercial banking institution with an effective machinery of branches spread throughout the country to stimulate banking development.[2] State Bank of India is playing a catalyst role in India's national building activity, by supporting various activities to alleviate the problems and distress of the people.[3] The progress of the State Bank of India is intertwined with the history of a newborn nation, growth and development of an emerging economy, and the beginning of a new banking system. Over the years, the State Bank of India has grown from strength to strength and lived up to its mission of being a premier commercial bank committed to service and national development.

4.1 HISTORICAL BACKGROUND

In the first half of the nineteenth century, three Presidency Banks were started in Madras, Bombay and Bengal with the financial participation of the government for conducting banking business and issue currency notes.[4] Towards the end of the 19th Century the cash balances of the government were kept in the government treasuries and the government shed its connections with the Presidency Banks. The Imperial Bank came into existence on the 27th January, 1921, by the Imperial Bank of India Act of 1920.[5] It was established by the amalgamation of the three Presidency Banks. The Imperial Bank was the biggest bank until 1935. It enjoyed powers and privileges as a special bank that had not been enjoyed by the other commercial banks in the country.

Until the establishment of the Reserve Bank of India in 1935, the Imperial Bank performed certain central banking functions, although it was purely a commercial bank. It acted as the sole-banker to the Government.[6] It was the custodian of public funds and Government cash balances and did all treasury work. It also held the cash balance of the Secretary of State. It assisted the Government in the floatation of new loans and the management of the public debt. It provided facilities to the public for the transfer of money between its branches at rates approved by the controller of currency. Most of the commercial banks kept their balances with the Imperial Bank and hence, it acted as the bankers bank.[7] It managed the clearing houses that were functioning in the principal cities of the country.

In addition to the central banking functions, the Imperial Bank performed the ordinary commercial banking functions. It accepted different kinds of deposits from the public and granted loans to the public on the basis of personal and collateral securities. It also rendered other commercial banking functions such as remittance of funds from one place to another receiving the customers' valuables for safe custody and other miscellaneous services.

By virtue of its high status, vast resources and wide connections, the Imperial Bank was regarded as the unofficial leader of the Indian money market. It rediscounted bills and played an important part in the internal trade of the country. It also provided liberal financial assistance to the co-operative movement in India.

As the Imperial Bank was operating as the government's bank and was occupying a unique position in the Indian money market, certain restrictions were imposed by the government on its ordinary commercial banking functions. It was not permitted to grant loans for periods exceeding six months or on the basis of immovable property or on the security of its own shares. It was prohibited from discounting or making loans against any bill unless it was guaranteed by at least two independent persons or firms. It was not permitted to grant unsecured overdraft in excess of Rs.1 lakh. It was officially prohibited from dealing in foreign exchange business except to the extent necessary to meet the needs of its own clients.

The establishment of the Reserve Bank of India in 1935, brought about a change in the status and working of the Imperial Bank. It ceased to function as the government's banker. The restrictions placed on its lending operations were removed. It was permitted to deal in foreign exchange business. It was authorised to grant loans for more than six months to accept immovable property and its own shares as collaterals for loans.

The Reserve Bank of India appointed Imperial Bank as Reserve Bank's agent to transact government banking business at places where the Reserve Bank had no office of its own. It also maintained currency chest and deposits of small coins on behalf of the government in those places where the Reserve Bank had no branches. As the sole agent of the Reserve Bank, it was permitted on behalf of the Government to pay, receive, collect and remit money, bullion and securities and to undertake and transact any other business which the Reserve Bank of India may entrust it with from time to time. Thus, the Imperial Bank was able to maintain its status and special position even after the creation of the Reserve Bank of India.

4.2 NATIONALISATION OF THE IMPERIAL BANK

Proposals for the nationalisation of the Imperial Bank had been under consideration since the attainment of Independence in 1947. In February 1948, the government accepted in principle for the nationalisation of Imperial Bank. The decision had been taken since several charges were levelled against the Imperial Bank. One of the major allegations was that the bank discriminated in favour of European companies as a result of which the Indian business concerns suffered[8]. After independence, it was pointed out that Indianization of superior posts was unduly delayed. Another criticism made against the bank was that of unfair competition with other commercial banks. It was pointed out that nationalisation would convert the Imperial Bank into a government owned institution with a direct field of operation and would considerably mitigate its anomalous position and help other commercial banks to expand and develop. The idea of nationalisation was vehemently opposed by the Central Board and the shareholders of Imperial Bank. As a result, in 1949, the government announced indefinite postponement of the issue of nationalisation.

The question of nationalisation of the Imperial Bank was again taken up by the government when the All India Rural Credit Survey Committee[9] appointment by the Reserve Bank recommended in 1952, the creation of a State Bank of India by amalgamating certain state owned banks with the Imperial Bank. In accordance with the recommendation of the committee, the State Bank of India Act was passed on 8th May, 1955 and the State Bank of India came into existence on 1st July, 1955.[10]

The State Bank was established, by the statutory amalgamation of the Imperial Bank and ten other State Associated Banks, *viz.*, the State Bank of Saurashtra, the Bank of Patiala, the Bank of Bikaner, the Bank of Jaipur, the Bank of Rajasthan, the Bank of Indore, the Bank of Mysore, the Hyderabad State Bank, the Bank of Baroda and the Travancore Bank. This was in line with the opinion expressed by the Rural Banking Enquiry Committee in 1950, which states that, "if these banks could be integrated into one institution, and if that one institution could be aligned to national policies then indeed, that would be an extremely important and extremely desirable line of development." The setting up of the State Bank was an important step towards the development of a strong commercial banking system in the country.

The major shareholder of the bank is President of India with 59.41 per cent shareholding (Figure 4.1). The other major shareholders include Life Insurance Corporation of India (9.56%), The Bank of New York (GDRs) (4.27%), ICICI Prudential Life Insurance Co. Ltd. (1.79%), Europacific Growth Fund (0.77%), Fidelity Management & Research Co. a/c FID Investment Trust–Fidelity diversified Intl. Fund (0.63%), General Insurance Corporation of India (0.54%), HDFC Standard Life Insurance Co. Ltd. (0.48%), Bajaj Alianz Life Insurance Co. Ltd. (0.44%) and Government of Singapore (0.35%).

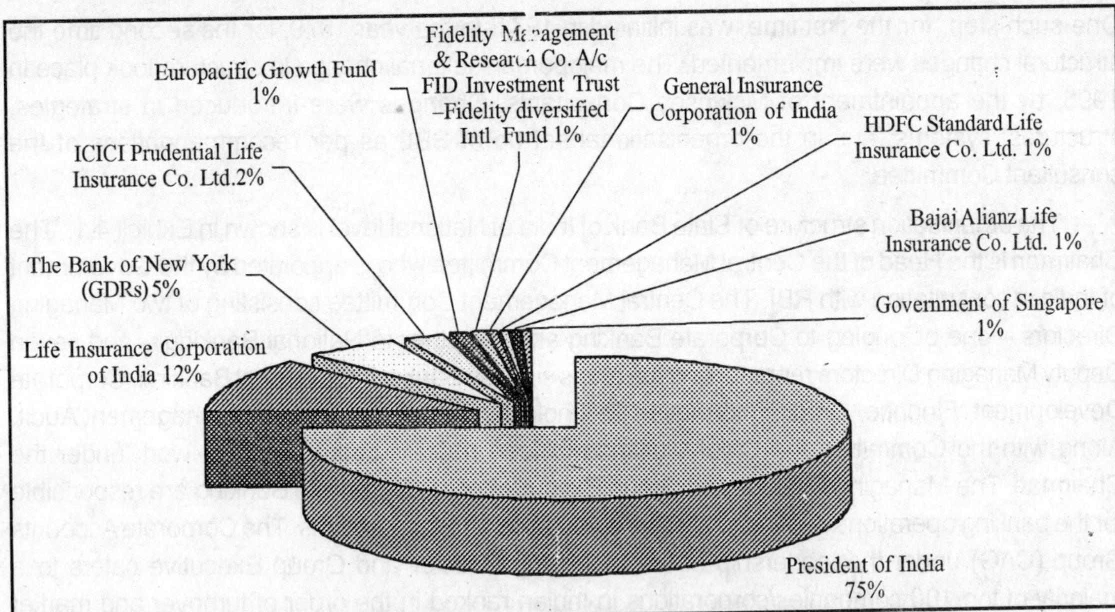

Fig 4.1 : Top Ten Shareholders of the Bank (as on 31-03-2009)

***Source*:** Annual Report of SBI, 2008-09.

4.3 ORGANISATION STRUCTURE AND MANAGEMENT

The management of the State Bank[11] vests in a Central Board of Directors which consists of;

- The Chairman, appointed under section 19(a) of SBI Act
- Two Managing Directors, appointed by the members of the Board under section 19(b)of SBI Act.
- Ten other directors on the Board including eminent personalities from academics. These included representatives of shareholders, nominee officials of Government of India and Reserve Bank of India and directors nominated by the Government of India under Section 19(d) of the State Bank of India Act, 1955.

The Chairman, the Vice-chairman and the Managing Director shall hold office for such terms not exceeding five years as the Central Government may fix when appointing them and shall be eligible for re-appointment. The directors elected by the shareholders and nominated by the Central Government will hold office for four years and are eligible for re-election or re-nomination. The other nominated directors shall hold office as per recommendations of the authority appointing them. Besides the Central Board, there are Local Boards of Management established at Kolkata, New Delhi, Kanpur, Ahmadabad, Bhopal and Patna. Each Local Board consists of the members of the Central Board residing in the area and directors not exceeding four elected shareholders whose names appear in the branch register.To keep the management free from politics, the Act stipulates that no member of the Central or State Legislatures shall be appointed as directors of the State Bank of India. Structural changes have been introduced by the bank in order to re-orient the business according to changing conditions in the market.

One such step, for the first time, was initiated in 1971. In the year 1979, for the second time the structural changes were implemented. The major organisational change in structure took place in 1995, by the appointment of Mckinsey Consultants. Changes were introduced in strategies, structures, systems, etc. in the organisational set up of SBI, as per recommendations of the consultant Committee.

The organisation structure of State Bank of India at National level is shown in Exhibit 4.1. The Chairman is the Head of the Central Management Committee who is appointed by the Government of India in consultation with RBI. The Central Management Committee consisting of two Managing Directors – one belonging to Corporate Banking and the other to National Banking – and seven Deputy Managing Directors representing the areas such as Banks, International Banking, Corporate Development, Finance, Credit, Information Technology, and Information and Management Audit. Along with the Committee the Chief Vigilance Officer at CGM cadre, will also work under the Chairman. The Managing Director and Group Executive of the Corporate Banking are responsible for the banking operations relating to big size companies and corporations. The Corporate Accounts Group (CAG) under the leadership of the Managing Director and Group Executive caters to a majority of top 100 companies/corporations in Indian ranked in the order of turnover and market capitalisation. The credit sanction of Rs.100 crore and above per company will fall under the jurisdiction of the managing director. The National Banking Group is headed by a Managing Director and Group Executive. This group consists of two distinct networks namely Development Banking and Personal Banking Network and Commercial Banking Network. About 90 per cent of the domestic deposits and 84 per cent of the domestic advances account for National Banking. The State Bank of India has seven Associate Banks and seven subsidiaries one of them is Banking Subsidiary and the other six are Non-Banking subsidiaries. One Deputy Managing Director will monitor the activities of all Associate Banks and Subsidiaries at the national level. Another Deputy Managing Director will co-ordinate and promote International Banking through a network of 92 overseas offices spread over in 32 countries covering all time zones. He is responsible for handling the country's foreign trade and related business and providing foreign currency resources to the Indian companies. The Deputy Managing Director (Corporate Development) is concerned with the development and growth activities of the bank. He is responsible for developing new products and schemes from time to time. The Accounting and Finance wing is headed by a Deputy Managing Director. He is also called Chief Financial Officer. The compilation of financial data, preparation of financial statement as per the regulations from time to time and monitoring the performance of the bank on the financial front are his responsibilities. One Deputy Managing Director will take care of Audit activities. The Deputy Managing Director, Information Technology is responsible for IT operations in the Bank. Considering the importance of IT to promote efficiency in banking, this new positions is created in the organisation system at the top management level. There is one Chief Vigilance Officer reporting to the Chairman. The officer will look after the activities including fraud detection and prevention of frauds. The disciplinary action against errant officials up to the level of DGM will be taken by this office.The Chief Vigilance Officer will maintain direct relations with Ministry of Finance, Government of India and Vigilance Committee of Reserve Bank of India.

The State Bank of India has 14 Local Head Offices, which are also called 'Offices at the Circles' located at state headquarters. The heads of all LHOs are directly responsible to the Chairman of the bank. The Circle Office has the jurisdiction of all Modules of the bank attached to it. The sanctions of above Rs.25 lakh and below Rs.100 crore are processed at the Circle Office. The Chief General Manager will be assisted by four Circle Officers at the DGM cadre in the areas of bank development, credit, finance and vigilance. The General Manager Personal and Development Banking is assisted by four Assistant General Managers (AGMs) in the areas of administration, personal, development and expansion.The General Manager, Commercial and International Banking is assisted by four AGMs in the areas of premises, computers, accounts and policy and decision making.

Exhibit – 4.1: Organization Chart at National Level

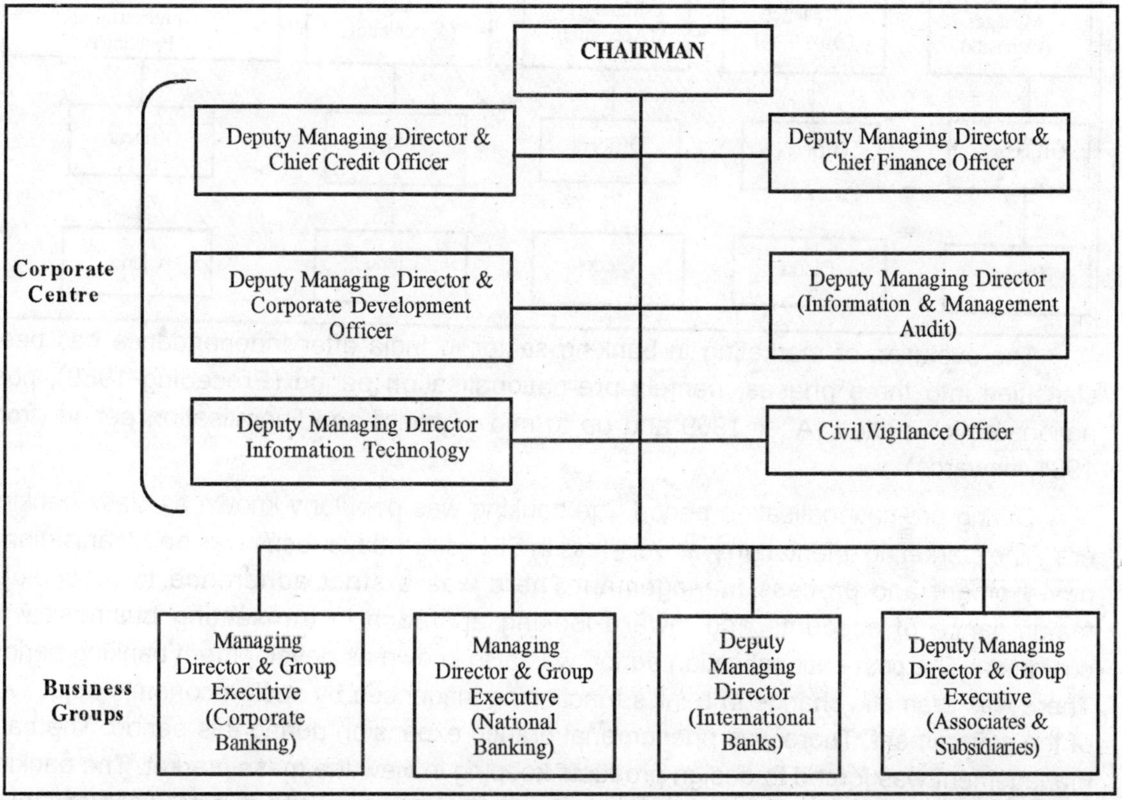

There are 58 Modules operated by the bank. Each module will be headed by Deputy General Manager. The Modules will co-ordinate the activities of the bank through regional offices. The heads of the regional offices and the branches headed by AGMs will directly report to the DGM of a Module.

The regional office will be headed by an Assistant General Manager and takes the responsibility of co-ordinating, developing and promoting the bank operations in a region. All Branch Managers in a region will report directly to the AGM. The functions such as credit support, sales planning, performance monitoring, general banking, personnel and HRD, and NPA management and recovery are managed at this office.

The organisation chart of a branch is shown in Exhibit 4.2. A branch is the first level office having direct interaction with large number of customers. The branch manager is the functional head of a branch. He/She is assisted by managers, officers and clerks and the size of the staff is based upon the volume of business.

Exhibit – 4.2: Organization Chart of a Branch

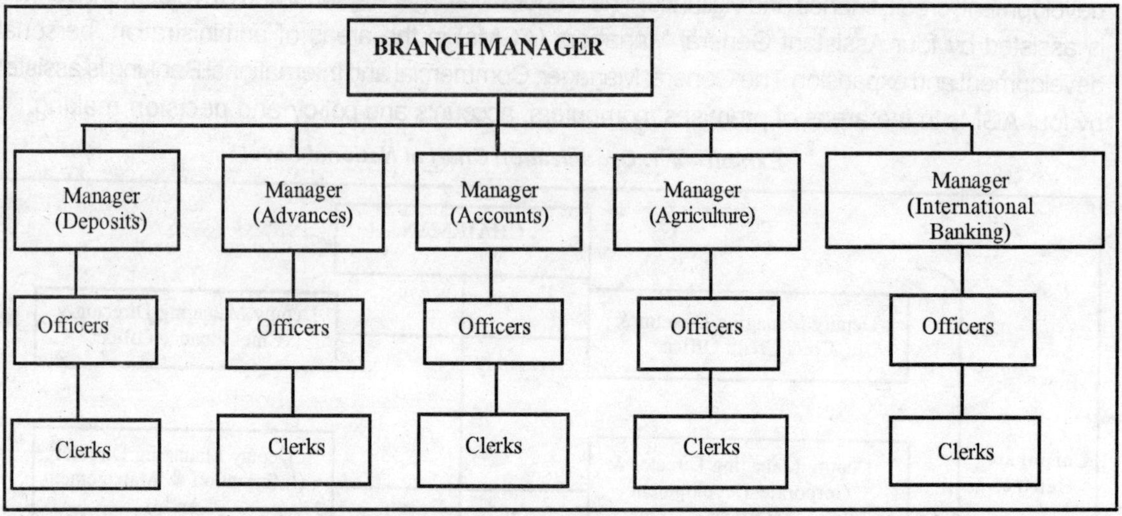

The evolution of marketing in banking sector in India after Independence has been classified into three phases, namely pre-nationalisation period (Preceding 1969), post nationalisation period (After 1969 and up to mid eighties) and liberalisation period (from 1991, onwards).

During pre-nationalisation period, the banking was popularly known as class banking era. The marketing orientation was very less in SBI as the major focus was on organisational development and process management.There was a strict adherence to meticulous maintenance of accounts and inward looking approach in transacting business with customers.The post nationalisation period was also known as development banking period. There was dramatic change in bank's functioning influenced by socio-economic objectives of the government. There was phenomenal branch expansion during this period. The bank management was forced to design products keeping in view the mass market. The banking habit of the people was nurtured and demand increased mostly due to word of mouth communication. The State Bank of India came out with schemes and innovative loan products like IRDP (Integrated Rural Development Program), DIR (Differential Interest Rates), crop loans, etc. During the period, the banking was almost a seller's market and a very little effort was made to know the market needs and wants in order to design suitable service products. The liberalisation period has also been called the bank marketing period. The State Bank of India and other nationalised banks were forced to change their orientation of business. Owing to the liberalised policy frame work, the competition from private banks and foreign banks got intensified. The management of SBI realised that unless market oriented functioning is introduced, it is difficult to retain its position and progress further.

The State Bank of India consulted Mckinsey Group regarding organization restructuring to promote customer focus in the year 1995. On the recommendations of the group, the SBI re-organised its structure by establishing Strategic Business Units (SBUs) in order to become closer to the customers in the identified market segments. They are (A) Global Markets Department, (B) Corporate Banking Group, (C) Mid Corporate Group, (D) National Banking Group, (E) Rural Business Group, (F) Marketing & Cross Selling Department, (G) Corporate Strategy & New Business, (H) International Banking Group, (I) Associates & Subsidiaries, (J) Asset Quality, and (K) Information Technology.

(A) Global Markets Department

Global Markets Department at the Corporate Centre handles the Bank's Treasury Operations across all time zones and covers activities in various markets, i.e., Forex, Interest Rates, Bullion, Equity and Alternative Assets.

B) Corporate Banking Group (CBG)

The Corporate Banking Group was constituted keeping in view the growing needs of large companies and the growing size of the market. It is also taken into consideration the need for specialized banking services of this segment. Accordingly, three SBUs were developed in the group. They are (1) Corporate Accounting, (2) Project Finance and Leasing SBU, and (3) Stressed Assets Management Group.

1. **Corporate Accounts Group (CAG):** The CAG is an exclusive outfit for large companies. The group focuses on relationship banking and provides one stop shopping for all finance related services to its customers, through a delivered credit process. Delivery of core products in a comprehensive, timely and cost efficient manner relative to competitors through branches is the main objective. The CAGs loan portfolio which was 30 per cent of the commercial and institutional non-food credit in 1998-99 decreased to 29 per cent in 2008-09. The share of CAG in total domestic credit portfolio has decreased from 16 per cent in 1998-99 to 15 per cent in 2008-09.

Transaction Banking Unit: The Transaction Banking Unit has been created in CBG with the Cash Management Product and Trade Finance wings under its fold to boost fee based income through Group Synergy.

Cash Management: Product with its brand name SBI-FAST has migrated to a centralized solution covering 379 branches to handle paper and e-collections as well as paper and e-payments for Corporate clients. The SBI-FAST, the cash management product in the group is a comprehensive cash management solution offering payments in addition to collections. The turnover of the product which was Rs.20,000 crore in 1998-99 increased phenomenally to reach Rs.5,06,752 crore in 2006-07 recording an increase of 2433.76 per cent. In order to capture the credit portfolio of vendors, the vendor financing activity is integrated with banking through internet platform. The Forex turnover has increased from Rs.1,50,525 crore in 1998-99 to Rs.5,11,712 crore in 2006-07.

2. **Stressed Assets Management Group (SAMG):** Stressed Assets Management Group (SAMG) was initially set up to take overall NPAs with outstanding of Rs.5 crore and above, for ensuring focussed efforts in resolution of NPAs. Now the policy has been modified to bring all NPAs of Rs.1 crore and above under the purview of SAMG. During the year ended March 2009, the gross reduction in NPAs of the Group was to the tune of Rs.1,187 crore.

3. **Project Finance and Leasing:** Project Finance Group is targeting the delivery of the entire range of project finance related services from project advice to domestic and cross border financing and syndication. Its attention is mainly focused on the fast growing infrastructure industries that were characterized by long gestation period and capital raising phases. The Project Finance-SBU focuses on funding core projects like power, telecom, roads, ports, airports, SEZ and others. It also handles non-infrastructure projects with certain ceilings on minimum project costs.

Leasing: Due to the dynamic changes in the financial market in India, during 90's competitive forces have lead to the compression of interest spread of banks. This has compelled banks to foray into activities generating stable non-interest income. Leasing provides an alternative source of finance for the banks corporate customers and also helps the bank in tax planning and tax efficient leasing products. In view of unfavourable climate and availability of alternative funding options at cheaper cost, the Bank decided not to write leases since 2003-04. As at the end of March 2007, the disbursements and capitalization were "NIL" and profit amounted to Rs.16.42 crore.

(C) Mid Corporate Group (MCG)

The Mid Corporate Group was created on 1st July 2004 with eight MCG Regional Offices controlling 53 branches with high concentration of Mid Corporate (MC) business.The MC business at all other branches at certain identified centres was also brought under the control of MCG under the off-site model. The entire Off-site MC business of all branches at 31 identified centres has been brought under the fold of the MCG. The average processing time of credit proposals is about 15 days and quicker decision making on credit proposals of the Mid Corporate units has resulted in grater customer satisfaction.

The focus of the MCG was to increase market share of the Bank in the emerging Mid-Corporate segment through relationship management and quicker credit processing. The initiative has been successful in as much as it has resulted in increasing the credit portfolio under Mid-Corporate segment substantially with attendant increase in earnings.

As of March 2008, 23 MCG branches have been migrated to Core Banking platform. New Technology products like RTGS, CINB, Multi-city cheque facility and Core Power have been introduced in all these branches. These technology products coupled with quick Turn Around Time (TAT) have enabled Mid Corporate Group to increase its business substantially and generate higher income, both interest and fee based.

Gold Banking: The number of branches for retail sale of gold coins has increased from 250 in 2008, to 518 in 2009. The Bank also undertakes supply of customised gold coins to corporate customers. The Bank has re-launched Gold Deposit Scheme at 50 branches to mobilise gold from domestic market for deployment as metal loans to jewellers.

(D) The National Banking Group (NBG)

The National Banking Group consists of three business groups, *viz.*, Personal Banking, SME, and Government Banking. The group provides basic banking services to customers spread over the country through its two distinct networks, namely development and personal banking network and the commercial network. As at the end of March 2009, the NBG had 14 administrative circles encompassing a vast network of 11,448 branches to reach out to customers, even in the remotest corners of the country.

The advances of Personal Banking Unit increased from Rs.82,296 crore in 2000-01, to Rs.1,06,954 crore in 2008-09, showing a growth of 30 per cent.

Small and Medium Enterprises (SME) Business Unit is implementing various strategies to maintain the Bank's leadership in SME financing. The Bank is continuously engaged in bringing out new products to meet SME customer expectations, developing sector specific value propositions, and doing intensive cluster financing.The group deposits increased from Rs.73,811 crore in 2003-04, to Rs. 2,20,468 crore in 2008-09, showing a growth of 198.67 per cent.

Bank created Government Business Unit with the objective of focusing exclusively on marketing for the business emanating from this segment in the face of stiff competition, particularly in high value revenue collections of both the Central Government and State Governments. "SBI e-Tax" an online tax payment facility for Direct & Indirect Taxes has been launched in the year 2005-06. "e-freight" facility for payment of railway freight has been extended to large Corporates on a pilot basis. Centralized Pension Processing Centers (CPPCs) have been established at all 14 LHO centres to provide excellent customer service to pensioners. With the establishment of the Government Business Unit and the consequent focus on marketing, business turnover of this segment has grown substantially. Government business turnover recorded a growth of 19.63 per cent in the year 2006-07, compared to 10.82 per cent in the year 2005-06. Growth in Government commission has been 8.17 per cent in 2006-07, (compared to a decline of 11.97 per cent in the year 2005-06) due to introduction of various e-payment initiatives, and Centralised Pension Processing Centres at all Circles.

(E) Rural Business Group (RBG)

In the year 2006-07, a new business group, *viz.*, Rural and Agri Business Group, has been created as a strategic initiative for maximum exploitation of the emerging rural banking opportunity. Rural Business Group, which deals with the business of the Bank at all rural and semi urban centres, handles a deposit portfolio of Rs.2,15,931 crore and a credit portfolio of Rs.1,20,617 crore, which is 32 per cent and 26 per cent of the Bank's total domestic deposit and credit portfolio respectively as on 31.03.2009.

Agri Business: The Bank launched the new products, namely, Krishi Plus, Arthias Plus, Dairy Plus and Rakshak Tractor Plus to increase the flow of credit to agriculture sector in the year 2003-04. The advances of Agriculture Business Group increased from Rs.1,360 crore in 2003-04 to Rs.54,678 crore in 2008-09 showing an increase of 3920.44 per cent.

Regional Rural Banks (RRBs): The year 2006-07 was a year of consolidation of RRBs. There was Bank specific amalgamation at each State level. Resultantly, Bank has got 17 RRBs post amalgamation with a network of 2,557 branches spread over 122 districts and 17 states in the country in 2008-09. The Bank has sponsored 25 RRBs spread over 102 districts in 16 States with a network of 2,350 branches. The aggregate deposits and advances of the sponsored RRBs stood at Rs.17,273 crore and Rs.10,242 crore respectively as on 31st March, 2009.During the financial year, the Bank's sponsored RRBs made a profit of Rs. 203.31 crore.The Bank has, up to March 2006, contributed Rs. 134.97 crore for recapitalisation of the 29 RRBs taken up for financial restructuring.

(F) Marketing and Cross Selling Department

Consistent efforts by the Bank have resulted in emergence of Cross Selling as an important source of income. Initiatives taken by the Marketing-Cross Selling Department particularly in insurance and mutual funds business has earned the Bank an income of Rs.166.45 crore during the financial year ending March 2009 despite the adverse economic scenario.

(G) Corporate Strategies & New Business

The New Businesses Department was created to formulate strategies for new businesses, incubate new business initiatives, pilot the same and on stabilization, handover to the concerned Business Group. Various new businesses like Pension Fund Management, General Insurance, Private Equity, Financial Planning & Advisory Services (FP&AS), Custodial Services, Payment Solutions, Depository Participant Services, and Online trading have been initiated by the department.

(H) International Banking Group (IBG)

The State Bank of India had a network of 92 overseas offices spread over 32 countries covering all time zones.The Bank also has correspondent arrangements with 527 Banks in 124 countries by the end of 2008-09. To cater to the needs of a large customer base of the Bank, and to also supplement the efforts of foreign offices in the area of International Banking, the Bank has developed a network of Correspondent Banks numbering 527 consisting of reputed International Banks spread over 124 countries. The Bank also has about 1626 Bilateral Key Exchange (BKE) arrangements for SWIFT, which facilitates a seamless flow of financial messages covering trade, remittances etc.

The bank is focusing on NRI Business and Treasury Management through its foreign offices.The domestic operations relating to the international banking group include export credit, project export finance, merchant banking, forex turnover, global link services, and correspondent relations.

(I) Associates and Subsidiaries

The State Bank Group with a network of 16,055 branches including 4,607 branches of its six Associate Banks dominates the banking industry in India. In addition to banking, the group, through its various subsidiaries, provides a whole range of financial services which includes Life Insurance, Merchant Banking, Mutual Funds, Credit Card, Factoring, Security Trading and Primary Dealership in the Money Market. SBI's six Associate Banks had a market share of 6.74 per cent in deposits and 6.95 per cent in advances by the end of 2008-09.

Along with the management of CBG, NBG, RABG, IBG and Associates and Subsidiaries, the State Bank of India has identified treasury operations, asset quality and information technology as the core operations to develop the Bank capable of facing the fast emerging changes in the banking sector.

Treasury Operations: State Bank of India recognized the growing importance of treasury operations due to changing global trends in forex market and changing regulations in domestic banking sector. The bank has taken several initiatives to strengthen the system and procedures, accounting and risk management to ensure continued reliance on treasury operations and increasing contributions to the bank profitability without risk profile adversely.

(J) Asset Quality

NPA Management: The Bank's NPA management has assumed critical importance and is receiving focussed attention at all levels. At the corporate level, a Task Force comprising top executives monitors all NPAs of above Rs.5 crore. At Local Head Office level, the Circle Management Committee monitors all NPAs of above Rs.1 crore. The NPA management policy lays stress, inter alia, on early identification of problem loans, effective response to early warning signals, and appropriate recovery strategy including one-time settlement. Other measures taken by the Bank include upgradation of appraisal skills of the officers dealing in credit through special training programs and an effective credit audit mechanism, which throws warning signals for taking action to prevent performing assets turning into non-performing ones. For close monitoring of cases with Debt Recovery Tribunals (DRT), the Bank has nominated nodal officers in the DRT cells in the LHOs. The Bank has nine specialized Rehabilitation and Recovery branches to focus on BIFR cases and large value accounts especially in doubtful and loss categories. As a part of cleansing its balance sheet, the Bank has written off NPA accounts with high level of provision and the outstandings are held in Advances under Collection Account for further follow up.

(K) Information Technology

The Bank has adopted and is pursuing effectively its IT policy with the aim of achieving efficiency in operations, meeting customers and market expectations and staying ahead in competition.

Introduction of Electronic NOSTRO Account Reconciliation (ELENOR) in December 2000 has helped fast, accurate and fully integrated reporting of Forex transactions and has made a major breakthrough in effectively tackling the NOSTRO reconciliation. It has enabled online reporting of forex transactions from 444 forex intensive branches. State Bank Electronic Payment Systems (STEPS), which became operational from January 2001, facilitates instantaneous electronic transfer of funds in 1,557 branches to 3,270[12] branches in 2009. Another product, e-realisation, has been introduced in October 2001 to facilitate expeditiously reconciliation of outstanding entries in DDP cheques/dividends at 972 branches. These projects were conceived, developed and implemented with in-house expertise and their success has been widely acclaimed. Apart from the above, 2000 corporate customers are using remote log-in facilities, which have been implemented in 200 branches. Tele-banking has been implemented at 106 branches, where customers can access their accounts through telephone from anywhere at anytime.

With the computerization of all[13] branches, the State Bank of India brought improvement in customer service, introduced features such as Networked ATMs, Internet Banking, Tele banking and Customer Enquiry Terminals. Computerization has helped in extension of business hours, faster remittances and speedier collection of instruments.

The SWIFT network has been extended to 450[14] domestic branches, as at end of March 2009. This has helped faster and automated message transmission. The Bank's SWIFT Gateway and software at SWIFT Operation Center (SOC) have been upgraded to SWIFT Alliance Access.

The RBI VSAT project, Indian Financial Network (INFINET) backbone is being used for ELENOR, CMP, STEPS and other messaging, which has resulted in greater efficiency in transaction processing and reporting. The Bank has a network covering 164 VSATs in 113 cities extending the coverage to almost the entire country in 2001-02 and cover 5,327 in 612 cities were connected in 2005-06.

SBI Home page, the Bank's website, has been redesigned to provide a wide range of information, including profile of all SBI branches. The Bank's Website has reported a jump in the hits from an average of 0.8 million a month in September 2000, to 7.5 million a month at present. 'Online SBI', the Bank's Internet banking service, introduced on 1st July, 2001, covering retail customers has been expanded to cover corporate customers also in March 2002. At the end of March 2007, this service covered 4,498 branches.

The State Bank Computer Centre at Navi Mumbai, the sole Application Software Solution Provider in the field of reconciliation, has implemented various technology-oriented projects to facilitate speedy reconciliation of inter office transactions and helped the Bank in achieving nearly 100 per cent reconciliation. The project e-recon, which is used for transmission of branch clearing and drafts accounts data for reconciliation through Internet, has been implemented in 2,849 computerized branches. The project also covers RTC and Agency Gearing Accounts.

Software has been developed in-house for conduct of government transactions in branches and for electronic reporting of the transactions from the dealing branches to focal point branch and from focal point branch to Government Accounts Department. The software has since been launched for implementation in branches across all circles.

Corporate communication in the Bank has a new look with video conference facility being available at 24 centres, thus reducing the need for travel of the executives and, in effect, saving time.

The Bank is pursuing an aggressive IT policy as a strategic initiative to meet the growing competition for business and market share, achieve efficiency in internal operations, and meet customer expectations. With this end in view, several initiatives were undertaken, viz. ATM Project, where ATMs are now also enabled to pay utility bills, and college fees, book air-line tickets, accept donations etc. Further, bilateral sharing of ATMs was extended to thirteen banks, covering 15,700 ATMs, and an MoU has been signed with the Indian Railways for installing ATMs at 682 Railway Stations.

Core Banking Solution (CBS) presently covers 72 million accounts, and more than 85 per cent of the bank's business. Financial Project for Treasury and Core Banking Solution has been implemented at 73 foreign offices in 22 countries, along with Internet Banking at all foreign offices. Further, Internet Banking has been implemented at 4,498 domestic branches, and used by retail banking customers for utility bill payment and booking of Rail and Air tickets.

Payment Systems Group is responsible for implementation of RTGS, (4,748 branches) NEFT (4,690 branches), setting up MICR Cheque Processing Centres (5 new) and adding ECS facility at Clearing Houses(22) managed by SBI.

IT Policy and IS Security Policy have been implemented after being benchmarked against best global practices. The Bank's Central Data Centre and Disaster Recovery centres were certified as ISO/IEC 27001:2005 Compliant, which is the new International Standard for Information Security Management System.

SBI Connect, the Wide Area Networking (WAN) project of the Bank, is capable of carrying data, voice and video. All applications requiring connectivity now ride on the SBI CONNECT backbone, in addition to 5,794 branches/offices of SBI and 4,820 branches/offices of Associate Banks being networked under the SBI Connect Project.

New IT Initiatives: SBI, assigned by KPMG Consulting, has drawn up a five year IT plan which envisages a) migration from distributed to centralised computing, b) implementation of an integrated Core Banking System with capability for on-line, real-time transaction processing, c) multiple delivery channels, such as ATM, and Internet banking, d) automated treasury and risk management systems integrated into the core banking system, e) data warehousing, data mining, and work-flow capabilities, and f) integration into an Inter-bank payment gateway.

Implementation of the plan is in progress with rolling out of Internet Banking facility for both retail and corporate customers and networked ATMs, for customers at branches across the country. Under the plan, to roll-out a Wide Area Network (WAN) connecting 1,500 branches in 49 cities across the country, the Bank has selected data craft. The WAN would enable implementation of the Centralised Core Banking solution, selected by the Bank, to be procured from FNS, Australia. The implementation of the Core Banking solution has been entrusted to TATA Consultancy Services. Bank has also selected Reuters- Unisys's solution for Treasury Operations and Oracle Financial for Asset Liability Management. Roll-out of these solutions is underway.

(L)Customer Service

A number of initiatives were taken up to intensify focus on customer service. These include conducting of Open House or Town Hall Customer Meets with participation by Circle Management; 'Operation Samay' at branches to ensure that counters open for business before time and drawing up of ground rules for customer service for operating staff. Customers were encouraged to provide frank and honest feedback on services at Open House Meets. The Bank became a member of the Banking Codes and Standards Board of India (BCSBI) in September 2006. The Bank has thereby adopted the BCSBI's Code of Bank's Commitments to Customers as the Fair Practice Code for implementation at all its branches. The Bank has also appointed Code Compliance Officers at all its Local Head Offices. The Bank places importance not only to redress customer grievances but also in identifying systemic/attitudinal issues, if any, that lead to a high frequency of complaints in particular areas and in rectifying them.

(M)Community Service Banking:

Apart from the normal Banking operations, the Bank, seeks to reinvest part of its profit in various community welfare projects to improve the quality of the life of the poor, neglected, weaker and downtrodden sections of society.

4.4 PROGRESS OF THE BANK DURING 1999-00 TO 2008-09

The progress of the State Bank of India is explained in terms of Assets, Deposits, Loans and Advances, Income, Expenditure, Net Profit, Branch Network, Number of Employees, Business per Employee, and Profit per Employee.

The data presented in Figure 4.2 shows the growth of assets during 1999-00, to 2008-09. The total assets of the bank valued at Rs.2,64,704.97 crore in 1999-00 registered an upward growth year by year and by the end of the year 2008-09 the value of the assets stood at Rs.9,08,888.12 crore. In other words, the assets of the bank registered a growth of 243.36 per cent during the decade. The assets of the bank are in the form of advances, investments, balance with bank and money at call and short term notice, cash in hand and balance with RBI, fixed assets and other assets. Advances constitute major part of the total assets. The share of which varied between 34.69 per cent and 59.54 per cent during the period. Particularly during 2005-06 and 2006-07 the share of advances increased phenomenally. Investments occupy second place with a share varied between 26.33 per cent and 45.85 per cent during the period. The share of this asset was the lowest in 2006-07. The share of cash in hand and balance with RBI varied between 3.39 per cent and 7.14 per cent during the period, while the share of balance with bank and money at call and short term notice varied between 2.21 pre cent and 13.37 per cent. The share of fixed assets was less than one per cent. The share of other assets varied between 4 per cent and 8.28 per cent.

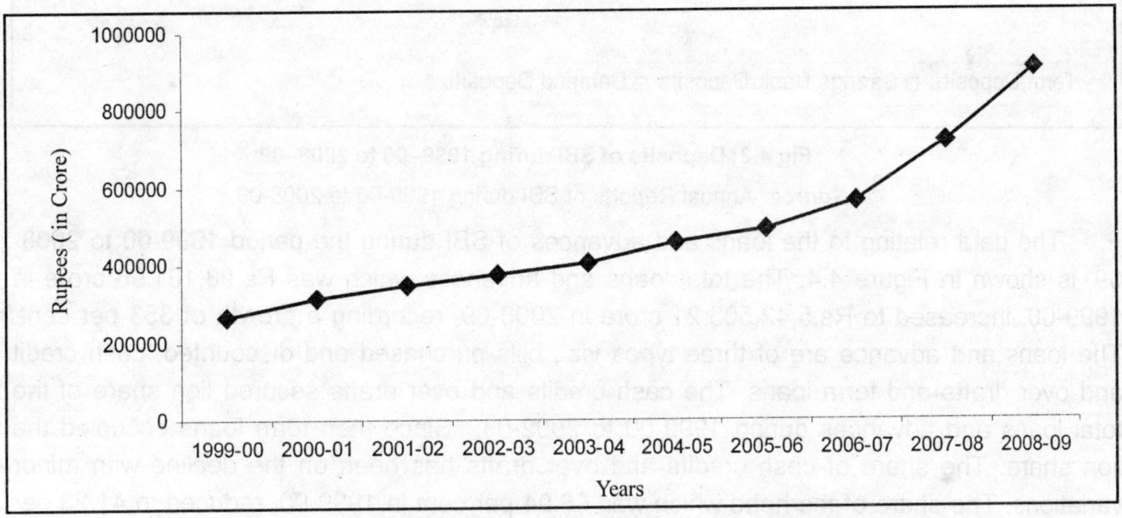

Fig 4.2 : Assets of State Bank of India during 1999–00 to 2008–09

Source: Annual Reports of SBI 1999-00 to 2008-09.

The deposits of SBI during the period of the study increased from Rs.1,96,821.07 crore in 1999-00 to Rs.74,2073.13 crore in 2008-09 recording a growth of 277.03 per cent. The bank has three types of deposits. They are; Term Deposits, Savings Bank Deposits, and Demand Deposits. Term deposits occupying major share compared to the other two categories. The share of term deposits varied between 63.67 per cent and 51.63 per cent during the period. The savings bank deposits occupy the second position and its share varied between 19.27 per cent and 29.71 per cent. The share of demand deposits varied between 14.92 per cent and 21.22 per cent during the period. Further, it can be seen that the share of term deposits is on the decline year by year from 2003-04 onwards, where as the share of saving bank deposits is on the increase except last two financial years.

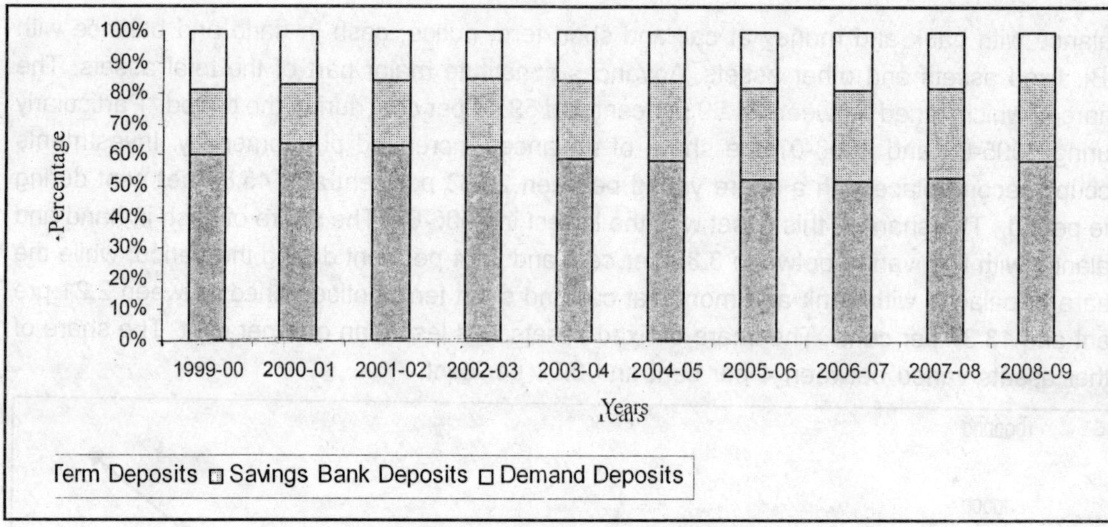

Fig 4.3: Deposits of SBI during 1999–00 to 2008–09

Source: Annual Reports of SBI during 1999-00 to 2008-09.

The data relating to the loans and advances of SBI during the period 1999-00 to 2008-09, is shown in Figure 4.4. The total loans and advances which was Rs.98,101.96 crore in 1999-00, increased to Rs.5,42,503.21 crore in 2008-09, recording a growth of 353 per cent. The loans and advance are of three types viz., bills purchased and discounted, cash credit and over drafts and term loans. The cash credits and over drafts secured lion share of the total loans and advances during 1999-00 to 2002-03. Since then term loans occupied the lion share. The share of cash credits and over drafts has been on the decline with minor variations. The share of the head which was 56.04 per cent in 1999-00, reduced to 41.23 per cent in 2008-09.

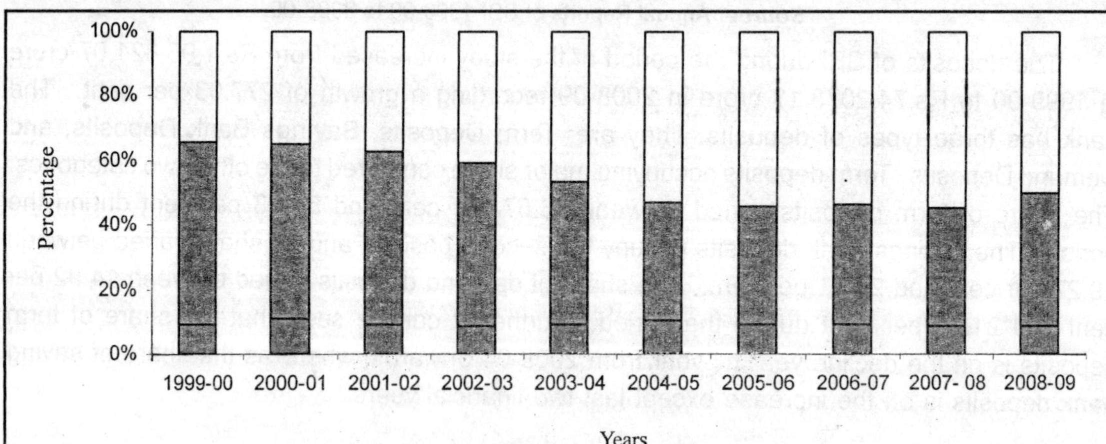

Fig 4.4: Loans & Advances of SBI during 1999–00 to 2008–09

Source: Annual Reports of SBI during 1999-00 to 2008-09.

The income earned by SBI during the period under the study has increased from Rs.25,770.25 crore in 1999-00 to Rs.76,479.22 crore in 2008-09 (Figure 4.5). In other words, the income of the bank was increased by 196.77 per cent. However, the growth over the previous year, though positive in all the years, highly fluctuated during the period. The year 2008-09, registered the highest growth rate (32.67 per cent), while the year 2003-04, registered lowest growth rate (3.38 per cent). The compound annual growth rate of the total income of the bank during the period was 11.49 per cent.

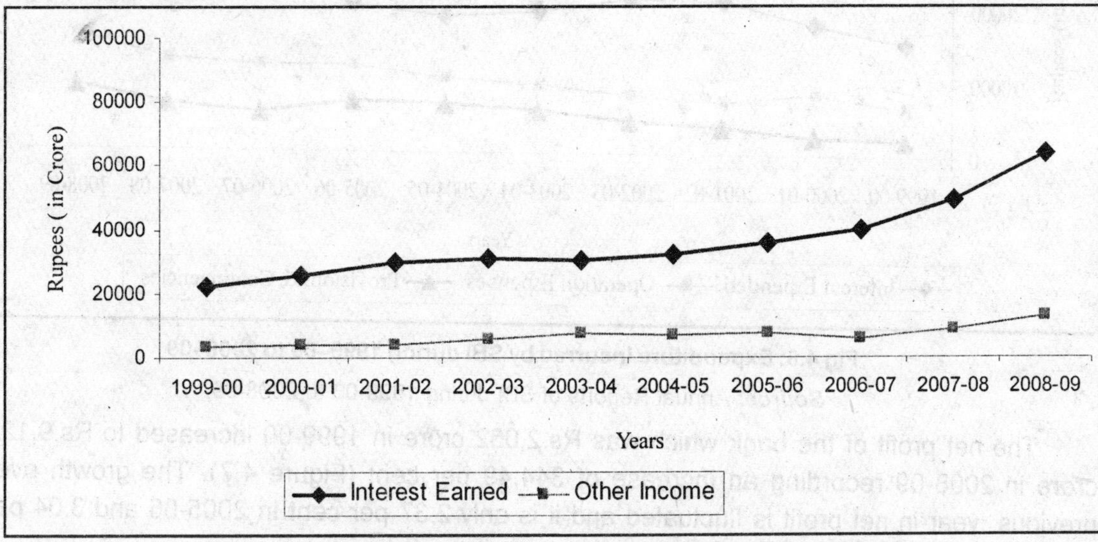

Fig 4.5: Income Earned by SBI during 1999–00 to 2008–09

Source: Annual Reports of SBI during 1999-00 to 2008-09.

The chief source of income of the bank is interest earned. The share of interest earned to the total income varied between 80 per cent and 87.72 per cent. The growth of income from interest earned over the previous year is fluctuative and varied between (-) 2.02 per cent and 30.31 per cent. The compound annual growth rate of the interest earned was 11.13 per cent. The share of other income varied between 12.28 per cent and 19.99 per cent. The growth of the income under this head over the previous year varied between (-) 21.29 per cent and 50.71 per cent. The compound annual growth rate of the other income was 13.52 per cent.

The details of expenditure incurred by the Bank during the period are shown in Figure 4.6. The total expenditure of the bank which was Rs.23,718.7 crore in 1999-00, increased to Rs.67,357.99 crore in 2008-09, recording an increase of 184 per cent. The expenditure increased every year during the period, but the percentage increase over the previous year varied between 1.99 per cent and 32.29 per cent. Interest expended is the major expenditure item, the share of which in the total expenditure, varied between 51.99 per cent and 65.70 per cent. The operational expenses occupy second position with a share varied between 22.85 per cent and 30.24 per cent. Provisions and contingencies is the other head of expenditure.

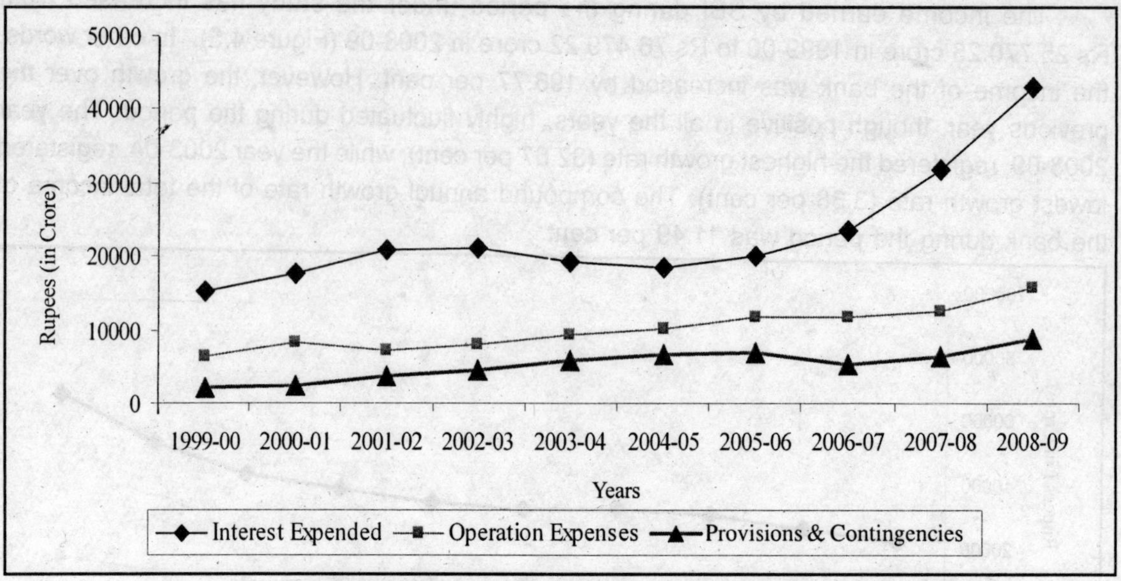

Fig 4.6: Expenditure Incurred by SBI during 1999–00 to 2008–09

Source: Annual Reports of SBI during 1999-00 to 2008-09.

The net profit of the bank which was Rs.2,052 crore in 1999-00 increased to Rs.9,121 crore in 2008-09 recording an increase of 344.49 per cent (Figure 4.7). The growth over previous year in net profit is fluctuated and it is only 2.37 per cent in 2005-06 and 3.04 per cent in 2006-07.

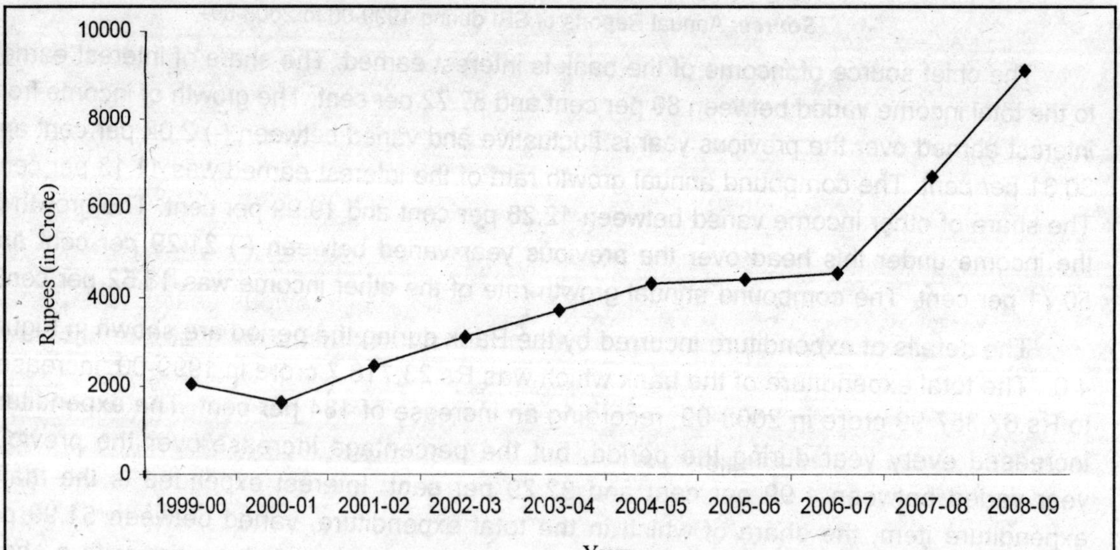

Fig 4.7: Net Profit of SBI during 1999–00 to 2008–09

Source: Annual Reports of SBI during 1999-00 to 2008-09.

The State Bank of India has a branch network spread over in all important locations in India. The total number of branches was 8,998 in the year 1999-00, which was increased to 11,448 in 2008-09 (Figure 4.8). The bank established branch network in foreign countries also. The number of Foreign branches increased form 52 in 1999-00 to 92 in 2008-09. In the year 2009, the Bank achieved another milestone by opening its 11,111th Branch at Sonapur (Kamrup District) in Assam. Apart from an addition of 461 branches on account of SBS merger, 807 new domestic branches were also opened (under NBG and RBG), and the Bank had a vast network of 11,448 domestic branches at the end of March 2009.

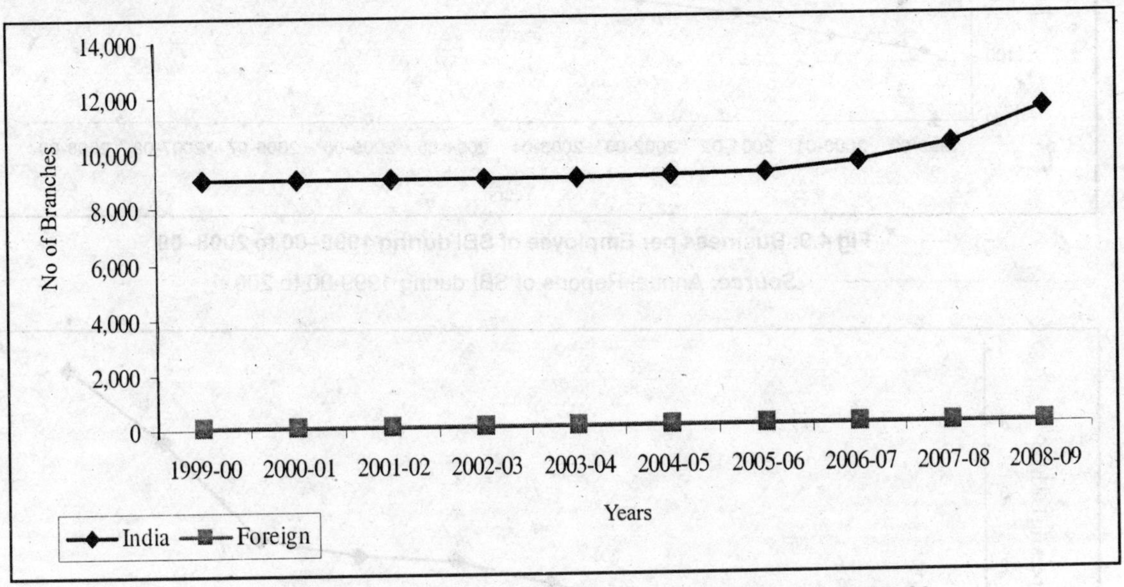

Fig 4.8: Total Number of Branches during 1999–00 to 2008–09

Source: Annual Reports of SBI during 1999-00 to 2008-09.

The data relating to business per employee and profit per employee achieved by the bank during 1999-00 to 2008-09, is shown in Figure 4.9 and Figure 4.10 respectively. The business per employee which was Rs.111 lakh in 1999-00, increased to Rs.556 lakh in 2008-09 recording an increase of 401 per cent. The business per employee is on the increase year by year though the percentage growth over previous year fluctuated and varied between 10.4 per cent and 26.28 per cent. The profit per employee also increased from Rs.0.8 lakh in 1999-00, to Rs.4.73 lakh in 2008-09, recording an increase of 444 per cent. Except 2000-01, negative growth rate over the previous year was registered, a positive growth rate was registered in all the other years.

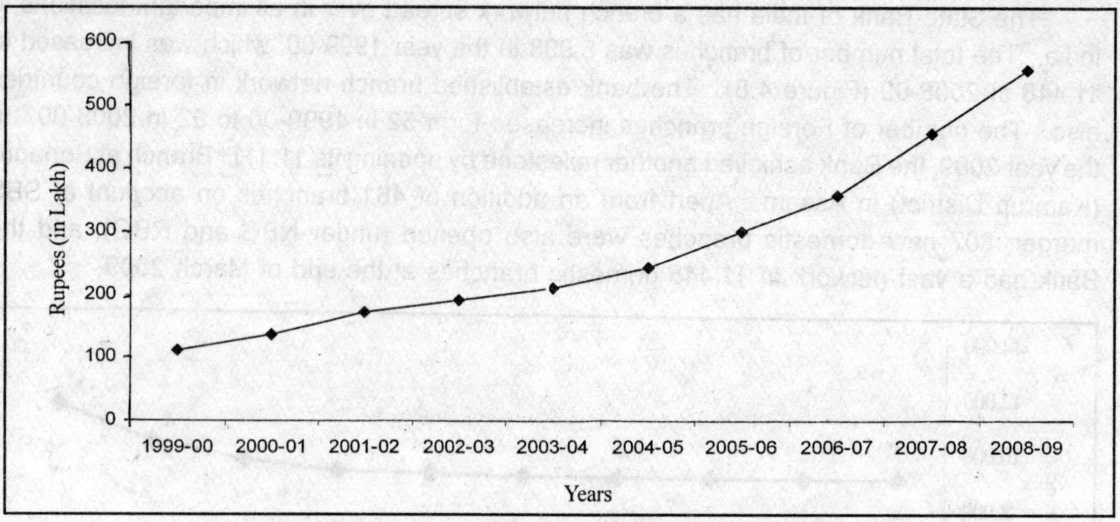

Fig 4.9: Business per Employee of SBI during 1999–00 to 2008–09

Source: Annual Reports of SBI during 1999-00 to 200.

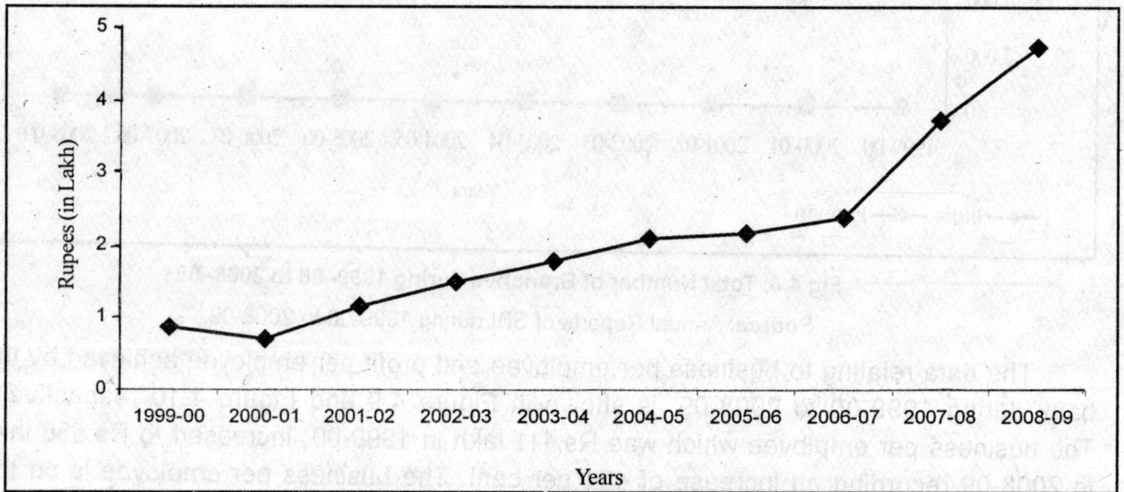

Fig 4.10: Profit per Employee of SBI during 1999–00 to 2008–09

Source: Annual Reports of SBI during 1999-00 to 2008-09.

Table 4.1 shows the key performance indicators of the bank during the period under the study. The return on average assets which was 0.87 per cent in 1999-00, increased to 1.04 per cent in 2008-09. The return on equity is highly fluctuated and varied between 11.92 per cent and 18.19 per cent during the period. The operating expenses to total income varied between 47.83 per cent and 67.66 per cent. The earning per share registered high fluctuation and varied between Rs.19.53 and Rs.143.77. The capital adequacy ratio varied between 11.88 per cent and 14.25 per cent. The net NPA to Net Advances which was 6.41 in 1999-00 decreased to 1.56 in the year 2006-07 and the declining per cent is 75.7.

Table 4.1: Key performance Indicators of SBI during 1999-00 to 2008-09

Indicators	1999-00	2000-01	2001-02	2002-03	2003-04	2004-05	2005-06	2006-07	2007-08	2008-09
Return on Average Assets (%)	0.87	0.57	0.73	0.86	0.94	0.99	0.89	0.84	1.01	1.04
Return on Equity (%)	16.89	11.92	15.97	18.05	18.19	18.1	15.47	14.24	17.82	15.73
Expenses to Income (%) (Operating Expenses to Total Net Income)	59.97	67.66	54.4	50.53	49.18	47.83	58.7	54.18	NA	NA
Earning per share (Rs.)	38.98	30.48	46.2	59	69.94	81.76	83.73	86.29	126.62	143.77
Capital Adequacy Ratio (%)	11.49	12.79	13.35	13.5	13.53	12.45	11.88	12.34	13.54	14.25
Net NPAs to	6.41	6.03	5.63	4.5	3.48	2.65	1.88	1.56	1.78	1.76

Source: Annual Reports of SBI during 1999-00 to 2008-09.

Highlights/Initiatives in the year 2008-09

- The rate of growth, both in deposits and advances, has been better than the growth rate of ASCB rural and semi urban branches. As a result, the Bank's markets share in rural and semi urban areas improved by 1.35 per cent in deposits and 1.27 per cent in advances between March and December 2008.
- High proportion (54 per cent of total deposits) of Current Account & Savings Account (CASA) deposits in the group contributes to its lower cost of deposits at 5.23 per cent, which is significantly lower than the Whole Bank average of 6.03 per cent.
- The business strategy envisaged setting up of multi pronged sourcing agents coupled with improved back end processing capacity.
- Front end sourcing force comprises, besides branches, alternate channels like Officers Marketing and Recovery (OMR) and Business Facilitators (BFs) and Business Correspondents (BCs).
- OMRs numbering around 4800 now source not only high value Agriculture segment loans but all types of deposits, loans and cross-selling products across all the segments.

- The Bank has appointed about 18,000 Customer Service Point (CSP)/outlets of Business Correspondents/Business Facilitators (BC/BFs). Some of the national level BC/BFs are India Post and ITC. During the year, the alliance with India Post has been scaled up nation wide and now covers more than 5,200 Post Offices across all States.
- To increase its outreach, the Bank has opened about 481 new branches in rural and semi urban areas during FY-09.
- To improve the processing capacity, 158 Rural Central Processing Centres (RCPCs) have been opened during FY-09.

4.5 SUMMARY

The management of the State Bank vests in a Central Board of Directors which consists of a Chairman and a Vice-chairman appointed by the Central Government in consultation with the Reserve Bank of India, Two Managing Directors, Six directors elected by the shareholders, and eight directors to be nominated by the Central Government. The State Bank of India has 14 Local Head Offices, which are also called 'Offices at the Circles' located at state head quarters. The heads of all LHOs are directly responsible to the Chairman of the bank. The Circle Office has the jurisdiction of all Modules of the bank attached to it.

There are 58 Modules operated by the bank. Each module will be headed by Deputy General Manager. The Modules will co-ordinate the activities of the bank through regional offices. The heads of the regional offices and the branches headed by AGMs will directly report to the DGM of a Module. The Regional Office will be headed by an Assistant General Manager and takes the responsibility of co-ordinating, developing and promoting the bank operations in a region. All Branch Mangers in a region will report directly to the AGM. The functions such as credit support, sales planning, performance monitoring, general banking, personnel and HRD and NPA management and recovery are managed at this office.

The State Bank of India consulted Mckinsey Group regarding organization restructuring to promote customer focus in the year 1995. On the recommendations of the group, the SBI re-organised its structure by establishing Strategic Business Units (SBUs) in order to become closer to the customers in the identified market segments. They are (A) Corporate Banking Group, (B) National Banking Group, (C) International Banking Group and (D) Associates and Subsidiaries.

The State Bank of India had a network of 83 overseas offices spread over 32 countries covering all time zones. The Bank also has correspondent arrangements with 525 banks in 126 countries by the end of 2006-07. To cater to the needs of a large customer base of the Bank, and to also supplement the efforts of foreign offices in the area of International Banking, the Bank has developed a network of Correspondent Banks numbering 525 consisting of reputed International Banks spread over 126 countries. The bank also has about 1100 Bilateral Key Exchange (BKE) arrangements for SWIFT, which facilitates a seamless flow of financial messages covering trade, remittances etc.

The State Bank Group with a network of 16,055 branches including 4,607 branches of its seven Associate Banks dominates the banking industry in India. In addition to banking, the Group, through its various subsidiaries, provides a whole range of financial services which includes Life Insurance, Merchant Banking, Mutual Funds, Credit Card, Factoring, Security Trading and Primary Dealership in the Money Market. SBI's seven Associate Banks had a market share of 6.74 per cent in deposits and 6.95 per cent in advances by the end of 2008-09.

4.6 REFERENCES

1. Vaish M.C., *Monetary Theory,* Vikas Publishing House, New Delhi, (1973): 685.
2. Vaish M.C., *Monetary Theory,* Vikas Publishing House, New Delhi, (1973): 685.
3. Panadikar S.G., *Banking in India,* Orient Longmans Ltd., Calcutta, (1951): 293.
4. Panadikar S.G., *Banking in India,* Orient Longmans Ltd., Calcutta, (1951): 293.
5. Subba Rao, B., Madhusudhana Rao, M. and Suryapraksh Rao, V., *Currency & Banking,*Tata McGraw-Hill Publishing Co., New Delhi, (1992): 188.
6. Mali Ram, *Currency and Banking,* Agarwal Press, Agra, (1958): 207.
7. Mali Ram, *Currency and Banking,* Agarwal Press, Agra, (1958): 208.
8. Varshney and Sundaram, *Banking Theory and Practice,* S. Chand & Sons, New Delhi, (1987): 263.
9. All India Rural Credit Survey Committee, appointed by *RBI* in (1951).
10. Bansal G.L. Banks since Nationalisation, *Birla Insurance of Scientific Research,* New Delhi, (1991): 12.
11. Varshney and Sundaram , *Banking Theory and Practice,* S. Chand & Sons, New Delhi, (1987): 264.
12. www.statebank.com/pdf/branches_alpha.pdf, dated 10-01-2010.
13. Report on Trend and Progress of Banking in India, 2006-07, RBI, p.358.
14. www.statebank.com/pdf/SWIFT.pdf, dated 10-01-2010.

□□□

Chapter 5 PRODUCT MIX

Marketing deals with identifying and meeting human and social needs.[1] According to American Marketing Association 'marketing is an organisational function and a set of processes for creating, communicating, and delivering value to customers and for managing customer relationships in ways that benefit the organisation and its stakeholders.[2] The objective of any firm is to satisfy its customer needs profitably, and in this the marketing role is to find out what the needs are, whether they are being met, and how to meet them better. Therefore, services marketing is a managerial process which ensures the efficient serving of the customers' needs.[3] A key ingredient of the marketing management process is insightful, creative marketing strategies and plans that can guide marketing activities. Developing the right marketing strategy over time requires a blend of discipline and flexibility. Firms must stick to a strategy but must also find new ways to constantly improve it.[4] Marketing strategy also requires a clear understanding of how marketing works.[5] Successful marketing thus requires companies to have capabilities such as understanding customer value, creating customer value, delivering customer value, capturing customer value, and sustaining customer value.[6]

5.1 SERVICES MARKETING MIX

Service characteristics add too many challenges in the market place over goods marketing. The traditional marketing mix that was developed, keeping in view the goals of marketing, may also be adapted to services marketing. But the service organisations cannot satisfy themselves with the use of the traditional marketing mix as they are to stay at sub-optimal performance in marketing.[7] Merely adopting marketing labels cannot resolve problems associated with the marketing of services. The four P's of traditional marketing mix (product, price, place and promotion) are controllable variables. It is believed that an effective combination of these four components will make an organisation have a competitive edge in getting preference by the target market. Marketing researchers have well identified the limitations and insufficiencies of the traditional marketing mix if applied to services also.[8] Booms and Bitner suggested in 1981, a seven P's marketing mix model to service firms. The seven P's were later supported by McGrath and other marketing specialists.

The marketing mix for service organisations are product, physical evidence, price, place, people, promotion and process.

5.2 PRODUCT MIX

The service offering, i.e., the service product, is the basis for marketing activity. According to Philip Kotler, product is anything that can be offered to a market for attention, acquisition, use or consumption that might satisfy a want or need.[9] A service product refers to an activity or activities that a marketer offers to perform, which results in the satisfaction of a need or want of a predominant target customer. It is the offering of a firm in the form of activities (intangible) that satisfy needs. The total range of services that a service firm offers to a variety of customers can be broken into subsets labeled as individual service products. The most important issue in the service product understands what benefits and satisfaction the customer is seeking from the service. According to Rama Mohana Rao, K.,[10] a service product is a package of a series of service elements executed in proper order in keeping with the needs and wants of the consumer, with an intention to maximise consumer satisfaction.

State Bank of India offers various products to suit the needs of the different clientele. Exhibit 5.1 presents the product mix of State Bank of India. The product mix of State Bank of India can be broadly categorised into eight product lines. Product line – I offers Personal Banking services, Product line – II offers Agricultural/Rural Banking services, Product line – III relates to Corporate Banking services, Product line – IV offers NRI services, Product line – V relates to Government Business, Product line – VI relates to various other services offered by the bank, Product line – VII offers International Banking services and Product line – VIII relates to services offered to Small and Medium Enterprises.

Exhibit 5.1: Product Mix of SBI

PRODUCT MIX		
Product line I	:	**Personal Banking**
Product line II	:	**Agricultural/Rural Banking**
Product line III	:	**Corporate Banking**
Product line IV	:	**NRI Banking**
Product line V	:	**Government Business**
Product line VI	:	**Services**
Product line VII	:	**International Banking**
Product line VIII	:	**Small-Medium Enterprise**

Exhibit 5.2: Product line – I

Personal Banking

Deposit Schemes

1 Savings Bank Account
- Savings Plus Account

2 Basic Banking – No Frills Account

3 Current Account

4 RICH Savings Account

5 Corporate Salary Package

6 Term deposits
- SBI Tax Savings Scheme, 2006
- Reinvestment Plan
- SBI MODS
- Recurring Deposits

Personal Finance

1 Loans to Employees to Purchase ESOPS of their Companies

2 Home loans
- SBI Flexi Home loans
- SBI Maxgain Home Lines
- SBI reality Housing
- SBI Freedom Home Loan
- SBI Optima Additional Home Loans

3 Prashasan Plus, Teacher Plus, and Oil Plus

4 Short-term Housing Loans

5 SBI Saral Personal Loan

6 Easy Travel Loan

7 Gram Nivas Scheme

8 Car Loan

9 Education loan

10 Property Loan

11 Loan Against Shares/Debentures

12 Loan for Earnest Money

13 Festival Loans

14 Medi-plus Scheme

15 Teacher Plus Scheme

16 Sainik Plus Scheme

17 Tribal Plus Scheme

18 Loan to Pensioners

19 Redit Khazana

20 Rent Plus

21 SBI Career Loan

5.3 PRODUCT LINE – I: PERSONAL BANKING

The list of products offered under Product line – I are presented in Exhibit 5.2. The personal banking products of State Bank of India can be broadly categorised in to two types. They are deposit scheme and personal finance.

Deposit Schemes

SBI offers different type of products under deposit schemes. A brief description of the products is presented hereunder.

Savings Bank Account: This account helps to plan and save for future financial requirements. Savings remain liquid, safe and earn moderate interest. Savings Bank Account earns an interest at the rate of 3.5% p.a., compounded half yearly. The other benefits are transfer of accounts between the wide network of branches without any charge, nomination facility and 25 cheque leaves free, in a year.

Savings Plus Account: This account brings to the best of both Savings Bank and Term Deposit Accounts. This provides the convenience of a Savings Bank Account along with higher interest of Term Deposit to the consumers.

Basic Banking – No Frills Account: This account can be operated with a very low minimum balance as well as low/nil charges, to cater to the needs of individuals from varied sections of population who are, otherwise, not fulfilling certain conditions of the existing Savings Bank account requirements. This service is offered to the individuals aged 18 years and above earning a gross income of Rs.5,000/- p.m. or less. The mode of operation may be single or joint. The initial deposit amount is Rs.50/- and the minimum balance is nil. This account provides cheque facility, ATM cum debit card facility, internet banking facility, pass book and nomination facility. The product is available at all branches except specialised branches. A customer will not be allowed to open more than one basic banking 'no-frills' account.

Current Account: This account holder is eligible for such services as unlimited number of payments, make payments by giving standing instructions, remit funds from anypart of the country to the account and upcountry cheque collection facility. The benefits of this account are Overdraft facility, Transfer of accounts between the wide banking network of branches without any charge, Nomination facility, Low minimum balance requirements, Internet banking and ATM Card facility.

RICH Savings Account: RICH Savings Account provides an enriched version of Savings Bank account consisting of various concessions and add-ons. !t is suitable for high net worth Individual/Mass Affluent customers.

Corporate Salary Package: The employees of a company, which is operating SBI for payment of salaries, will receive instant credit of salaries.

Term Deposit: This deposit provides for earning a higher interest on surplus funds for the investing customer. It also provides security, trust and competitive rate of interest. The period of term deposit may vary from 7 days to 10 years.

SBI Tax Savings Scheme, 2006: This product is designed to cater to the needs of the Income Tax assesses.The distinctive features of this product are to enable customers to place long term deposits to earn higher rate of interest and also to avail the tax benefits under section 80C of Income Tax Act, 1961. The minimum deposit is Rs.1,000/- or multiples thereof and the maximum deposit should not exceed Rs.1,00,000/- in a year.

Reinvestment Plan Deposits: The scheme is offered for individuals including Minors, Proprietorship or Partnership Firm, Clubs/Associations, Companies, Co-operative Societies, Banks and Financial Institutions. The period of this deposit vary from 6 months to 120 months. A minimum amount of Rs.1,000/- and thereafter in multiples of Rs.100/- has to be deposited. Customers are allowed to take advance against this deposit. This scheme is available at all branches in the country. Other facilities like automatic renewal facility, safe custody facility are available at free of charge. The account can be closed prematurely.

Multi Option Deposit Scheme: The Multi Option Deposit (MOD) Account is a combination of Savings Bank or Current Account with Term/Special Term Deposit Accounts, so that one can securely write cheques up to the balance in the MOD account or up to the drawing power available as overdraft in the Current account. The features of this deposit scheme are complete liquidity, convenience of overdraft, earns a higher rate of interest on deposit, without the dilemma of locking it for a long period. At the time of need for funds, withdrawals can be made in units of Rs.1,000/- from the deposits by issuing a cheque from Savings Bank account or through overdraft facility from Current account. The period of Term Deposit vary from 1 year to 5 years. An MOD account can be opened with SBI for a minimum amount of Rs.10,000/- only. The scheme is available at all SBI branches.

Recurring Deposit: Recurring Deposit provides the customers the element of compulsion to save at high rates of interest applicable to Term Deposits along with liquidity to access that savings any time. One can have this deposit with SBI for a minimum monthly instalment of Rs.100/- only. Monthly instalments can be deposited on any working day of the month. Delayed monthly installments attract penalty.

Personal Finance

Under this head SBI offers wide range of products. The following is the brief description of the products offered under the head personal finance.

Loans to Employees to Purchase ESOPs of their Companies: To assist employees for purchasing shares of their own companies under the Employee Stock Option Scheme (ESOP).

Home Loans: The purpose of these loans are to purchase/construction of house/flat, purchase of a plot of land for construction of house, extension/repair/renovation/ alteration of an existing house/flat and purchase of furnishings and consumer durables as a part of the project cost, takeover of an existing loan from other banks/housing finance companies.

- **'SBI-Flexi' Home Loans:** A customised product designed to enable borrowers to hedge home loan against unfavorable movement in interest rates. The product gives a one time irrevocable option to choose one of the three customised combinations of fixed and floating interest rates and also to choose the order in which the fixed and floating rate will be availed.

- **'SBI-Maxgain' Home Loans:** This product enables to earn optimal yield on savings and minimises interest burden on home loans, with no extra cost. The loan is granted as an overdraft facility with the added flexibility to operate home loan account like SB or current account. The product serves to minimise interest cost by enabling to park surplus funds in 'SBI-Maxgain' (with the benefit to withdraw the surplus funds whenever require), specially in the wake of low yields from other deposit/investment avenues.
- **'SBI-Reality' Home Loans:** This product is to purchase a plot of land for house construction. The loan is available for a maximum amount of Rs.20 lakh (relaxation considered on case to case basis) and with a repayment period of up to 15 years. Customers are also eligible to avail another housing loan for construction of house on the plot financed by the bank with the benefit of running both the loans concurrently.
- **'SBI-Freedom' Home Loans:** This product is to provide financial support to the customers to invest in without mortgaging the property. Customers also have an option to take the loan by way of mortgage of the property and pledge financial securities in lieu of margin money.
- **'SBI-Optima' Additional Home Loans:** This product is intended to meet expenditure towards major repair, renovation, addition to customer house/flat, purchase of furniture, fixtures and consumer durables.

'Prashasan Plus', 'Teacher Plus' and 'Oil Plus': These schemes offer concessional interest rate of 0.25% below the applicable interest rates on home loans to niche client groups like Government Employees, Teachers, Employees of Public Sector Oil Companies, etc.

Short-term Housing Loan: This scheme is intendment to support purchase or construction of a new house/flat or purchase an existing (old) house/flat or for extension, repair, renovation or alteration of a house/flat.

SBI Saral Personal Loan: The loan is offered for any legitimate purpose whatsoever (e.g. expenses for domestic or foreign travel, medical treatment of self or a family member, meeting any financial liability, such as marriage of son/daughter, defraying educational expenses of wards, meeting margins for purchase of assets etc.).

Easy Travel Loans: Loans are offered to all customers to meet any kind of travel expense such as cost of ticket, hotel stay, visa, airport tax, etc.

Gram Nivas Scheme: Objective of this scheme is to comprehensively cater to the needs of the village community with special focus on poorest of the poor for housing loans keeping in view the peculiarity of the ownership title in rural areas, social habits, type of construction and other related needs.

Car Loans: Car loans are offered to all consumers depending on their repayment availabilities. The purpose of this loan is to offer financial support for the purpose of a new car, jeep or Multi Utility Vehicles (MUVs), a used car/jeep (not more than 5 years old) and take over of existing loan from other bank/financial institution.

Education Loan: A term loan granted to Indian nationals for pursuing higher education in India or abroad where admission has been secured. All courses having employment prospects are eligible. The loan is offered to Graduation courses/Post graduation courses/Professional courses, other courses approved by UGC/Government/AICTE, etc.

Property Loan: This is an all purpose loan, i.e., the loan can be obtained for any purpose whatsoever. If amount of loan is Rs.25 lakh and above then purpose of loan will have to be specified along with an undertaking that loan will not be used for any speculative purpose whatever including speculation on real estate and equity shares.

Loan against Shares/Debentures: For meeting contingencies and needs of personal nature, loans are offered for subscribing to rights or new issue of shares/debentures against the security of existing shares/debentures. However, loans will not be sanctioned for (i) speculative purposes, (ii) inter-corporate investments, and (iii) acquiring controlling interest in company/ companies.

Loan for Earnest Money Deposit: This product addresses the financial requirements towards Earnest Money Deposit to book residential plots/built-up houses/flats being sold by Government Housing Agencies, Urban Development Authorities like PUDA, HUDA, and Housing Boards.

Festival Loans: The purpose is to meet any kind of festival related expenses.

Medi-plus Scheme: Loans are offered for individuals to avail specialised expensive medical treatment e.g. coronary by-pass, Hip and Knee replacement surgery, cochlear implants (surgical) for the hearing impaired, etc.

Teacher-plus Scheme: Teacher Plus is a special scheme for teachers placed under State and Central Governments as also under the deemed universities. Concessions in the rates of interest, processing charges and margin amounts are offered.

Sainik Plus Scheme: SBI offers Sainik Plus with special discounts on processing fees, interest rates and margin amounts on various finance schemes. This is available for all Non Commissioned Officers (NCOs) and Jawans of Indian Army. The concession schemes are Personal Loan, Festival Loan and Housing Loan.

Tribal-plus Scheme: The scheme is a special housing finance scheme for Hill/Tribal areas of North East India and areas around Chandigarh, Bhopal, Lucknow, Patna and Bhubaneswar.

Loan to Pensioners: The purpose of the loan is to meet personal expenses. The customers are Central or State Government pensioners drawing pension through one of the branches of the bank and are of not more than 72 years of age. Customers can avail a loan of up to a maximum of 12 months pension, subject to a ceiling of Rs.1,00,000/-.

Credit Khazana: This scheme offers housing loan to customers concessions in interest rates and margins are offered to those who subsequently avail car loan, education loan, personal loan or tractor loan.

Rent Plus: This product is intended to meet liquidity mismatch of the applicants.

SBI Career Loan: This product is specially intended to the customers who take Pilot training courses or Airhostess Training courses in India and abroad, from institutes recognised by the Ministry of Civil Aviation/DGCA.

5.4 PRODUCT LINE – II: AGRICULTURE/RURAL BANKING

The details of Product Line – II are presented in Exhibit 5.3. The Agricultural/Rural Banking products of State Bank of India can be categorised in to three types. They are Agriculture Banking, Micro Credit and Regional Rural Banks.

Exhibit 5.3: Product Line – II

AGRICULTURE/RURAL BANKING

Micro Credit

- Self Help Groups
- Financial Inclusion

Agricultural Banking

- Agricultural Term Loans
- Farm Mechanisation Scheme
- Kisan Credit Card Scheme
- Land Development Scheme
- Loan against Warehouse Receipts / Cold Storage Receipts
- Financing of Combine Harvesters
- Crop Loans
- Land Purchase Scheme
- Krishi Plus Scheme
- Produce Marketing Loan Scheme
- Kisan Gold Card Scheme
- ARTHIAS Plus Scheme
- Dairy Plus Scheme
- Broiler Plus Scheme
- Finance to Horticulture
- Minor Irrigation Scheme

Regional Rural Banks

Micro Credit

Self Help Groups (SHG): SBI has taken up SHG movement as a mission. Micro Credit is offered to the self help groups as a noble mission to reach those families who were hitherto having no access to the credit by any formal financial institution and, therefore, were depending on informal sources and moneylenders.

Financial Inclusion: Under this scheme, the extension of banking services through business facilitators/business correspondents is provided. The main objective of the scheme is to extend micro finance services for uplifting the poor and to extend banking facilities in untapped/unbanked areas through the use of existing branch network and new technology in combination with outsourcing.

Agricultural Banking

State Bank of India's branches have covered several agricultural activities like crop production, horticulture, plantation crops, farm mechanisation, land development and reclamation, digging of wells, tube wells and irrigation projects, forestry, construction of cold storages and godowns, processing of agri-products, finance to agri-input dealers, allied activities like dairy, fisheries, poultry, sheep-goat, piggery refurbished second hand tractors, loans against pledge of warehouse receipts, loans against produce stored by the farmer at his/her own premises, loans against book debts of Arthias, mulberry cultivation, rearing of silk worms and grain ages. In fact, the Bank can cover any other agricultural related activities undertaken. The following are the 16 specific products offered by the bank under the head.

Agricultural Term Loans (ATL): Agricultural term loans are provided for the purchase of assets, farm machinery, bullocks, sheep, etc., creation of assets (orchard development, poultry, dairy development etc.) connected with rural activities under agriculture, horticulture, plantation, sericulture, animal husbandry, fisheries etc., where the loan amount is repayable over a period of time not exceeding 3 years. All categories of farmers and agricultural labourers are eligible. Loan amount Rs.50,000/- up to 100% of the cost of the asset/project cost is provided as loan. Above Rs.50,000/- up to 85% of the cost of the asset/project is given as loan.

Farm Mechanisation Scheme: This scheme is intended to provide credit for purchase of farm equipment and machinery for agricultural operations. It covers activities ranging from purchase of tractors and accessories, trailers, power tillers, combine harvesters, power sprayers, dusters, threshers etc. Farmers owning more than minimum acreage of perennially irrigated lands are eligible (for power tillers 2 acres, for tractors 4 acres for > 35 HP and 6 acres for above 35 HP and for combine 8 acres). Eligibility for purchase of other farm equipment is decided on the income generated by the agri activity. Loan amount Rs.50,000/- up to 100 per cent of the cost of the asset is provided as loan. Above Rs.50,000/- up to 85 per cent of the cost of the asset provided as loan.

Kisan Credit Card Scheme (KCC): The purpose of this scheme is to extend adequate and timely support to farmers for their short term credit needs. Farmers with excellent repayment record for 2 years, and new farmers with sizeable deposits with the bank branches for 3 to 4 years are eligible.

Land Development Scheme: This scheme offers credit solutions for land development projects in the form of direct finance to cultivators for better productivity. Loans under this head cover various activities like land clearance(removal bushes, trees, etc.), land leveling and shaping, contour/graded bonding, bench terracing for hilly areas, contour stone walls, staggered contour trenches, disposal drains, reclamation of saline/alkaline soils and fencing etc. All farmers owning agricultural land are eligible. Loan amount Rs.50,000/- up to 100 % of the cost of the asset/project cost is provided as loan. Above Rs.50,000/- up to 85 % of the cost of the asset/project is given as loan.

Loan against Warehouse Receipts/Cold Storage Receipts: The bank extends financial assistance to farmers' storing produce in private/government warehouse/cold storages against pledge of warehouse/cold storage receipt to prevent distress sale. The maximum repayment period of the loan is 6 months. The loan amount will be 60 % of the value (minimum support price) of the produce stored.

Financing of Combine Harvesters: Under this scheme financial support is provided to farmers for the purpose of combined harvesting. Farmers owning a minimum 8 acres of perennially irrigated land, non-farmer entrepreneurs capable of utilising combine harvester for custom hiring work and those who can put the combine harvester with a minimum productive workload of 1000 hours are eligible for the loan.

Crop Loan: The purpose of this loan is to provide financial assistance to meet cultivation expenses for various crops. Agriculturists, Tenant farmers and Share Croppers who actually cultivate the lands are eligible for these loans. All categories of farmers - Small/Marginal (SF/MF) and others are included. Loan amount is based on the cost of cultivation incurred for each crop per acre of crop cultivated and 90 % of the cost of cultivation is given as loan.

Land Purchase Scheme: This scheme is to give loans to small and marginal farmers/landless labourers for purchase of agricultural land. Small/marginal farmers, tenants, share-croppers owning less than 5 acres of un-irrigated/2.5 acres irrigated land in their own name and landless agricultural labourers, with record of prompt repayment of loans, are eligible to avail this loan. Maximum loan amount under the scheme will be Rs.5 lakh.

Krishi Plus Scheme: The purpose of the scheme is to finance for purchase of tractor to Rural Youth for custom hiring. The tractor to be financed should be in the approved list of tractors circulated to the branches by the bank. As much as 85 per cent of the cost of the asset is provided as loan subject to a maximum amount of Rs.4 lakh.

Produce Marketing Loan Scheme: The Bank extends financial assistance to help farmers storing produce in their own premises to prevent distress sale. This facilitates immediate renewal of crop loans for next season.

Kisan Gold Card Scheme: The scheme sanctions hassle free term loans to farmers having excellent repayment record. Consumption loan to meet domestic expenses like children's education, marriage, medical expenses, etc., are also included to the extent of 20 per cent of limit.

ARTHIAS Plus Scheme: This scheme is to finance commission agents against their receivables of farmers. The loan amount should be repaid within a period of 6 months.

Dairy Plus Scheme: Loans are offered for Purchase of milch cattle/milking machine/ construction of shed/chaff cutter and other equipments. Farmers who are member of milk procuring societies or located on milk route, owners of small dairy with less than 10 milch animals and owning a minimum of 0.25 acres for every 5 animals, large dairy units with 10 milch animals and more owning a minimum of 1 acre of land for cultivation of fodder for every 5 animals are eligible for loan.

Broiler Plus Scheme: Under the scheme, loans are available to farmer for construction of broiler sheds or any other development work required and equipment needed for broiler farming.

Finance to Horticulture: This scheme offers, loans for the development of fruit orchards like mango, chikoo, guava, grapes, pomegranate, apple, lechee, etc., as well as short term fruit crops(banana, pineapple, etc.), flowers in open and green houses (roses, carnation, chrysanthemums, jasmine, etc.) and vegetable crops (potato, tomato, brinjal, gourds, peas, etc.).

Minor Irrigation Scheme: This scheme provides credit for creating irrigation facilities from underground/surface water sources. All structures and equipments connected with it are also financed. The loans cover various activities like digging of new wells (open/bore wells), deepening of existing wells (traditional/in well bore), energisation of wells (oil engine/ electrical pump set), laying of pipe lines, installing drip/sprinkler irrigation system and lift irrigation system.

Regional Rural Banks

State Bank of India has sponsored 30 RRBs, which operate in 102 districts of 16 States viz. Andhra Pradesh, Arunachal Pradesh, Assam, Bihar, Chhattisgarh, Himachal Pradesh, Jammu & Kashmir, Jharkhand, Karnataka, Madhya Pradesh, Meghalaya, Mizoram, Nagaland, Orissa, Uttaranchal and Uttar Pradesh, with a network of 2,336 branches. This forms 16% of the total bank branch network in the country. As many as 2,020 of these branches (86%) are located in remote rural areas of the country.

5.5 PRODUCT LINE – III: NRI BANKING

State Bank of India provides customised services with a global footprint to suit customer banking needs. Exhibit 5.4 presents the details of NRI services offered by the bank.

Deposits

NRIs can open any of the following eight types of accounts to deposit their funds.

NRI Rupee Account: The account can be opened only by Non Resident Indians (NRIs), open jointly only with another NRI (in case customer wish to open the account jointly with spouse (s), he/she should also be an NRI). For the account holders, ATM cards will be issued and Internet Banking facility is available. A minimum balance of Rs.1000/- is to be maintained in the account.

Current Account: The bank issues ATM cum Debit Card to this account holder. It provides access to the wide network of ATMs across the country to withdraw cash, enquire about balance, etc. Customers can also withdraw cash from Maestro endorsed ATMs of other banks under bilateral sharing, at a nominal fee. The other benefits of this account are overdraft facility, transfer of accounts without any charge, nomination facility and low minimum balance requirements. This account operation is very useful to the customers because of unlimited number of payments, payments by standing instructions to the bank, remittance of funds from any part of the country to the account and upcountry cheque collection facility.

NRI Term Deposit: The deposit is for a minimum period of one year and a maximum period of 5 years. Interest can be drawn quarterly on Term Deposit Receipts (TDRs) or compounded quarterly Special Term Deposit Receipts (STDRs). No interest is payable for deposits of less than 12 months.

Exhibit 5.4: Product Line –III

NRI BANKING

Deposits

- NRI Rupee Account
- NRI Term Deposits
- Current Account
- Non-Resident Account
- SBI Special Platinum Account
- Super Saver Term Deposit
- Foreign Currency Non Resident Account
- Resident Foreign Currency Account

NRI Car Loan Scheme

NRI Home Loan

Remittance to India

Miscellaneous

- Facilities for Returning Indians
- Investment Scheme for NRI
- Tax Benefit for NRI

Non-Resident (Ordinary) Account: The account holders of their service can withdraw money for making local payments in rupees. Investments are allowed in shares/securities/ immovable properties on non-repatriation basis with general or specific permission from the RBI. Balances can be repatriated for any bonafide purpose, subject to payment of taxes, duly certified by a Chartered Accountant up to a maximum of US$ one million per calendar year. Income Tax at a flat rate of 30 per cent will be deducted at source on interest earned in the NRO accounts irrespective of the amount of interest. Advance against NRO term deposits is permissible. Income in India can be credited to NRO accounts.

SBI Special Platinum Term Deposit: This is a special term deposit product to customers with higher rate of interest.

Super Saver Term Deposit Scheme: The purpose of this scheme is to offer higher rate of interest for long term deposits. The minimum deposit is Rs.10,000/- and in multiples of Rs.1000/- thereafter. There is no maximum deposit limit. The tenure of this deposit varies from 4 years to 10 years and available in all branches of the SBI. The other facilities are nomination facility, loan facility and transferability among branches.

Foreign Currency Non Resident Account (FCNR): FCNR accounts can be opened only by an NRI and also open jointly with another NRI. Nomination facility is also available (nominee can be a resident Indian also). Deposits can be opened in US$, Euro, Sterling Pounds, Canadian Dollars, Australian Dollars and Japanese Yen. The minimum period of deposit is one year and maximum period is 5 years. Premature withdrawal is permissible subject to one per cent penal interest. No interest is payable if the deposit is closed within a year. Rupee loans can be taken in India against the security of the deposit. Foreign currency loans can be availed abroad against the security of FCNR deposits.

Resident Foreign Currency Account: NRIs returning to India for permanent settlement can open RFC accounts. RFC accounts are at present being opened in US dollars only.

NRI Car Loan Scheme: State Bank of India presents a special product in car loans to cater to overseas Indians. To meet their specific needs, bank has launched a new car loan scheme titled as 'NRI-Car Loan'. Under the stated scheme, the borrower will be a resident Indian who is a close relative of sponsoring NRI/PIO who would be the guarantor. Under the NRI – Car Loan Scheme the NRI/PIO will be the guarantor and the NRI's /PIO's nominee will be the principal applicant. The car loan will be granted at the request of the guarantor (NRI/PIO).

NRI Home Loan: Loans to NRIs & PIOs can be extended for several purposes. The purposes include purchase/construct a new house/flat, to repair, renovate or extend an existing house/flat, to purchase an existing house/flat, to purchase a plot for construction of a dwelling unit and to purchase furnishings and consumer durables, as a part of the project cost.

Remittances to India

State Bank of India offers the following services under the head remittances to India.

- Drafts in Indian rupees can be purchased from exchange companies or the correspondents and mailed to the branch where customer has their account.
- Telegraphic or wire transfers can be made through bank branches abroad or Bank correspondents to branches having SWIFT/TT drawing arrangements.

- Cheques can be deposited for credit of customer accounts. These will be collected and credited to customer accounts.
- Traveler's cheques can be tendered by personally during their visit to India.
- If branch is SWIFT enabled, customer can transfer funds from anywhere by SWIFT.
- For speedy credit to accounts from Gulf, customer can use SBI Express.

Miscellaneous

The following are the other services offered to NRI's by the bank.

Facilities for Returning Indians

- Customers are free to maintain their assets acquired or inherited abroad.
- NRIs/PIOs on return to India can freely maintain and operate their foreign currency accounts with Banks abroad.
- Balances in NRI/FCNR accounts can be credited to RFC accounts in US Dollars.

Investment Schemes for Non Resident Indians: NRIs are permitted to invest in

- Government Securities and Treasury Bills.
- Schemes of Domestic Mutual Funds.
- Equity shares of PSUs on disinvestment (subject to terms and conditions in notices inviting bids).
- Bonds issued by PSUs.
- Non-convertible debentures of Indian Companies.

Tax Benefits for NRIs

- Interest on NRE and FCNR deposits are free of income tax.
- Tax @ 30 per cent will be deducted at source on all interest income in NRO accounts.

On permanent return to India, income on all investments out of foreign exchange funds would be eligible for a flat tax rate of 20 per cent (excluding surcharge) till maturity of the investments.

5.6 PRODUCT LINE – IV: INTERNATIONAL BANKING

International banking services of State Bank of India are delivered for the benefit of its Indian customers, non-resident Indians, foreign entities and banks through a network of 83 offices/branches in 29 countries, spread over all time zones. The network is augmented by a cluster of Overseas and NRI branches within India and correspondent links with over 522 banks, the world over. Bank's Joint Ventures and Subsidiaries abroad further underline the Bank's international presence.

The International Banking services include corporate lending, loan syndications, merchant banking, handling letters of credit and guarantees, short-term financing, collection of clean and documentary credits and remittances. The specific products offered by the bank under International Banking are shown in Exhibit 5.5.

Exhibit 5.5: Product Line–IV

INTERNATIONAL BANKING
Trade Finance
• Export Avenue
• Import Avenue
Merchant Banking
Project Export Finance
Export Gold Card
Treasury

The Bank has carved a niche for itself in the Euro land with branches located in Antwerp, Paris and Frankfurt. Indian banks and corporates are able to avail single-window Euro services from the Bank's Frankfurt branch.

Trade Finance

SBI offers the financial solutions to all Trade Finance related fund needs (both in Indian rupee and foreign currencies). The gamut of services includes credit for both pre shipment and post shipment activities.

Export Avenue: The trade finance cell of SBI offers both Pre shipment and Post shipment credit in rupee denominated terms to exporters having firm export orders or confirmed letters of credit.

Import Avenue: This service is ideal for both Indian importers and their foreign suppliers. SBI offers credit to foreign suppliers of Indian importers by purchasing the import bill for its full value through one of the bank's overseas offices. The tenure of this form of supplier's credit does not exceed 180 days.The supplier gets 100 per cent of the invoice value immediately, making his/her deal practically a cash sale.

Offshore Banking Unit

State Bank of India has opened the first Offshore Banking Unit (OBU) in India at the SEEPZ Special Economic Zone, New Bank Building, Andheri (East) Mumbai on 17th July, 2003 - another landmark in the history of India's financial sector. The OBU will be deemed as an overseas branch of the bank and undertake the activities such as raising funds in convertible foreign currency as deposits and borrowings from Non Residents sources, transactions in foreign exchange with residents in India who are eligible to enter into or undertake such transactions in terms of various rules and regulations as framed under Foreign Exchange Management Act, 1999.

Merchant Banking

SBI's Merchant Banking Group is positioned to offer perfect financial solutions to business. The bank specialised in the arrangement of various forms of foreign currency credits for corporates.

Project Export Finance

State Bank of India is an active participant in the area of finance of project export activities. These activities will mainly involve financing the fund based and non fund based requirements of the project exporters.

Exporters Gold Card

State Bank of India has launched "*SBI exporters gold card scheme*" to meet the working capital needs of exporters with good track record and credit worthiness, subject to their fulfilling the specified eligibility norms. The salient features of the scheme are; assessment norms have been simplified and for units with export turnover up to Rs.100 crore, simplified assessment in terms of Nayak Committee norms will be made within specified time not exceeding 25 days in case of new sanctions and 15 days in case of renewals.

Treasury

SBI's relationships with over 700 correspondent banks are also leveraged in extracting maximum value from treasury operations. SBI's treasury operations are channeled through the Rupee Treasury, the Forex Treasury and the Treasury Management Group (TMG). The Rupee Treasury deals in the domestic money and debt markets while the Forex Treasury deals mainly in the local foreign exchange market. The TMG monitors the investment, risk and asset-liability management aspects of the bank's overseas offices.

The Treasury Management Group (TMG) is a part of the International Banking Group (IBG) and functions under the Chief General Manager (Foreign Offices). As the name implies, the department monitors the management of treasury functions at SBI's foreign offices including asset liability management, investments and forex operations. The Portfolio Management Services Section (PMS) of State Bank of India has been set up to handle investment and regulatory related concerns of Institutional investors functioning in the area of social security.

5.7 PRODUCT LINE – V: CORPORATE BANKING

In Corporate Banking, the products are grouped under four categories such as Corporate Accounts Group, Mid Corporate Group, Project Finance and Services (Exhibit 5.6). The following are the details.

Corporate Accounts Group (CAG)

CAG is Strategic Business Unit of SBI, set up exclusively to cater to the specialised banking needs of top corporate clients of the country. It was the direct outcome of SBI's structural reorganisation in the light of deregulation, globalisation and liberalisation of the banking industry. It was launched in the year 1995.

Core Credit Products: The core credit products are Rupee loans, Project cape loans, Export Credits and foreign Currency loans.

Exhibit 5.6: Product Line –V

CORPORATE BANKING

Corporate Accounts Group

- Core Credit Product
- Structured Products
- Fee Based Products
- Cash Management Products
- Other Products

Mid Corporate Group

Project Finance

Products and Services

- Industrial Sector
- Trade and Service Sector

Structured Products

(a) Short-term Corporate Loans: For shoring up net working capital, ongoing capital expenditure, repayment of high cost debt, R&D expenditure, implementation of VRS.

(b) Securitised loans- in association with SBICAP: Up fronting of assured cash flow emanating from future receivables, *viz.*, rentals, royalties, debtors, Lease rentals, etc.

Fee Based Products: The products offered under this head are LCs, Guarantees and DPG. While SBI is the most widely accepted Indian Bank across the world with correspondent relationship extending to a spectrum of international banks, the LCs, Guarantees and DPGs are issued at the most competitive rates. SBI is the only Indian Bank whose guarantee is accepted by most of the Export Credit Agencies globally without seeking confirmation.

Cash Management Product: State Bank of India provides cash management services to Corporate Clients under the brand name SBI-FAST (Funds Available in Shortest Time) from 320 collecting locations across the country with pooling facility at different branches as per client's choice, which is physically connected to the central hub at Mumbai. Under SBI-FAST, funds are transferred directly to the client's main account (at any one or more of the 65 pooling centres) from various collection centres on the same day that they are cleared at the centres. SBI-FAST also offers disbursement/payment services through a separate debit transfer module to facilitate payments at various expenditure centers and plant locations. SBI is the acknowledged leader in the collection services, which basically aims at collection of sale proceeds electronically for companies having a wide market network spread all over the country.

Other Products

Treasury and Forex Products: SBI being the largest Forex and money market player in the country, an array of treasury and Forex products are offered at very competitive rates.

Efficient delivery platform: For effective delivery of the products, exclusive and totally technology driven CAG outlets have been opened at the 4 metros and Ahmedabad with state-of-art communication facilities.

MID Corporate Group

Mid Corporate Group (MCG) has been set up in the bank under Corporate Banking Group to cater to the various banking requirements of Mid-Corporates. It provides business solutions to its customers through its 28 dedicated branches all over the country. A Mid-corporate has been defined as a business entity having annual turnover between Rs.25 crore and Rs.350 crore or an entity having a minimum fund based limit of Rs.5 crore (including term loans).

Project Finance

This product is a one-stop-shop of financial services for new projects as well as expansion, diversification and modernisation of existing projects in infrastructure and non -infrastructure sectors. The SBI has formed a dedicated Project Finance Strategic Business Unit to assess credit proposals from and extend term loans for large industrial and infrastructure projects. Apart from this, project term loans for medium sized projects and smaller clients are delivered through the CAG and the NBG.

Products and Services

Industrial Sector: The following are the products offered to the industrial sector.

- **Working Capital Finance:** SBI offers working capital finance to meet the entire range of short-term fund requirements that arise within a corporate's day-to-day operational cycle.

- **Deferred Payment Guarantees:** SBI can extend deferred payment guarantees to industrial projects for obtaining imported equipment. The DPG is a standby credit guaranteeing deferred payments, usually for payments for capital goods, turnkey contracts, etc.

- **Structured FInance:** SBI structured finance involves assembling unique credit configurations to meet the complex fund requirements of large industrial and infrastructure projects. Structured finance can be a combination of funded and non-funded facilities as well as other credit enhancement tools, to fit the multi-layer financial requirements of large and long-gestation projects.

- **Dealer Financing:** SBI extends financial support to the corporate distribution networks, by providing both working capital finance and term loans to select dealers of identified companies. This gives dealers to leverage their business relationship with major corporates to avail low cost credit. Also, this type of financial solutions allows the corporate negotiate a better price with dealers. Dealer financing may be extended in the bill discounting form or simply as cash credit.

- **Channel Financing:** Channel financing is an innovative finance mechanism by which the bank meets the various fund necessities along supply chain at the supplier's end itself, thus helping to sustain a seamless business flow along the arteries of the enterprise.

- **Equipment Leasing:** The SBI has deployed a dedicated Strategic Business Unit for lease financing that is richly experienced in arranging lease contracts for procuring expensive equipment for projects or plants. SBI, arranges lease agreements as stand alone contracts or as part of a structured package.

- **Loan Syndication:** The SBI leverages its vast network of relationships to arrange syndicated credit products for corporate clients and industrial projects.

Trade and Services Sector: To finance new trucks/tankers/trailers/tippers/luxury buses including take over of existing similar loans from other banks/institutions, SBI offer products under this head.

5.8 PRODUCT LINE – VI: SERVICES

SBI offers a wide range of services other than deposits and loans and advances. The following are the auxiliary services offered by the bank (Exhibit 5.7).

Exhibit 5.7: Product Line –VI

SERVICES

Viswa Yatra Foreign Travel Card
- FTC Gift card

Payroll Card

Gift Cards

Locker

eZ-trade@sbi

DEMAT Services

Gift Cheques

ATM Services
- SBI Gold International Debit Cards
- Cash-plus Scheme

Internet Banking

RBI-EFT

e-Rail

e-Pay

Foreign Inward Remittance

Viswa Yatra Foreign Travel Card (FTC): This is a prepaid plastic card issued in association with VISA International.

FTC Gift card: This Gift Card is a pre-paid plastic card supported by magnetic-strip based technology. It is usable at all VISA enabled merchant establishments and POS by signature/PIN. It is a substitute for gift vouchers sold by many retail houses as its use is not restricted to any particular merchant establishment/point of sale.

Payroll Card: It is a prepaid plastic card issued in Indian rupees in association with VISA international. Periodical payments like salary, payment of TA/medical/incentives etc. can be loaded on to the card from a single point and the funds are available to the employees immediately.

Gift Cards: It is a pre-paid plastic card supported by magnetic-strip based technology.

Locker: For the safety of valuables the bank offers customers safe deposit vault or locker facilities at a large number of branches. There is a nominal annual charge, which depends on the size of the locker and the centre in which the branch is located.

eZ-trade@sbi: This service is an online trading platform to cater to all trading (*presently available to Indian residents only*) needs. This service provides with a 3-in-1 account which is an integrated platform of Bank Account, Demat Account and an Online Trading Account to give a convenient and paper free trading experience under one roof.

DEMAT Services: This service is an open linked 3-in-1 account viz. a SB a/c, DeMat a/c or DP a/c and Trading a/c. The linked account offers 24x7 investing, security, no paper work, easy transfer of funds, instant order confirmations, speed and transparency.

Gift Cheques: SBI offers Gift Cheques at all its branches in denominations of Rs.101/-, Rs.201/-, Rs.501/- and Rs.1001/-. Gift Cheques do not attract any charges and come with an attractive free envelope.

ATM Services: State Bank offers the convenience of more than 11,300 ATMs in India, the largest network in the country and continuing to expand fast.

- ***SBI Gold International Debit Cards:*** SBI Gold Debit Cards have come with a variety of add-on features besides higher daily cash withdrawal limits at ATMs. The Gold International Debit cards are issued in association with MasterCard as well as VISA International and are available with all core banking branches.
- ***Cash-plus Scheme:*** This scheme offers ATM-cum-Debit Card - named as State Bank Cash plus - offers services for personal banking customers. Cash plus also provides online access to savings or current account and has a tie-up with master card international (Maestro Card).

Internet Banking: www.onlinesbi.com is the Internet banking service of the State Bank of India. Customers can check their account balances, view account, request for cheque book, drafts, bankers cheques, stop cheque payment and issue standing instructions. They also can transfer funds to other accounts at the branch, request for third party transfers, invest and renew Term Deposits.

RBI-EFT: Inter-bank Electronic Funds Transfer facility of the Reserve Bank of India (RBI - EFT) is available with SBI branches in the clearing zone of Service Branches at Kolkata, Mumbai, New Delhi and Chennai.

e-Rail: The facility has been launched in 2003 in association with IRCTC. The scheme facilitates Booking of Railways Ticket Online.

e-Pay: Bill Payment@OnlineSBI (e-Pay) will let customer to pay his/her Telephone, Mobile, Electricity, Insurance, and Credit Card bills electronically over Online SBI website http://www.onlinesbi.com. If the biller presents bills online, can also give Auto Pay instructions and the bank will pay the bills as and when it falls due. The service is available for select local billers at Ahmedabad, Bangalore, Bhopal, Bhuvaneshwar, Chandigarh, Chennai, Delhi, Guwahati, Hyderabad, Kolkata, Lucknow, Mumbai, Patna and Thiruvanathapuram. The national billers like LIC, SBI Cards, SBI Life Insurance, etc., can be paid at any centre across the country.

Foreign Inward Remittance: Sending remittances to India for credit to the account with the bank or for family is made simple and convenient through this service with wide foreign offices network and correspondent banking arrangement with about 600 banks worldwide. Wherever in the world customer may be, there is the bank office or a bank having corresponding banking arrangement with SBI to provide facilities of remittances.

Real Time Gross Settlement System (RTGS) & National Electronic Fund Transfer System (NEFT): Bank offers Real Time Gross Settlement System (RTGS) & National Electronic Fund Transfer system (NEFT) which enables an efficient, secure, economical and reliable system of transfer of funds from bank to bank as well as from remitter's account in a particular bank to the beneficiary's account in another bank across the country.

The other regular services of the bank are payment of cheques, bills of exchange, drafts subscriptions, traveler cheques, foreign exchange, and custodian service.

5.9 PRODUCT LINE – VII: GOVERNMENT BUSINESS

State Bank of India is a public sector bank and the bank has an obligation to serve the banking needs of the government and involved in the process of economic and social development of the country. State Bank of India's linkage with government business is widespread (Exhibit 5.8). It is significant that out of 11,448 branches in India, about 9,116 branches are conducting Government Business. The large network of the branches provides easy access to the common man to deposit the government dues and pension payments.

Exhibit 5.8: Product Line –VII

GOVERNMENT BUSINESS
SBI – e-Tax
Government Accounts
Public Provident Fun
Senior Citizen Savings Scheme

SBI e-tax – Online Tax Payment Facility: This is an online tax payment facility that saves time, is convenient, hassle free and paperless. It is available on a 24x7 basis and enables to pay taxes online, with ease and simplicity. Direct/Indirect taxes can be paid through SBI e-tax.

Government Accounts Department: The Government Accounts Department (GAD) oversees the handling of government business undertaken by SBI branches as sub-agent of Reserve Bank of India. It is a co-ordinating agency between the branches dealing in Central Government transactions and Reserve Bank of India, CAS, Nagpur, on the one hand and Accounting Authorities of Department of Central Government on the other.

Public Provident Fund – 1968: This scheme was introduced by Central Government in 1968. The scheme enables the members of the public to make contributions to the fund and obtain Income Tax rebate under the relevant provisions of the Income Tax. Customers can operate this scheme through SBI.

Senior Citizens Savings Scheme: Government of India has decided to operate the scheme through all branches of Public Sector Banks which are operating PPF Scheme, 1968.

5.10 PRODUCT LINE – VIII: SMALL AND MEDIUM ENTERPRISES

State Bank of India has been playing a vital role in the development of small scale industries since 1956 (Exhibit 5.9). The Bank has financed over 8 lakh SSI units in the country. It has 55 specialised SSI branches, 99 branches in industrial estates and more than 400 branches with SBI divisions. The bank finances for Small Business activities which are of special significance to a large number of people as many of these activities can be started with relatively lower investment and with no special skills on the part of the entrepreneurs.

Traders Easy Loan Scheme: This scheme is launched by SBI to provide hassle free loan to Traders. Any business man/entrepreneur/professional and self employed person can avail this loan. Loan under the scheme can be availed to meet normal business requirements and is sanctioned against equitable mortgage of property.

SSI Loans: State Bank of India provides several financing options for SSIs.

- **General Purpose Term Loans:** State Bank of India grants term loans to small scale industries for meeting general commercial purposes like substitution of high cost debt, research and development, shoring up net-worth and funding business expansion. The tenure of the loan normally is three years, and the pricing is fine-tuned to suit the risk profile of the borrower. The repayment is structured in monthly or quarterly installments, according to the cash generation cycle.

- **Liberalised Credit for SSI:** State Bank of India extends production-linked credit facilities to small-scale industries, ancillary industrial units and village and cottage industrial units on liberal terms and conditions. Under this scheme, the quantum of advances is not linked to the security furnished, but the genuine requirements of the unit.

- **Entrepreneur Scheme:** State Bank of India grants financial assistance to technically qualified, trained and experienced entrepreneurs for setting up new viable industrial projects. Loans are extended to technocrats who are unable to meet the normal margin requirements under the liberalised schemes.

Exhibit 5.9: Product Line – VIII

SMALL-MEDIUM ENTERPRISES

Traders Easy Loans

SSI Loans

- General Purpose Term Loans
- Liberalised Credit for SSI
- Entrepreneur Scheme
- Equity Fund Scheme
- Stree Shakti Package

Business Current

Open Term Loans

Retail Trade

Doctor Plus

Dental Doctor Plus

SBI Shoppe

Cyber Plus

SME Credit Plus

Small Business Credit Card

Auto Clean

Dal Mill Plus

Paryatan Plus

Transport Plus

Flexi Loan

Swarojgar Credit Card

Auto Loan

Artisan Credit Card

Rice Mill Plus

School Plus

- **Equity Fund Scheme:** Under the Equity Fund scheme, the SBI grants financial assistance to entrepreneurs who are not able to meet their share of equity fully, by way of interest-free loans repayable over a long period. This type of assistance fills in the gap between the margin requirements in the project and the capital contributed by the promoter. The Equity Fund assistance can be normally repaid over 5 to 7 years after the moratorium period.

- **Stree Shakti Package:** The Stree Shakti Package is a unique scheme run by the SBI, aimed at supporting entrepreneurship among women by providing certain concessions. An enterprise should have more than 50% of its share capital owned by women to qualify for the scheme. The concessions offered under the Stree Shakti Package are the margin will be lowered by 5% as applicable to separate categories, the interest rate will be lowered by 0.5% in case the loan exceeds Rs.2 lakh and no security is required for loans up to Rs.5 lakh in case of tiny sector units.

Business Current Accounts: The accounts are Sahaj current account, Standard current account, Power gain current Account and Power pack current account. The Sahaj current account provides basic banking facility and ATM cum Debit Card facility limit up to Rs.15,000/-, and minimum quarterly average balance is Rs.1,000/- for this account. Standard Current account provides inter-core transaction facility and internet banking facility. Minimum daily balance required is Rs.10,000/-. Power Gain current account provides unlimited free cash deposit, free domestic ATM cum Debit Card facility, free bankers cheques, free internet banking facility, etc. The minimum quarterly average balance is Rs.1,00,000/-. Power pack current accounts provides free international ATM cum Debit card, unlimited free cash deposit, cheque return protection facility up to Rs.1,00,000, free inter-core transaction facility, free cheque books, etc. The minimum quarterly balance is Rs.5,00,000/-.

SBI Open Term Loan: The loan can be utilised for any genuine commercial purposes in line with the regular business activity of the customer.

Retail Trade: The bank offers working capital products as well as loans for purchase, renovation and repairing of equipment. Retail trade finance is normally capped at Rs.5 lakh. Any individual or a firm (partnership or proprietorship) engaged primarily in buying and selling mercantile goods is eligible for this mode of finance.

Doctor Plus: The purpose is to finance qualified medical practitioners of any discipline.

Dental Doctor Plus: The purpose is to provide financial support for dental equipment under tie-up arrangement.

SBI Shoppe: This scheme helps to purchase new/old shops/establishments/offices, modernisation/expansion of establishments/shops, etc., and all furniture/fixtures, electrical fittings and other accessories required for shops/showrooms/offices.

Cyber Plus: This service is intended to finance for setting up of internet/cyber cafes especially at rural and semi-urban centers with potential for such a facility.

SME Credit Plus: The idea behind the product designed is to meet the unforeseen and sudden expenditure of SMEs.

Small Business Credit Card: A hassle free, convenient and novel Small Business Credit Card Scheme launched for easy credit delivery to SSI and SBF segments.

Auto Clean: This loan is intended for those who want conversion of petrol operated vehicles to CNG/LPG operated vehicles by fitting CNG/LPG Kit.

Dal Mill Plus: Under this service, finance is provided for acquisition of machinery, modernising the factory or setting up of additional facilities.

Paryatan Plus: This scheme provides construction/renovation/modernization /expansion of hotels, rest houses, yatri niwas, construction of office premises, purchase of office equipment and computers by travel agents/tour operators, purchase of vehicles (Luxury buses, Coaches, Cars, Vans) at tourist sites, and purchase of house boats and luxury boats, setting up of restaurants/coffee houses/ice-cream parlours/fast food centres, amusement parks/rope ways, health clubs/spas, etc.

Transport Plus: The objective of this service is to finance new trucks/tankers/trailers/ tippers/luxury buses including take over of existing similar loans from other banks/institutions, subject to applicability of bank's take-over norms.

Flexi Loan: This loan is offered for general purposes like; holding of stocks/book debts, acquisition of land and building, building construction/up gradation and renovation of offices, showrooms, godowns, etc. substitution of high cost debt, shoring of networking capital and computerisation expenditure.

SWAROJGAR Credit Card: This card is to provide timely credit (working capital or block capital or both), to meet the investment needs of the self-employed persons.

Auto Loan: This product is for the purpose of purchase of new car/jeep/MUV of any model by non individuals and also to purchase old vehicles (not more than 4 years old).

Artisan Credit Card: The purpose of this card is to meet working capital requirements and investment needs (tools and equipment required for manufacturing) of artisans.

Rice Mills Plus: The purpose of this product is to finance for the acquisition of machinery/ factory building for modernisation and working capital needs of rice mills.

School Plus: The purpose of the scheme is to finance schools for construction of new buildings, repair and renovation of old building and also to purchase of electronic and lab equipment, books, manuals, furniture and fixture, etc.

Though a public sector bank, it has set in motion a series of steps to transform itself into a modern, technology enabled customer-centric, world-class banking organisation, meeting best global practices and standards in banking and service delivery. The bank has maintained its record of profitability, while adjusting to the changing circumstances and interest rate environment. Despite intense competition and pressure on spreads it has maintained and improved its NIM. Major innovations and initiatives are in the arena of technology, banking products and processes, service delivery channels and human resource to efficiently serve bank customers across the globe. The bank maintains its drive on the technology front to enhance customer service, increase productivity, and manage risk better. After having computerised all its branches, it has been moving swiftly to implement real time on-line banking.

The bank has formed a new department to draw up a blueprint for the cutting-edge segments in financial sector services. Private equity, point of sale, cards business (gift cards, payroll cards and other cards) pension, general insurance, merchant acquisitions and gold banking are a few areas SBI is looking at for developing its profile as a modern 21st century bank. With the new initiative, SBI is determined to capture its lost market share.

State Bank of India offers large number of products to the market. Each product has a specifically defined target market. The wide variety of the products under different product lines explains the market coverage of the bank and its social and commercial objectives. However, the interviews with officers of the bank revealed that the bank is not making product wise profitability analysis. Many branch managers revealed that they understand that some of the products offered by the bank are not profitable. There is limited support from external marketing to make the new products successful. Many new products are not known to the consumers. They revealed that even a large number of employees are not aware of the total details of many products. Therefore, internal marketing and external marketing shall be given importance by the bank to make all the products accepted by the market. It is also necessary to have product specific cost and profit analysis to identify problems and to take necessary steps to solve them.

New Products introduced during 2008-09

The bank has introduced the following new products during the year 2008-09.

- Import factoring, a new product, was launched in association with SBI Factors & Commercial Services Ltd.

Gold Banking

- The Bank has taken several initiatives to undertake bullion business in a big way.
- The number of branches for retail sale of gold coins has increased from 250 in 2008 to 518 in 2009. The Scheme will be extended to cover all important centres of the country in 2009-10 by increasing the number of branches selling gold coins to about 1100. The Bank also undertakes supply of customised gold coins to corporations.
- The Bank has re-launched Gold Deposit Scheme at 50 branches to mobilise gold from domestic market for deployment as metal loans to jewelers.
- The Bank is in the process of setting up a dedicated Bullion branch at Mumbai to undertake bullion business in a focussed manner.

5.11 SUMMARY

State Bank of India offers various products to suit the needs of the different clientele. The product mix of State Bank of India can be broadly categorised into eight product lines. Product line – I offers Personal Banking services, Product line – II offers Agricultural/Rural Banking services, Product line – III relates to Corporate Banking services, Product line – IV offers NRI services, Product line – V relates to Government Business, Product line – VI relates to various other services offered by the bank, Product line – VII offers International Banking services, and Product line – VIII relates to services offered to Small and Medium Enterprises.

State Bank of India offers large number of products to the market. Each product has a specifically defined target market. The wide variety of the products under different product lines explains the market coverage of the bank and its social and commercial objectives.

However, the interviews with officers of the bank revealed that the bank is not making product wise profitability analysis. Many branch managers revealed that they understand that some of the products offered by the bank are not profitable. There is limited support from external marketing to make the new products successful. Many new products are not known to the consumers. They revealed that even a large number of employees are not aware of the total details of many products. Therefore, internal marketing and external marketing shall be given importance by the bank to make all the products accepted by the market. It is also necessary to have product specific cost and profit analysis to identify problems and to take necessary steps to solve them.

5.12 REFERENCES

1. Philip Kotler and Kevin Lane Keller, *'Marketing Management'*, 12e, Pearson Education, New Delhi, (2006): 5.
2. Philip Kotler and Kevin Lane Keller, *'Marketing Management'*, 12e, Pearson Education, New Delhi, (2006): 6.
3. Ronald T. Rust, Antony J. Zoharik and Timothy I. Keming Ham, *'Services Marketing'*, Addition Wesley Longman, New Delhi, (1999): 15.
4. Keith H. Hammonds, *'Michael Porter's Big Ideas'*, Fast Company, (March 2001), 150-154.
5. http://www.h&m.com, and Eric Sylvers, 'Cut-Rate Swedish Retailer Enters the Italian Market', *New York Times*, (August 27, 2003) W1.
6. Philip Kotler, and Kevin Lane Keller, *'Marketing Management'*, 12e, Pearson Education, New Delhi, (2006): 39.
7. Rama Mohana Rao, K., *'Services Marketing'*, Pearson Education, New Delhi, (2005): 62-63.
8. Rama Mohana Rao, K., *'Services Marketing'*, Pearson Education, New Delhi, (2005): 62-63.
9. Philip Kotler, *'Marketing Management - Analysis, Planning, Implementation and Control'*, Prentice Hall of India Pvt. Ltd., New Delhi, (1987): 463.
10. Rama Mohana Rao, K., *'Services Marketing'*, Pearson Education, New Delhi, (2005): 123.

□□□

Chapter 6

PRICING POLICIES AND STRATEGIES

Pricing is an essential and one of the most important decision areas of marketing. It is a major determinant of the market demand. Either a buyer or a seller may propose a price, but it does not become one until accepted by the other.[1] Price affects the firms competitive position and its share of the market. As a result, price has considerable influence on the revenue of the business. "Price is the mechanism for translating quantitative terms into the perceived value of the product to the consumer. Price is one of the main considerations for the consumer for making the final choice."[2] Pricing plays a dominant role in the determination of the present as well as the future revenues of a concern. "Prices not only determine what can be obtained for goods or services which are already produced or being served, but also influence plans for future production and future marketing."[3]

In the banking sector pricing decision reflects in terms of interest rates for loans and advances and on deposits, and service charges for various support services performed by banks. The pricing decision of any scheduled bank will be in accordance with the RBI guidelines that are in force. The flexibility in pricing is very much limited to the Banks. The interest is the payment for the use of funds over a period of time. The rate actually charged will depend on such factors as the term of loan/deposit, type of loan/deposit, the credit worthiness of the borrower, the amount of collaterals and the tax treatment of interest for both parties.

6.1 THE SYSTEM OF ADMINISTERED INTEREST RATES

The central fact about bank interest rates in India is that they are far from being determined by market forces, but they are determined by market authorities. Deposit interest rates were regulated for the first time in 1966, through inter bank agreements. Since 1969, RBI has taken a responsibility of fixing interest rates for banks. The RBI fixed different deposit interest rates and lending interest rates for different types of banks, *viz.*, larger banks, smaller banks, co-operative banks and regional rural banks. The controller of capital issues fixes the ceiling on the coupon rates on industrial debentures and preference shares. The Indian Banks Association used to fix the ceiling on call rates since 1973, up to October 1988. The call rates were freed from ceiling in 1988. The Government fixes the interest rates on treasury bills and long term Government securities. They also regulate the fixation of interest rates on long term loans of financial institutions. The RBI fixes different interest rates on loans to different categories of borrowers and on loans for different purposes. The government and RBI fix interest rates on different financial instruments such as commercial bills. Co-operative societies are required to accept deposits at higher rates and to lend at lower rates than the rates of other commercial banks. Thus, the ruling level and structure of interest rates in India in any given period was an administered one.

6.2 REASONS FOR REGULATION

The regulation of interest rates basically is intended to control wide fluctuations which may de-stabilize the financial system. In many countries including India, low interest rates had been regarded desirable in order to induce a higher growth of fixed capital formation. The belief in the theories of economic development which gave paramount importance to the high rate of capital formation was the critical development factor in shaping such a policy.

The requirement of funds for Government had been another major consideration. In a planned economy the Government and the public sector have huge financial requirements. The interest rates are used as a means with an expectation that if interest rates are kept low and stable through direct controls, the cost of public debt will be kept low, and stability is maintained in the government securities market which is conducive to debt placement and management. In a planned economy, the priorities and objectives of development are determined by the Governmental authorities. If the course of development is to be in keeping with these priorities, the provision of credit with certainty and at a low cost in the desired direction becomes necessary.[4] The money and capital markets in India are characterised by a variety of imperfections. As a result, certain types of borrowers are discriminated against with regard to the availability, cost and other terms of finance. The discretionary control of cost and availability of finance was regarded necessary to remove such discrimination against the disability of certain borrowers, where such a policy was said to help in improving the distribution of income in favour of low income and the disadvantaged groups in society.[5]

6.3 DEREGULATION OF INTEREST RATES

In order to develop and to make the banking sector more competitive and market oriented, the Reserve Bank of India initiated a shift from administrated pricing to free and flexible pricing system.

The Chakravarthy Committee which was appointed in 1985, to review the working of monetary system, strongly recommended that the administered system should be modified in such a manner that the deficiencies so far referred to were eliminated substantially. The committee recommended that the ceiling on interest rates on bank loans and call loans should be abandoned and that the interest rates on treasury bills, Government securities and bank deposits should be appropriately raised so as to yield realistic and reasonable returns to the holders of these claims. The committee also mentioned that the higher interest rates are not really against the goal of social Justice and in fact they help small savers who are not in a position to take advantage of fiscal concessions. The recommendation of the committee was approved by the Reserve Bank of India.

6.4 TRENDS DURING 1990S AND THE DEREGULATION

Major financial sector reforms were undertaken in the nineties with a view to fostering competitive efficiency in the banking sector. One of the major objectives of the banking sector reforms has been to eliminate financial repression, which has been inherent in the administered interest rate structure.[6] The Narasimham committee which was appointed in 1991, by RBI recommended that the real interest rates should be positive and that concessional interest rates should be done away with. In acceptance of the recommendation, interest rate reforms were undertaken in money, credit and government security markets. Beginning from the year 1992-93, the structure of interest rates for the commercial banks was altered to a more simplified one. As a step towards progressive rationalisation of the banks lending rate structure, the six categories of lending rates were reduced to four in April 1992 and were further reduced to three in April 1993. Effective October, 1994, interest rates on loans above Rs.2 lakh were freed and banks were permitted to determine their prime lending rates.[7] Successive credit policy pronouncements of the RBI during the last decade have brought substantial deregulation and flexibility for banks in evolving their price strategy.

The complexities of interest rate prescription rose through 1970s and early 1980s, was done away with during 1990s. In acceptance of the recommendations by the Chakravarthy Committee, interest rate reforms were undertaken in money, credit and government security markets. The structure of interest rates for commercial banks was altered to a more simplified one. Besides, the reduction in number of slabs, bank rate was reactivated in April, 1997. With inflation rate under control, monitory policy was directed towards reducing the minimum lending rate.[8] The gradual introduction of a loan system in the place of cash credit system has facilitated banks in planning their cash flows better. The restrictions on project financing by banks have been increasingly liberalised to enable banks to extend term loans. Further, a gradual scaling down of preemptions in the form of reserve requirements and SLR prescriptions have enabled banks to manage their assets better.[9]

6.5 PRIME LENDING RATE (PLR)

In a deregulated set up, each of the major commercial banks and term lending institutions has begun fixing and announcing their respective PLRs. The PLR is the rate, which the lender charges to the borrowers of a high credit standard.

The practice of fixing PLRs has resulted in the emergence of multiple PLRs. The banks and financial institutions fix Short-term Prime Lending Rate (STPLR), Medium-term Prime Lending Rate (MTPLR) and Long-term Prime Lending Rate (LTPLR). From February 1997, the RBI has allowed Banks to fix two sets of STPLR, one for the cash credit and the other for the loans. The PLR for cash credit is usually higher by one per cent basis point than the PLR for loans. This is expected to encourage borrowers to switch over from cash credit to loan delivery system.

Deregulation and rationalisation of the interest rate structure has been a key component of the financial sector reform process initiated since the early 1990s. All interest rates, barring select rates such as savings deposits, non-resident India (NRI) deposits, small loans up to Rs. 2 lakh and export credit, have been deregulated.

The interest rate on savings bank deposits is regulated by the Reserve Bank and is prescribed at 3.5 per cent per annum since March, 2003. Depending on the monetary and macroeconomic developments, the ceilings on interest rates on non-resident external rupee deposits (NRE) and Foreign Currency Non-Resident (Bank) [FCNR(B)] deposits are linked to the LIBOR/SWAP rates and are reviewed regularly from time to time. The interest rate ceiling on NRE deposits for one to three year maturity was reduced by 50 basis points each on 31st January, 2007 and on April 24, 2007 to LIBOR/SWAP rates for US dollar of corresponding maturities. The interest rate ceiling on FCNR(B) deposits was reduced by 25 basis points to LIBOR/SWAP rates minus 25 basis points for the respective currency/maturities on 31st January, 2007 and further by 50 basis points to LIBOR/SWAP rates minus 75 basis points for the respective currency/maturities on 24th April, 2007.

On 12th July, 2007 the Government announced a package of measures to provide relief for a temporary period in terms of interest rate subvention of 2 percentage points per annum on rupee export credit availed of by exporters in nine categories of exports, *viz.*, textiles (including handlooms), readymade garments, leather products, handicrafts, engineering products, processed agricultural products, marine products, sports goods and toys and to all exporters from SME sectors defined as microenterprises, small enterprises and medium enterprises. Accordingly, it was decided that banks would charge interest rate not exceeding Benchmark Prime Lending Rate (BPLR) minus 4.5 per cent on pre-shipment credit up to 180 days and post-shipment credit up to 90 days on the outstanding amount for the period 1st April, 2007 to 31st December, 2007 to all SME sectors and the nine sectors as indicated above. The Government of India partially modified the interest rate subvention to exporters to extend the scheme by three months up to 31st March, 2008 and increased the coverage of the scheme to include jute and carpets, processed cashew, coffee, tea, solvent extracted de-oiled cake, plastics and linoleum.

According to demanding trends in the market and as per the instructions of RBI, the SBI follows flexible interest policy. As and when the credit policy of RBI is announced, the SBI changes its interest rates accordingly. In view of decline in the spreads, the Bank has been concentrating more on deposit mobilisation and disbursements by marketing its activities focusing on safety and liquidity.

State Bank of India changed interest rates many times during the period under study (Table 6.1). Interest rates on term deposits were changed 28 times during the decade. In 2002-03, the bank changed interest rate on deposits 5 times. On the other hand, the interest rates on savings deposits were changed only 2 times during the period. The interest rates on advances were changed 19 times during the period under study. In 1997-98 and 2005-06, the interest rates on advances were changed 4 times each.

TABLE 6.1: Interest Rate Changes in SBI during 1997-98 to 2007-08

Year	Advances	Deposits	
		Savings	Term deposits
1997-98	4	-	3
1998-99	3	-	2
1999-00	-	1	1
2000-01	3	-	4
2001-02	2	-	3
2002-03	-	1	5
2003-04	2	-	3
2004-05	-	-	1
2005-06	4	-	1
2006-07	1	-	3
2007-08	-	-	2

Source: Report on Trend and Progress of Banking in India during 1997-98 to 2007-08.

6.6 SUMMARY

In the banking sector pricing decision reflects in terms of interest rates for loans, and advances and on deposits, and service charges for various support services performed by banks. The pricing decision of any scheduled bank will be in accordance with the RBI guidelines that are in force. The flexibility in pricing is very much limited to the Banks. The interest is the payment for the use of funds over a period of time. The rate actually charged will depend on such factors as the term of loan/deposit, type of loan/deposit, the credit worthiness of the borrower, the amount of collaterals, the tax treatment of interest for both parties.

The central fact about bank interest rates in India is that they are far from being determined by market forces, but they are determined by market authorities. Deposit interest rates were regulated for the first time in 1966, through inter bank agreements. Since 1969, RBI has taken a responsibility of fixing interest rates for banks. The RBI fixed different deposit interest rates and lending interest rates for different types of banks, *viz.,* larger banks, smaller banks, co-operative banks and regional rural banks. The controller of capital issues fixes the ceiling on the coupon rates on industrial debentures and preference shares. The Government fixes the interest rates on treasury bills and long term Government securities. They also regulate the fixation of interests rates on long term loans of financial institutions. The RBI fixes different interest rates on loans to different categories of borrowers and on loans for different purposes. The Government and RBI fix interest rates on different financial instruments such as commercial bills. Co-operative societies are required to accept deposits at higher rates and to lend at lower rates than the rates of other commercial banks. Thus, the ruling level and structure of interest rates in India in any given period was an administered one.

State Bank of India changed interest rates many times during the period under study. Interest rates on term deposits were changed 28 times during the decade. In 2002-03, the bank changed interest rate on deposits 5 times. On the other hand, the interest rates on savings deposits were changed only 2 times during the period. The interest rates on advances were changed 19 times during the period under study. In 1997-98 and 2005-06, the interest rates on advances were changed 4 times each.

6.7 REFERENCES

1. Edward W. Candif, Richard R. Still and Norman A.P. Eovani, *'Fundamentals of Modern Marketing',* Prentice Hall of India, New Delhi, (1980): 288.
2. Sudarsana Rao, G., 'Marketing of Services - A Study of Marketing Operations of Andhra Pradesh State Electricity Board ', Unpublished Thesis, Andhra University, Visakhapatnam, (1991): 216.
3. Mamoria C.B. and Joshi, R.I., *'Principles and Practice of Marketing in India',* Kitab Manal, Allahabad, (1984): 218.
4. Reserve Bank of India, Report on Current and Finance, The Author, *Reserve Bank of India Publications,* Mumbai, (1998-99): VI-14.
5. Reserve Bank of India, Report on Current and Finance, The Author, Reserve Bank of India Publications, Mumbai, (1998-99): VI-16.
6. Report on Currency and Finance, *RBI Publications,* Mumbai, (1998-99).
7. Report on Currency and Finance, *RBI Publications,* Mumbai, (1999-00).
8. Reserve Bank of India, Report on Current and Finance, The Author, *Reserve Bank of India Publications,* Mumbai, (1998-99): VI-13.
9. Reserve Bank of India, Report on Current and Finance, The Author, *Reserve Bank of India Publications,* Mumbai, (1998-99): VI-13.

Chapter 7 DISTRIBUTION SYSTEM

Distribution is an important element in the marketing mix of any organisation. It is the facilitating function for the interaction of producer and consumer for the exchange to take place. Distribution or the place element of the marketing mix is concerned chiefly with two main issues, i.e. accessibility and availability. Accessibility must be a component of the actual service offering for it to have value. Additionally, the perishable nature of services means it is essential for the service to be available to customers – in the right place and at the right time. The services cannot be stored until a later date and must be available for consumption at the point of production.[1] Decisions about marketing channels, which help producers deliver goods and services to their target market, are among the most critical issues the management facing because the channels that are chosen intimately affect all the other marketing decisions.[2]

Distribution of services differs significantly from that of manufacturing goods.The nature of the service both influences and shapes distribution strategy. It is through delivery systems that the supplier provides service to the customer. With mature services, improvements may take the form of incremental enhancements to improve the efficiency or attractiveness of the delivery system. The thrust of the so-called experience economy, often consists of enhancing the experience associated with delivery processes as opposed to improving the core product[3].

The special characteristics of services such as intangibility, inseparability, variability, perishability and customer participation require specific form of distribution system. Service products are mostly those where no transfer of ownership takes place and the service is simply rented or consumed. But it is essential that it must be available and accessible before its consumption. This needs a distribution system. The distribution system may be defined as the channels, or means used by which the services provider gains access to potential buyer of the service product.[4]

Service characteristics limit the application of channel know-how and warrant adaptations to cope with the specific problems. Services are intangible, often inseparable from provider and cannot be stored or transported. That being so, unlike goods they cannot be produced in one place and transported to another place for sale. Therefore, services must be sold at multiple outlets which combine promotion and production activities.[5]

Designing a distribution system in a services organisation (whether it be for profit or non profit) involves two tasks. One is to select the channels of distribution, and the other is to provide physical facilities for the distribution of the services.[6] A service marketing organisation may choose either direct marketing or channels of distribution. Direct marketing involves no intermediaries and the service producer sells directly to the customers. In the case of channels of distribution, a number of intermediaries are involved between the producer and the customer. When intermediaries are involved in distribution there will be two marketers-one is a service principal and the other is a service deliverer.The service principal is the service originator and the service deliverer is the distributor. The service deliverer fulfils the promises of the service principal given to the customers. The service intermediaries, apart from fulfilling promises, also provide time, place and convenience utilities to the target customers.The intermediaries may perform services of many service principals and thereby, providing a retailing functions for customers.[7]

Basically, quality in service occurs in the service encounter between customer and employee of the service firm. Maintaining standards of performance at the service outlet is always challenging to the service provider. If such job is assigned to middlemen, there may be a danger of decrease in value of offering and bad reputation to the organisation. However, if the distributor has ability and willingness to offer such services, the risk of failure and damage to the company image get minimized.[8]

7.1 BRANCH NETWORK OF STATE BANK OF INDIA

The State Bank of India follows direct marketing to provide banking services to the target market. The production and distribution outlets of the banking services are the branches and ATMs established in various parts of the country. It has achieved a phenomenal growth in terms of branch network since its inception. It has the largest network of bank branches in the country.

The State Bank of India is a public sector bank and as such it plays a vital role in the development of the economy as a whole. The bank committed itself in developing market for banking services in rural areas by cultivating banking habits in rural population. The underlying principle behind the expansion of branches in the rural areas was the extension of the banking services to the areas that are poorly served and particularly to stimulate banking in rural areas where the commercial banks in private sector are reluctant to extend their services. The bank is under obligation to mobilize savings from the rural population of the country through opening new branches in rural India.

The data presented in Figure 7.1 shows the State Bank of India has been expanding its branch network in India. The total number of branches in India which was 8,859 in 1999-00, increased to 11,472 in 2008-09, recording an increase of 29.8 per cent. The bank has its presence through its branch network in rural, semi-urban, urban, and metropolitan of the country. It is significant to note that the major part of its branch network is located in rural areas. The share of the rural branches, out of the total varied between 46.47 per cent and 38.06 per cent during the period. It reveals further the number of branches in rural areas declined year by year with an exception of 2004-05 and increased form 2005-06, onwards; the branches in Semi-Urban areas have registered a marginal growth of 37.16 per cent during the decade. The branches in urban areas registered 47.59 per cent growth during the period. The branches in the Metropolitan areas registered a highest percent growth during the study period.

It can be inferred from the above that the bank is planning to strengthen it's branch network in metropolitan and urban areas and reduce the number of branches in rural areas.

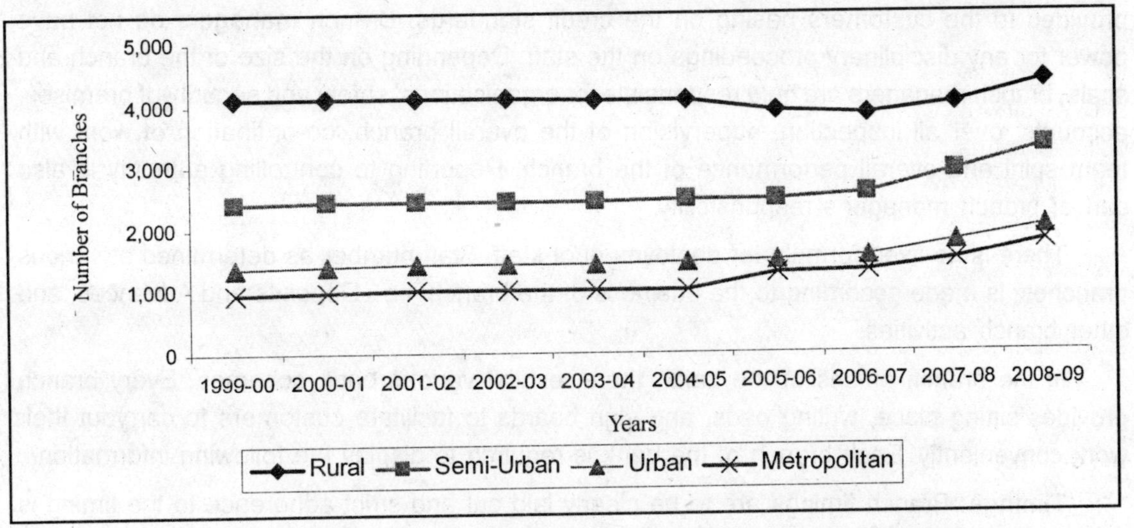

Fig 7.1: Number of Branches of SBI in India during 1999-00 to 2008-09.

Source: Annual Reports of SBI during 1999-00 to 2008-09.

The State Bank of India has established branches in foreign countries also. The number of branches established abroad which was 52 in 1999-00, increased to 92 in 2008-09 (Figure 7.2). In other words, the number of branches increased to 77 per cent during the period under study. The State Bank of India has branches in Australia, Bahrain, Bahamas, Bangladesh, Belgium, Canada, France, Germany, Hongkong, Israel, Japan, China, Maldives, Oman, Singapore, South Africa, Sri Lanka, U.K., U.S.A., etc.

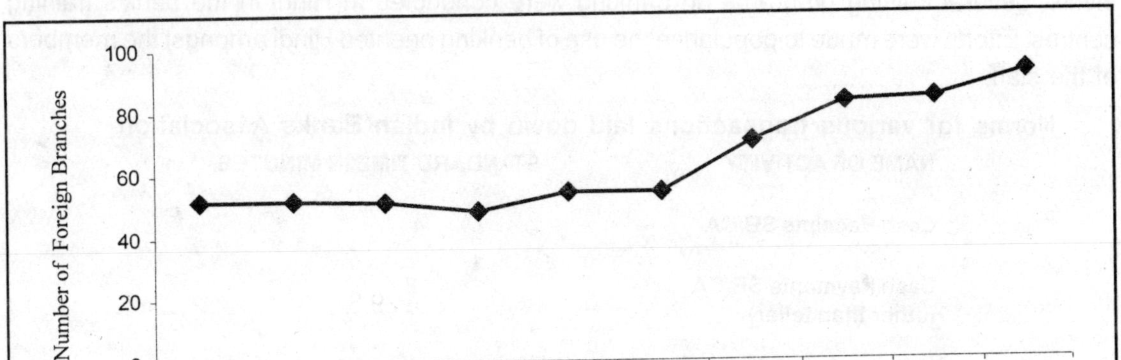

Fig 7.2: Number of Foreign Branches of SBI during 1999-00 to 2008-09.

Source: Annual Reports of SBI during 1999-00 to 2008-09.

7.2 BRANCH MANAGEMENT

Branch managers are vested with discretionary powers according to the size of the branch and scale. Loan sanctions will be made by the branch manager at his/her discretion within the broad framework of the bank. Depending on the size of the branch, loans and advances are provided to the customers basing on the credit standards. Branch managers do not have power for any disciplinary proceedings on the staff. Depending on the size of the branch and scale, branch managers are held responsible for organisations' safety and security of premises, accounts, over all inspection, supervision of the overall branch, co-ordination of work with team spirit and overall performance of the branch. Reporting to controlling authority is also part of branch manager's responsibility.

There is no fixed formula for deployment of staff. Staff number as determined at various branches, is made according to the business of the branch, i.e., Deposits and Advances, and other branch activities.

In the branch offices of the bank, there, exhibit various bank schemes. Every branch provides sitting place, writing pads, and sign boards to facilitate customers to carryout their work conveniently. Each branch of the bank is required to display the following information.

Timings: Branch timings are to be clearly laid out and strict adherence to the timing is required while discharging duties in the branch.

Holidays: Holidays are to be clearly displayed in the Branches.

Name: Branch Manager's name, AGM's name, Name of the bank and branch are to be invariably displayed.

Official language: The bank complied with the statutory requirements relating to the official language policy.

A number of training programs/workshops/seminars were conducted for officials at various levels. Several training programs on banking were conducted in Hindi in the bank's training centres. Efforts were made to popularise the use of banking oriented Hindi amongst the members of the staff.

Norms for various transactions laid down by Indian Banks Association

NAME OF ACTIVITY	STANDARD TIME IN MINUTES
Cash Receipts SB/CA	4
Cash Payments SB/CA (other than teller)	8
Issue of cheque book	8
Opening of SB account	16
Issues of draft	12
Payment of draft	8

Branch Layout

The branch layout of State Bank of India is made as per the availability of space. It is made convenient to the customer to have access to different areas such as cash section, accounts section, and teller section. There is no specific layout design. The authority concerned in the module i.e. the panel engineer, visits the branch and in consultation with security officer make suggestions on branch layout. From the bank's point of view, the primary motive is to safeguard '*Cash chest*'.

7.3 MANAGEMENT INFORMATION SYSTEM (MIS)

The bank's MIS aims at providing timely and accurate information to the management with the help of advanced information technology. With the introduction of the Management Information System for Loans and Advances (MISLA) in over 7,000 branches, the bank is now capable of more in-depth analysis of borrowed accounts, which would facilitate better credit management. The introduction of the Relational Database Management Systems (RDBMS) would strengthen monitoring process. In order to make information available easily to the functionaries at the corporate centre, 'Intranet' has been put into operation by the bank.

7.4 REDESIGNING OF BRANCHES

State Bank of India has taken up business process reengineering to simplify transaction process and administration work load after identifying that the operations and administration accounting for about 40 per cent of the time. As a part of this, it has taken up branch redesign. The branch redesign involves two types of changes in a branch. The first is change in roles of various functionaries of the branch and the second is change in internal layout to facilitate functioning of role holders of a redesigned branch. The branch redesign aims at providing multiple benefits to both – customers as well as staff. Clear communication of roles of the employees, increased focus on sales and shifting of non-customer facing activities out of the branch are the three major principles of the redesign.

The bank has taken the following measures towards clear communication of roles.

- Single Window Operators (SWOs) to handle all service transactions where transaction time is of prime importance.
- Customer Relations Officers (CROs) to handle transactions with significant interaction and opportunity to cross-sell.
- Service Manager (upgraded role of Accountant) in charge of the service section of the branch. Case Managers added if the work of Service Manager exceeds one man-day.
- Full time cash officer in currency chest branches. In hand balance branches, role to be played by the senior SWO.
- Grahak Mitra as first touch point for customer.

To achieve increased focus on sales the bank introduced the following changes.

- Branch Manager to build relationships with top customers of branch and spend around 60 per cent of his time in proactive sales and marketing activities, in addition to acquisition of new valuable customers.
- CROs to spend 20 per cent of their time in proactive sales and marketing.

Further, many changes were introduced at the branch level to orient the branch towards more sales. The redesign focused on;

- Moving non-customer facing operations as far as possible (e.g., reconciliation, returns, major part of audit) out of the branch;
- Centralising administration work (e.g., AMCs, MIS, statutory reports) to regional offices;
- Relieving the branch of credit appraisal and monitoring by creating a local/regional loan processing centre;
- Creating capability to sell full range of products through the branches, including "third party products like Mutual Funds, Insurance and Credit Cards;
- Making branches 'sales and service hubs/financial centers' with employees in customer-facing roles, focusing on sales, service or transactions;
- Migrating large proportion of cash withdrawals to ATMs;
- Encouraging use of cheque drop box for cheque deposits;
- Increasing use of internet/ATM for funds transfer and enquiries;
- Creating call centers as a viable service/transaction channel;
- Installing a fully functional CBS in the branch;
- Networking branches;
- Redefining processes in detail to support the new architecture; and
- Defining clear role guidelines and streamline delegation of authority.

These changes are intended to benefit all the three important pillars of bank marketing *viz.*, customers, employees and the bank. The benefits of the customers included help and guidance from Grahak Mitra at the entry point in branches, reduction in waiting time, convenience of completing all transactions at a single counter (SWO/CRO), increased and friendlier customer area, and more professional look/better ambience as non-customer facing activities are not visible to customers.

The employees are benefited by way of greater specialisation of skills due to separation of sales and service related activities in the branch, development of multi skills in employees (both clerical and supervising staff) will lead to self enrichment and self-confidence, fewer roles in the branch leading to greater clarity of roles of branch functionaries, and better team spirit amongst staff.

On the implementation of the new design, sudden absenteeism of staff does not impact customer service. Multi skilling of staff helps in balancing work load and improving productivity.

Branch Manager is freed up to focus on sales due to creation of Service Manager's roles. As per the new design, the branches are recognized into six types.

a. Core Sales and Service Branch (SSB)
b. SSB with affluent module
c. SSB with SME module
d. A self assisted outlet – Mini Branch
e. Sales focused outlet
f. Product specific outlet such as home loan center, locker center, etc.

a. Core Sales and Service Branch (SSB) is relatively a lean branch (Figure 7.3). It will cater to a broad spectrum of customers including mass and mass affluent p-segment customers and small enterprises. The branch will have staff comprising of officers and employees engaged primarily in sales and marketing roles.

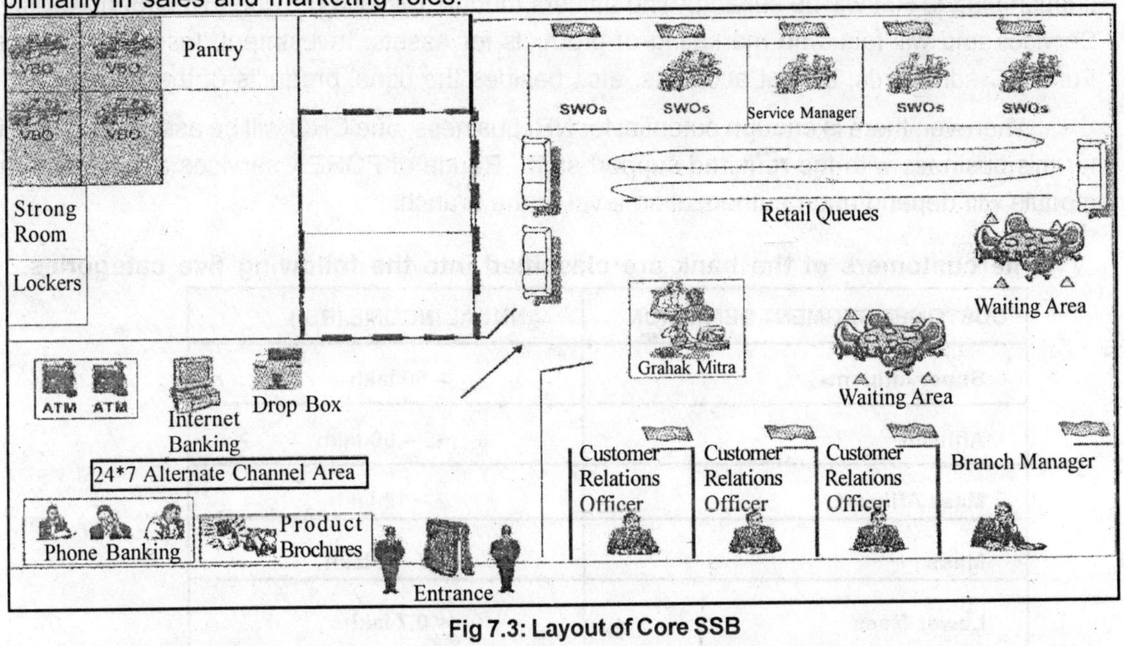

Fig 7.3: Layout of Core SSB

A clerical staff, called "Grahak Mitra" will be positioned near the entrance and will address simple queries, provide product information and literature, guide the customers and encourage them to use alternate channels.

Officers called "Customer Relations Officers (CROs)" will open new accounts and engage in consultative selling with promising prospects/customers and market liability products, loan products and third party products (such as SBI Life, SBIMF etc.). Single Window Operators (SWOs) will serve the customers on their routine transactions.

Each and every member of the branch will have definite role. With reduction in the number of staff to 10-15, the branches will have customer friendly layout with around 70 per cent of banking hall open for customers. The furniture design, colour combination of the interior and signage will be made uniform to further strengthen brand image of the bank.

In addition to the Core SSB format, modules focusing on affluent and SME customers will be added on branch formats *viz.*, "SSB with Affluent Module" and "SSB with SME Module" respectively.

b. Core SSB with affluent module: This branch will have the same format as that of Core Sales and Service Branch with addition of an Affluent Module. This module will be required at a branch serving affluent/mass affluent people predominantly. These categories of customers prefer relationship based banking.

The Relationship Manager (RM) of the branch will own high value customers of the branch. The Manager will be outbound for about 60 per cent of the time, to meet/select top customers/potential customers at the place of their choice. He/she will endeavor for up-selling/ cross-selling of retail assets, mutual funds, insurance etc. For providing services to the visiting high value customers a separate area within the Core SSB will be created, where RM and one support staff to RM will be serving. The affluent module will also provide Investment Advisory Services and will focus on marketing of products for Assets, Investment, Insurance, Mutual Funds, Credit Cards, Demat accounts, etc., besides the usual products of the bank.

Wherever, there is enough potential for NRI business, one CRO will be assigned specially for this business with the required support staff. Range of FOREX services available at the module will depend upon authorization level of the branch.

The customers of the bank are classified into the following five categories.

CUSTOMER SEGMENT DEFINITION	ANNUAL INCOME (RS.)
Super Affluent	**> 50 lakh**
Affluent	**12 – 50 lakh**
Mass Affluent	**2 – 12 lakh**
Mass	**0.7 – 2 lakh**
Lower Mass	**< 0.7 lakh**

c. Core SSB with SME module: This branch has all the capabilities of a Core SSB with the usual functionalities along with additional module to service SMEs (Small and Medium Enterprises). Figure 7.4 shows the Core SSB with SME module. The module will basically perform the sales and service functions in respect of the SME customers. Depending on the potential of the area, the module will be attached to a suitable branch. The Medium Enterprises (ME) will be served through relationship banking model by a team comprising Relationship Manager (ME) and Credit Support Officer (CSO).The Relationship Manager for Medium Enterprises (RMME) will provide personalized services to the ME customers. He/she will also acquire new customers. The Small Enterprises will be served by dedicated Customer Relation Officer (CRO). The module will have a dedicated service platform for the SMEs comprising of separate Credit Support Officer (CSO) as well as SME Service Desk and Bulk Cashier. Depending on the volume of trade finance as well as the cash management products, Trade Finance front desk can also be added in the module, if there are large numbers of SME customers.

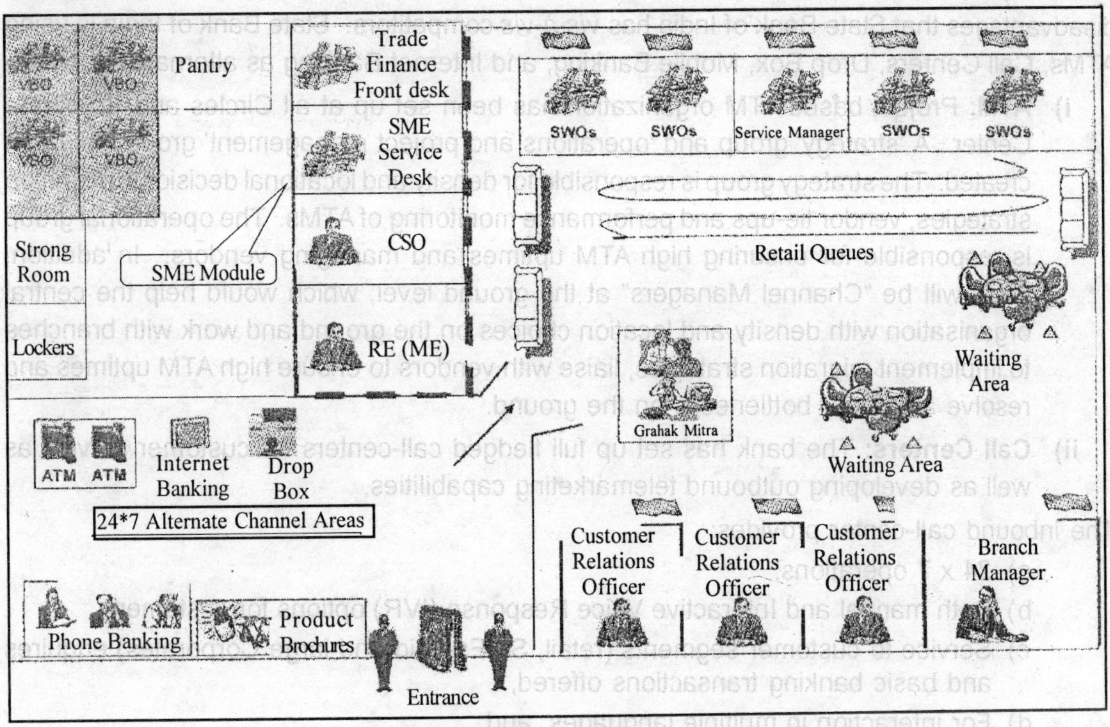

Fig 7.4: Layout of Core SSB with SME module

SME has two components i.e. Small Enterprise (SE) and Medium Enterprise (ME) which is business units defined on the basis of their turnover. The units having turnover up to Rs.5 crore are treated as Small Enterprises whereas the units having more than Rs.5 crore and less than or equal to Rs.50 crore are treated as Medium Enterprises.

Other branch formats: The following are the other branch formats.

a. A self assisted outlet (Mini Branch) operated by 1-2 staff and supported by a full suite of alternative channel access devices (ATMs, call center link, internet kiosk, etc.).

b. SBI Financial Centre, which is a sales outlet, located in high traffic areas.

c. Product specific outlets such as home loan center, locker center, etc.

Branches are further clustered into micro markets. A micro market is a well defined geography within which most of the customers are willing to travel to do their banking transactions. An official in the rank of AGM, who will have direct business responsibility for the branches under him, will head the micro market. Micro markets, like branches are free from any administrative tasks. Administrative tasks will be performed from Zonal Offices. The micro market head will also have a small sales team attached to him.

7.5 ALTERNATE CHANNELS DESIGN

The growth and expansion of alternate channels are important because it greatly increases customer convenience, reduces the cost to serve customers and eliminates the service disadvantages that State Bank of India has *vis-à-vis* competitors. State Bank of India is using ATMs, Call Centers, Drop Box, Mobile Banking, and Internet Banking as alternate channels.

i) **ATM:** Project based ATM organization has been set up at all Circles and Corporate Center. A 'strategy' group and 'operations and project management' group has been created. The strategy group is responsible for density and locational decisions, migration strategies, vendor tie-ups and performance monitoring of ATMs. The operational group is responsible for ensuring high ATM uptimes and managing vendors. In addition, there will be "Channel Managers" at the ground level, which would help the central organisation with density and location choices on the ground and work with branches to implement migration strategies, liaise with vendors to ensure high ATM uptimes and resolve any other bottlenecks on the ground.

ii) **Call Centers:** The bank has set up full fledged call-centers for customer service as well as developing outbound telemarketing capabilities.

The inbound call-center provides:

a) 24 x 7 operations,

b) Both manual and Interactive Voice Response (IVR) options for customers,

c) Service to customer segments (retail, SMEs, mid and large Corporates) enquires and basic banking transactions offered,

d) For interaction in multiple languages, and

e) For routing calls to call-centers through State Bank of India net work.

The bank has extended the services of internet banking offerings to retail and corporate segment in addition to mobile banking and smart card based processes to widen the scope of using alternate channels by the customers.

iii) **Drop Box:** The Drop Box facility was introduced in the year 2002 and subsequently the scope of the Drop Box was enlarged in the year 2004 on the recommendations of the Committee on "Procedures and Performance Audit on Public Services" headed by Dr. S.S. Tarapore.

Drop box offers a hassle free service to customers for cheque deposit by allowing instant and 24 x 7 access. It frees up staff engaged in issuing counterfoil, and their services can be utilized elsewhere. It has three slits for Outstation Collection, Clearing and On-Branch instruments. Slits are colour coded for easy identification. Cheques for DDP/local purchases and cheques against Government Challans will continue to be tendered across counters. Decision regarding high value clearing cheques may be taken at branch level.

The process time which was one hour in traditional branch system to open an account has been reduced to 8 to 10 minutes in branch and CPC based setup. The following table illustrates the process simplification.

Process Redesigned to provide superior service to customer in branch

(Example to open an account)

FROM BRANCH BASED ...

- Application form filling and receipt
- KYC Verification
- Receipt of cash
- Authorisation of receipt
- Customer and account set up
- Authorisation of customer and account set up
- Receipt of cheque book from VPIS (Valuable Paper Inventory Systems)
- Set up of cheque book
- Authorisation of cheque book
- Set up of passbook
- Authorisation of passbook account
- Delivery to customer
- Scanning of signature and linking to account
- Intimation to GE for ATM card
- Filling of document

... TO COMBINATION OF BRANCH AND CPC

At Branch

- Receipt of application and KYC verification
- Customer and account set up only *"minimum details"*
- Receipt of cash
- Hand over the welcome kit comprising cheque book and unnamed ATM Cum Debit Card to customer
- Day end verification (post checking)
- Forward application to CPC

At CPC

- Completion of all remaining data entry
- Scanning and linking of signature
- Filing of document
- Preparation of welcome kit (in bulk) and dispatch to branch

7.6 BRANCH IMAGE BUILDING

With a view to enhance its branch image, State Bank of India has introduced a uniform "look and feel" for their branches. A standardised visual identity in terms of exterior facade, interior decor, the colour scheme, the design as well as the dimensions of the counters, furniture and fixtures, lighting, ceiling and flooring, and the quality specifications for the materials to be used for the above purpose. An Architect/Interior design firm has been engaged for preparing a Design Manual for two different formats, i.e., standard and premium.

7.7 MODEL BRANCH

As per the guidelines of the Reserve Bank, the State Bank of India has identified 220 branches to be developed as Model Branches. Selection of branches is made by representing a proper mix of metropolitan, urban, semiurban and rural branches from all over the country. The parameters for selecting a branch as a Model Branch are layout, workflow, health and recovery of advances, profitability and productivity in addition to the quality of customer service rendered by the bank branches.

7.8 PERSONALISED BRANCH NETWORK

Through the Personalised Branch Network, SBI provides a range of services under one umbrella. The ambience of these branches is intended to provide comfort, convenience and pleasantness to the customers.The personalised branches are opened for the sake of customers who need completion of transactions within the shortest possible time. The customers who come under personalised branch network are highly valuable customers.They have to maintain a minimum cash balance of Rs.10,000/- at these branches.

7.9 POLICY ON UNECONOMICAL BRANCHES

SBI identifies uneconomical branches in which the expenditure incurred is very high as regards salaries of the personnel, rent and maintenance charges of the premises, where as the business and revenue generated is far less than the expenditure incurred.The bank cannot close these branches in rural areas as per the policy of RBI to serve the poor.But in order to minimise losses, these uneconomical branches are being shifted to nearby places where they can get some business.

7.10 SUMMARY

The State Bank of India follows direct marketing to provide banking services to the target market. The production and distribution outlets of the banking services are the branches and ATMs established in various parts of the country. It has achieved a phenomenal growth in terms of branch network since its inception. It has the largest network of bank branches in the country.

The State Bank of India has established branches in foreign countries also. The number of branches established abroad which was 52 in 1999-00 increased to 92 in 2008-09. In other words, the number of branches increased to 77 per cent during the period under study. The State Bank of India has branches in Australia, Bahrain, Bahamas, Bangladesh, Belgium, Canada, France, Germany, Hongkong, Israel, Japan, China, Maldives, Oman, Singapore, South Africa, Sri Lanka, U.K., U.S.A., etc.

State Bank of India has taken up business process reengineering to simplify transaction processing and administration work load after identifying that the operations and administration accounting for about 40 per cent of the time. As a part of this, it has taken up branch redesign. The branch redesign involves two types of changes in a branch. On the implementation of the new design, sudden absenteeism of staff does not impact customer service. Multi skilling of staff helps in balancing work load and improving productivity. Branch Manager is freed up to focus on sales due to creation of Service Manager's roles.

As per the guidelines of the Reserve Bank, the State Bank of India has identified 220 branches to be developed as Model Branches. Selection of branches is done by representing a proper mix of metropolitan, urban, semi- urban and rural branches from all over the country. The parameters for selecting a branch as a Model Branch are layout, workflow, health and recovery of advances, profitability and productivity in addition to the quality of customer service rendered by the bank branches.

SBI identifies uneconomical branches in which the expenditure incurred is very high as regards salaries of the personnel, rent and maintenance charges of the premises, where as the business and revenue generated is far less than the expenditure incurred.The bank cannot close these branches in rural areas as per the policy of RBI to serve the poor. But in order to minimise losses, these uneconomical branches are being shifted to nearby places where they can get some business.

7.11 REFERENCES

1. Shajahan. S, *'Services Marketing'*, Himalaya Publishing House, Mumbai, (2001):.34.
2. Philip Kotler, *'A Framework for Marketing Management'*, Pearson Education, (Singapore) Pvt. Ltd., Indian Branch, New Delhi, (2002): 235.
3. Christopher Lovelock, *'Services Marketing'*, Addition Wesley Longman (Singapore) Pvt. Ltd., Delhi, (2001): 338.
4. Ramphal M.K. and Gupta S.I., *'Services Marketing'*, Galgotia Publishing Company, New Delhi, (2000): 20.
5. Upah, Gregory, 'Mass Marketing in Service Retailing', A Review and Synthesis of Major Methods, *Journal of Retailing*, Pal (1980): 60-61.
6. William J. Stanton, Michael J. Ezel and Brace J. Walker, *'Fundamentals of Marketing'*, Tata Mc-Graw Hill Publishing Co. Ltd., New Delhi, (1994): 550.
7. Rama Mohana Rao K., *'Services Marketing'*, Pearson Education, New Delhi, (2005).
8. Rama Mohana Rao K., *'Services Marketing'*, Pearson Education, New Delhi, (2005).

□□□

Chapter 8

INTERNAL MARKETING

The concept of internal marketing states that the employees of the organisation form the first market and the goods and services as well as specific external marketing campaigns have to be marketed to employees before they are marketed externally. According to Gronroos[1], the internal marketing concept states that the internal market of employee is best motivated for service mindedness and customer-oriented performance by an active marketing like approach, where a variety of activities are used internally in an active, marketing like and coordinated way. Internal marketing in all its forms was recognised as an important activity in contributing to the people element of the marketing mix and in developing a customer focused organisation. In practice, it is concerned with communications, developing responsiveness, responsibility and unity of purpose. The fundamental aims of internal marketing are to develop internal and external customer awareness and remove functional barriers to organisational effectiveness.[2]

There is concrete evidence to the effect that satisfied employees can make satisfied customers and satisfied customers can in turn reinforce employees' sense of satisfaction in their jobs. Some have even gone so far as to suggest that unless service employees are happy in their jobs, customer satisfaction will be difficult to achieve.[3] Among the most demanding jobs in service business are the so-called boundary – spanning positions, where employees are expected to be fast and efficient in executing operational tasks and be courteous and helpful in dealing with customers. As a result, many service encounters have the potential to be a threecornered fight among the needs of partially conflicting parties; the customer, the server and the service firm. If the job is not designed carefully or the wrong people are picked to fill it, there is a real risk that the employees may become stressed and unproductive.[4] The purpose of internal marketing is to integrate multiple functions of the firm and operate through service firm as the holistic management process. Internal marketing ensures that all employees understand and experience various business activities and campaigns and also prepare and motivate them to act in a service oriented manner. The necessary condition is that the internal exchange between the organisation and its employees must be operating effectively before facing external markets.[5] Service marketers need to develop a high level of interpersonal skills and customer-oriented attitude in employees for the reason that employees in services are key to the service experience.[6]

The kind of effort service firms put in for designing a service product for the external market to respond, they have to make efforts for designing a product for internal market too. While customer satisfaction is the orientation for external market, employee satisfaction should be orientation for internal market. The needs and wants of the employees should be studied carefully along with their expectations, to design a package of benefits that are capable of satisfying them. The internal product consists of a job and a work environment which motivates the employees to respond favourably to management's demand for customer orientation and good interactive market performance as part time marketers and which moreover attracts and retains good employees. In order to ensure proper design of internal service product, there is a need to make the concept of internal marketing as a part of the strategic management philosophy. Internal marketing is a philosophy of managing personnel and developing and enhancing a service culture systematically. The activities of internal marketing should promote service mindedness and customer orientation. Most of the internal marketing activities are part of human resource management and development. The strategies adopted for internal marketing includes:

A. Hire the right people
B. Develop people to deliver service quality
C. Provide needed support system
D. Retain the best people

8.1 HIRE THE RIGHT PEOPLE

The growth and goal achieving capability of any organization largely depend upon the dynamism, competence, motivation and effectiveness of its employees. State Bank of India has a working force in different categories to serve the clientele and the society at large. The staff pattern of State Bank of India consists of officers, clerks and sub-ordinates. The bank has been making efforts to develop the conventional skill and to concentrate on better attitudinal orientation of staff.

Recruitment to the officer's cadre is done by conducting all India level competitive examination and also through internal promotions to the experienced and talented people named management trainee officers. The selection is based upon the written test. The final selection is made basing on written test performance, group discussion, and personal interview. After selection, the officers are put on probation for about a period of two years.

The SBI used to select people for the clerical cadre basing on written test conducted by the State Bank separately till 1990's. Later, the test was conducted by the Banking Service Commission until it was abolished. Advertisement for recruitment used to be given in all the leading news papers to make it known to the large populace. For employees of clerical cadre, after giving advertisement and receipt of applications from the respondents, the bank conducts a written test to check the candidates' ability with respect to arithmetical accuracy and analytical power. The written test is followed by personal interview through which the bank checks the candidate's communication skills, attitudes and other behavioural aspects. Finally, the selected candidates will be placed in respective jobs after initial induction program.

There is no selection process for the sub-ordinate staff. Initially, they will be taken on temporary basis and basing on work satisfaction, permanence in employment will be provided. Subordinates are recruited into the bank by the discretion of the bank manager and be placed in employment on temporary basis. Generally, candidates with good manners and polite behaviour are chosen as subordinates.The recruitment/probation for three categories of employees – officers, clerks and subordinates are as follows.

The Central Board of the Executive Committee makes all appointments and promotions for the official cadre in State Bank of India. There are three channels through which officers are recruited in the bank.

a) Direct recruitment - probationary officers and rural development officers.
b) Promotion as trainee officers.
c) Promotion as junior management officials from the clerical cadre.

Recruitment

1) The probationary officers are recruited through the Central Recruitment Board.
2) The trainee officers and the junior management officials are recruited from the clerical cadre. The minimum period for qualifying for promotion to the junior management grade ranges from 5 to 10 years.

Probation

1) A person appointed as probationary officer/rural development officer shall be on probation for a period of two years.
2) Any other employee of the bank promoted as an officer to the junior management grade shall be on probation for a period of one year.
3) The period of probation will be for two years in the case of appointments made in the bank for the posts like Law Officer, Security Officer, Engineer, etc.

Training

1) The probationary officers/trainee officers are given specialized training at Staff College during the 2 years period of the job training. All the general banking work including specialised work is taught at various branches and also at administrative offices during the period.
2) The junior management officials are given on the job training for a period of six months and also in service training in the training centers.

Promotion

A. **Merit Channel:** Promotion to different grades of officers in the bank shall be made in accordance with the policy laid down by the Central Board of Executive Committee from time to time. In State Bank of India, promotions are based on the marks obtained by the officers in the various processes of selection after suitable conversion as per weightage given in the test.

B. Seniority Channel

1) Officers in the Junior Management Grade scale I who have put in certain number of minimum years of service in JMG scale I will be eligible for consideration for promotion. The number of years of service would depend upon the number of vacancies to be filled in under this category and also the availability of the officers with adequate seniority. A merit list will be prepared on the basis of the set selection criteria.

Seniority	:	**40 marks (5 marks for each year of service after six years)**
C.A.I.I.B.	:	**10 marks (part I - 4 marks, both parts 10 marks)**
Performance Appraisal	:	**30 marks**
Interview	:	**20 marks**
Total	:	**100 marks**

2) Sixty-five per cent of the total vacancies will be reserved for promotion under the seniority channel.

3) Promotion of the Rural Development officers and Technical officers will be governed by the two channel policy explained in A and B above.

Promotion from MMG scale II to MMG scale III

Promotion to MMG scale III is based on a system of performance appraisal and interview of the eligible officers. The eligibility criteria are to be reckoned with reference to a date of eligibility to be stipulated yearly by the Central Office. The eligibility criteria are:

a) The officer should be in MMG scale II on or before the date of eligibility.

b) The officers as on the date of eligibility should have passed both parts of the C.A.I.I.B. examination and completed 7 years of confirmed service, in MMG scale II.

Promotion from MMG scale III to SMG scale IV

Promotion to SMG scale IV is made on the basis of service record and past performance on the basis of an appraisal system. Officers who have completed 4 years of service in MMG scale III will be eligible for promotion to SMG scale IV.

Promotion from SMG scale IV to SMG scale V

Promotion to SMG scale V is a crucial filter point and great emphasis is placed on merit/ suitability and potential. The performance of the officers in their current and immediately preceding assignments is carefully assessed on the basis of service record and appraised material. The eligibility criterion is 3 or 4 years service in SMG scale IV.

Policy for Promotion from Clerical to Junior Management Cadre

i. **Regular channel (merit cum - seniority)**: A test will be conducted for clerical cadre employees for the purpose of promoting them to the junior management cadre. The following are the details of the test.

Eligibility: All clerical cadre employees with a minimum qualification of matriculation (excluding record keepers, record keepers-cum-cashiers, godown keepers, bill collectors) and with a minimum service as shown below will be eligible to appear for the test.

i.Minimum service:	**General: 14 years**	**SC: 12 years**	**ST: 6 years**
ii.Upper age limit:	**General: 50 years**	**SC/ST: 55 years**	

iii.There will be no limit on the number of chances. A candidate may appear for the test any number of times till he/she reaches the prescribed age limit.

iv.Allocation of Marks

(a) Written test	:	**60 marks**
(b) Performance appraisal	:	**10 marks**
(c) Interview	:	**10 marks**
(d) Length of service	:	**20 marks (2 marks for every completed year of service beyond 15 years subject to a maximum of 20 marks)**
Total	:	**100 marks**

Bonus for rural service: 1 mark for every completed year of service put in by the candidate in a rural branch subject to a maximum of 5 marks.

ii. **Seniority Channel:** 10 per cent of the posts earmarked for promotion under merit cum-seniority channel will be set aside for an exclusive seniority channel. Promotions against these posts will be made through an interview to be conducted for the candidates who cross the stipulated upper age limit of 50/55 years as the case may be. The upper age limit shall be 52 and 57 years for General and SC/ST candidates respectively.

iii. **Merit Channel:** Promotions as trainee officers are on the basis of following criteria

1) Minimum service 4 years
2) Minimum qualifications
   (a) Graduation and part I of C.A.I.I.B.
   (b) Matriculation with both parts of C.A.I.I.B.
   (c) Graduation with a pass in intermediate examination of ACA/ICWAI/ACS
   (d) ACA/ICWAI/ACS

The upper age limit for this cadre is 40 and 45 years for General and SC/ST categories respectively and there is no limit on the number of chances. The allocation of marks is as shown below

Written test	70 marks
C.A.I.I.B.	5 marks
Professional qualifications such as ACA/ICWAI/ACS	5 marks
Performance appraisal	10 marks
Interview	10 marks
Total	100 marks

Based on the performance in the written test, candidates who secure the qualifying marks of 28 out of 70 in the written test are called for an interview.

Policy for promotion from subordinate to clerical cadre:

A test is conducted at regular intervals for promoting subordinate staff to clerical cadre. The following are the details of the test.

I. Merit Channel

1. Eligibility: Permanent full time employees with 5 years of service. However, service put in on a permanent part time employee prior to full time appointment will be reckoned proportionately by notionally converting part time service into full time service, in case such full time employee has less than 9 years service.
2. Qualification: Matriculation or equivalent examination.
3. These will be no limit on the number of chances.

ALLOCATION OF MARKS

(a) Written Test	:	70 marks
(b) Additional qualification Graduation and/or C.A.I.I.B.	:	10 marks
(c) Performance appraisal	:	10 marks
(d) Interview	:	10 marks
Total	:	100 marks

Bonus for rural service: 1 mark for every completed year of service put in by the candidate in a rural branch subject to a maximum of 5 marks.

II. Regular channel (merit-cum-seniority): Promotions are given to sub-ordinate staff basing on merit cum seniority.

(a) Eligibility: Permanent full time employee with 8 years service.

(b) Minimum qualification 8th standard.

(c) No limit as to the number of chances.

(d) Allocation of marks.

(a) Written test	:	60 marks
(b) Length of service	:	20 marks (2 years for every completed year of service beyond 9 years with a maximum of 20 marks)
(c) Performance appraisal	:	10 marks
(d) Interview	:	10 marks
Total	:	100 marks

III. Seniority channel:

Ten per cent of the posts earmarked for promotion under merit-cum-seniority channel will be set aside for an exclusive seniority channel. Promotion will be made based on interview conducted for the purpose.

8.2 DEVELOP PEOPLE TO DELIVER SERVICE QUALITY

Training is an important tool to develop human resource and it facilitates the transition to a more sustainable world. It should have a job specific focus, aimed at filling gaps in knowledge and skill that would help individuals find employment and be involved in development work. Training programs should promote a greater awareness of developmental issues on a way of learning process.Training is the major approach for developing the employees of the organisation to perform efficiently and to deliver service quality. In State Bank of India, the newly selected and existing employees are given training in different aspects according to changing market conditions and needs. SBI training experience spreads over more than four decades and is based on an in-depth understanding of the business and banking environment, domestic as well as international.

Training in State Bank of India

State Bank of India aims to enhance knowledge, develop skills and re-orient attitude of the employees to keep pace with the changing environment. The Bank's training network consists of 4 apex level colleges viz., State Bank Staff College, Gurgaon; State Bank Staff College, Hyderabad; State Bank Institute of Rural Development and State Bank Institute of Information and Communication Management and over 50 learning centers located across the country. In addition to providing training, the colleges conduct research on relevant topics. With a view to providing on site training to employees working in the branches, the bank has a visiting faculty scheme, under which faculty from training centres visit branches and conduct training sessions to the employees taking into consideration the local factors also.

Identification of training needs

Identification of training needs is the basic exercise on which the entire edifice of a training program is built. A specialised as well as individualised view of training of different categories of employees performing various jobs is essential for designing appropriate training programs.The State Bank of India recognised the need for training for each category of employees, sub-ordinates, clerks, and officers and developed adequate infrastructure for the purpose.

Training Philosophy

"Training in the State Bank is a proactive, planned and continuous process as an integral part of organisation development. It seeks to impart knowledge, improve skills and re-orient attitudes for individual growth and organisational effectiveness."

Training System Goals

In view of the developments that are taking place in the economy, particularly in the banking sector emphasis was laid on the planned shift in the strategic goals, structures, systems and process of the organisation to cope with the change.Preparing the people working in the bank to anticipate and cope with these changes effectively became the focus for training in the bank. The training in the bank is conducted as a change agent to reorient the attitudes for better management and marketing.The following are the goals of the training system.

1. **Training**
   - updating, maintenance and renewal
   - proactive, progressive, preparative, and educative
   - reorienting attitudes for better management and marketing
   - a change agent
   - feedback to corporate office to assist in policy formulation, product development
2. **To act as a think-tank**
3. **An internal consultant**
4. **Organisational development interventions**
5. **To conduct customised on-site programs at the branches**
6. **Interventions at branch level for organisational development**
7. **Research and Development**
8. **Course Design:** The details of the basis of course design, program objectives, course content, session plans, reading and reference materials are presented here under.

   Basis of course design
   - Bank's mission, policies and guidelines
   - Regulatory and market factors
   - Feedback of the users
   - Individual development and user needs
   - Development of expertise and preparation for future in the context of competition and change
9. **Program objectives**
   - Each program has clearly defined objectives
   - Course design/content flow from the objectives
   - Trainees feedback on achievement of objectives

10. **Course content**
    - Choice of inputs as appropriate for the program
    - Sequenced to facilitate smooth and easy flow
11. **Session plans**
    - Sessions are inter-linked and sequenced in such a way as to optimize learning
12. **Reading and reference material**
    - Pre-course material relevant to the program is supplied to the trainees at the beginning
    - Separate material for different subjects as needed

Programs Conducted: The following are the themes on which the training programs are conducted by the SBI for its employees.

1 **Credit management**
- Credit appraisal and management
- Project appraisal and project finance
- Risk management
- NPA management and industrial rehabilitation

2 **International banking**
- Foreign exchange and Euro-markets
- Course programs and workshops
- Trade finance, trade settlements, and financing techniques
- Derivatives

3 **Management development programs**
- Branch management program
- Executive development programs
- P.O./T.O. (management trainee) programs
- Leadership and motivation
- Time management
- Counseling skills
- Professional effectiveness
- Stress management
- Role clarity/role efficacy
- Quality circles

4 **Special capsule programs**
- Foreign currency funding options
- Financial markets and products
- Leasing and hire purchase
- Assessing and managing risk
- Industry-specific programs
- Gold banking

- Asset - liability management and treasury management
- Housing finance
- Profit planning
- Joint ventures
- Bench marking for service quality

5 **Personnel Management and Industrial Relations**

6 **Inspection and audit**

7 **Marketing**

8 **Faculty development programs**

9 **Behavioural Science programs (focus on personal growth leading to personal efficacy in the organisational context)**

10 **Programs for the officials of other commercial banks, especially designed to meet their specific needs**

Training Methodology: The methods adopted in training for imparting knowledge, developing skills, formulation of attitudes are as following;

1 **Imparting Knowledge**
- Lectures
- Exercises
- Questionnaires
- Quiz
- Group work
- Interface/panel discussions

2 **Development of Skills**
- Case studies
- Exercises
- Group work

3 **Attitude formation**
- Small group work
- Role play
- Exercises
- Interface/panel discussions
- Customer interaction

4 **The training colleges/centers are equipped with Audio-visual teaching aids and computer aided learning systems.**

Faculty

SBI makes a constant rotation of talent between operations and training to ensure a continuous process of renewal and also to anchor the system to the realities of practical banking. For the purpose of training, the bank adopted the following selection process.

Selection is done by experts after a skill demonstration.Selected faculty members are put through structured faculty development training to give further needed skills and attitude. In-house and external training is given for advanced specialization in the relative subjects.

Training Colleges

The State Bank of India established four apex level colleges. They are State Bank Staff College, Gurgaon; State Bank Staff College, Hyderabad; State Bank Institute of Rural Development (SBIRD), Hyderabad; and State Bank Institute of Information and Communication Management (SBIICM), Hyderabad.

Training Centres

Training needs are also recognised for various other employees in the junior officer's cadre, clerks and sub-ordinates. The training focus is mainly on adaptation to changes in the work procedures, to update constantly the knowledge on continuous changes in the policies of government and their impact on bank's working. For this purpose training centers were established at various parts of the country. The training at these centers also focuses on ensuring systems and procedures in the bank matching with the changing business environment and continuous review and updation of systems and procedures. Emphasis has also been laid on the awareness of changes and to improve the skills in employees and also towards facilitating attitudinal changes.

The bank is providing training to the employees mostly on general banking, core banking, foreign exchange, customer service, etc. The focus was not adequately given on emerging changes, service packages of the bank and more specifically on customer interactive skills. Therefore, the bank needs to redesign its training programs to suit the employees' needs. The bank shall establish more training centers to provide training to more employees and also to reduce periodicity.

8.3 PROVIDE NEEDED SUPPORT SYSTEM

The bank has established the needed support systems to provide necessary information to the employees. For internal communication, the theme of SBI has been 'the customer is the king, he/she is not at mercy'. The employees are also enlightened about various issues on contemporary developments in economy, the trends in the banking all over, and also the achievements of employees in the business. The media used for internal communication includes:

- SBI Monthly review
- Gurukula
- SBI Economic Newsletter
- Choyanika, etc.

SBI monthly review published by Economic Research Department highlights various issues through articles on the financial sector reforms and their impact on banking sector, issues on rural credit and agricultural development, top cs concerning the economy, agriculture, industry, finance, the monetary or external sector, international economic development including human resources management, etc. This enlightens the knowledge of the employees which is helpful in the day to day activities.

Gurukula from State Bank Academy, Gurgaon provides information on the training needs and also about the development of the various programs during the training period.This constantly updates the knowledge of the staff in response to the demands of the customers. This also motivates the employees to pursue further training in new developments that are taking place in the banking system.

Economic Newsletter provides information about the policy changes of Government and RBI and their implications on bank's performance.The activities of the bank and the impact of the same on the resources of the bank are communicated through this news letter. Choyanika is published from State Bank Staff College. It provides information on employee empowerment, motivation and the compensation packages. It also provides information about the work force, and the employees' union level deliberations.

8.4 RETAIN THE BEST PEOPLE

The Bank, in order to retain the talented and potential employees offers financial packages and also provides welfare facilities.

The Financial benefits

The financial benefits to the employees are offered in the form of monthly salary. The pay scale revision is done for every four years. Changes in cost of living are affected through Dearness Allowance. The pay structure is under three categories; officers, clerical and cash department and sub-ordinate staff.

In the officers cadre there are seven grades: JMGS I, MMGS II, MMGS III, SMGS VI, GS V, TEGS VI and TEGS VII with different pay structure as shown in Table – 8.1.

Table 8.1: Pay Scale of Officers as on 31-03-2007.

Scale I	Rs.10000 – 470/6 - 12820 – 500/3 – 14320 – 560/7 - 18240
Scale II	Rs.13820 – 500/1 – 14320 – 560/10 - 19920
Scale III	Rs.18240 – 560/5 – 21040 – 620/2 - 22280
Scale IV	Rs.20480 – 560/1 – 21040 – 620/5 - 24140
Scale V	Rs.24140 – 620/4 - 26620
Scale VI	Rs.26620 - 680/4 - 29340
Scale VII	Rs.29340 – 680/2 – 30700 – 900/1 – 31600 – 1000/1 – 32600

The second category of employees is clerical/cash department staff who conducts counter services to the customers. The salary scales are shown in Table – 8.2.

Table 8.2: Pay Scale of Clerical Staff as on 31-03-2007.

Clerk and Cash Department Staff	4410 - 215/3 – 5055 – 335/3 – 6060 - 470/4 – 7940 – 500/3 – 9440 – 560/4 – 11680 – 970/1 – 12650 – 560/1 – 13210

Third category of employees is sub-ordinate staff who assist the clerical staff, cash department staff and officers in the performance of their respective duties. The salary pay structure of sub-ordinate staff is shown in Table 8.3.

Table 8.3: Pay Scale of Subordinate Staff as on 31-03-2007.

Subordinate Staff	4060 - 195/4 – 4270 – 115/2 – 4500 – 135/2 – 4770 – 165/3 – 5265 – 195/4 – 6045 – 325/3 – 6750 – 270/3 – 7560

The pay scales of officer's cadre were revised two times during the period of study. The first revision took place in the year 1997 and the second revision took place in the year 2002. The minimum term for pay scale revision for officers cadre was 4 years. During the period of study the pay scales for clerks cadre were revised two times, first time in the year 1997 and the second time in the year 2002. The pay scales of the sub- ordinate staff were also revised two times between 1997-98 to 2006-07. The first revision took place in the year 1997 and the second revision in the year 2002.

Welfare Facilities

To retain talent and professionalism in the bank, the following welfare activities are provided by the Bank.

Award of Educational Scholarships: State Bank of India awards scholarships, for any full time Degree, Diploma courses recognised by the Government besides the ordinary courses viz., B.A., B.Com., B.Sc., M.A., M.Com., M.Sc., professional courses in Medicine, Engineering, Architecture, Law, Management Studies, etc., are also covered under the scheme.

The Scholarships are as Under

	FOR DAY SCHOLAR	FOR BOARDERS
(A) At Intermediate level	100	300
(B) At Graduate /Post Graduate level for ordinary courses of B.A., B.Com., M.A., M.Com.	150	400
(C) Professional Courses	200	500

Promotion of Canteens: The State Bank of India allocates amount to staff welfare fund. The fund is created out of profits of the bank. Outside the scope of the staff welfare fund, the wages of canteen employees on a uniform scale on monthly basis are paid out of bank's charges account.

Library: The expenditure needed for running library is provided by State Bank of India. The non-recurring expenses for books, furniture and the recurring expenses for newspapers, periodicals are met by the bank.

Holiday-cum-Convalescent Homes: The bank has established at various centres the Holiday-cum-Convalescent Homes for the use of the employees. Employees in one circle are allowed to make use of the Holiday-cum-Convalescent Homes established in other circles by advance reservation. The rental charges are very nominal which will be recovered from the employees.

Sports: State Bank of India encourages sports activity among its employees. It provides Table-Tennis boards at the work places depending on availability of space. It also provides Balls, Bats, Shuttle Cocks, Kits, Nets, Carom boards in connection with games.

Advances to Staff: In order to help employees to come out of their financial problems, the State Bank of India provides various types of advances to the staff. The following are the various types of advances which are provided to the staff.

TYPE OF ADVANCE	AMOUNT OF ADVANCE	INTEREST CHARGE
Against gold ornaments, Government securities, LIC policies, Units of UTI, State Bank of India Magnum, NSC, Share on Banks, own Term Deposits		**Maximum interest paid on Staff TDR or receivable on which ever is higher security**
Against Kisan Vikas Patras		**Vary with maturity** **5 years – 14%** **5 ½ years – 13.0%** **6 years – 12%** **6 ½ years – 11.5%**
Car loan	**Upto Rs.80,000** **Above Rs.80,000 – 1,60,000**	**8.5%** **12.0%**
Scooter – Motor Cycle	**Upto Rs.15,000** **Above Rs.15,000 – 30,000**	**7.5%** **12.0%**
Housing Loan	**Upto Rs.1.10 lakh** **Above Rs.1.10 – 5 lakh** **Above Rs.5 lakh**	**8.5%** **11.0%** **12.0%**
Soft loan	**Maximum 10 basics** **Subordinates Rs.40,000** **Assistants Rs.80,000** **Officers Rs.1,20,000**	**0.5 above PLR**

Perquisites: State Bank of India offers various perquisites in order to motivate and retain the talent in the organisation. The following are the details of the perquisites offered by the bank to its employees.

Officiating Allowance: Every employee in the officer cadre is eligible for an allowance of 6 per cent of the basic pay for aggregate of 7 days in a month not exceeding Rs.250/-.

Deputation Allowance: The bank pays deputation allowance for employees deputed to various training centre/BSRB and locally established organisations. The allowance is 6 per cent of basic pay subject to the maximum of Rs.500/-, when deputation is within the bank. If employees are deputed outside the bank, the allowance is 12 per cent of basic pay subject to the maximum of Rs.1,000/-.

Conveyance Allowance: The Bank provides conveyance allowance to the officer whenever they incur such expenses on bank's work.

Car Allowance: The officers are eligible for 45 liters to 55 liters of petrol depending upon the service in the scale.

Two Wheeler: The officers are eligible for two wheeler allowance depending on the service which varies from 20-30 liters and on production of utilisation certificate for Rs.425-575.

Out of Pocket Allowance: The bank pays half halting allowance of Rs.100/- to an officer who is deputed locally for at least 4 hours subject to at least 15 km from office and 5 km. from residence or *vice versa.*

Halting Allowance: The Bank pays halting allowance at the following rates to the employees cadre.

EMPLOYEE	MAJOR 'A' CLASS CITIES	PLACES IN AREA – I	OTHER PLACES
JMSI, M II & M III	Rs.220	Rs.190	Rs.165
SMG IV & above	Rs.275	Rs.220	Rs.190

Hotel Charges: The bank pays hotel charges to employees whom the bank nominates for bank dealings.

EMPLOYEE	ELIGIBILITY	MAJOR 'A' CLASS CITIES (RS.)	PLACES IN AREA – I (RS.)	OTHER PLACES (RS.)
TEG (VI & VII)	IV Star Hotel A/c	3,500	1,750	1,500
SMGS (IV & V)	III Star Hotel A/c	1,600	1,195	1,050
MMGS (II & III)	II Star Hotel (non A/c)	825	700	600
JMS (I)	I Star Hotel (non A/c)	500	425	300

(For Delhi/Mumbai 125% of the maximum for TEG – VI & VIII)

Allowances for transfer including Insurance packing local transfer of goods, is Rs.4,000/- for JMS (I) and MMGS and Rs.5,000/- for SMGS IV to TEG.

Residential Telephone: The Bank pays telephone charges incurred at the following ways. S.T.D. facility is allowed to all officers in SMG IV and above, all TEGs and other functionaries who are permitted by competent authority.

Reimbursement for Traveling by own conveyance for employees who came by their own cars - conveyances are paid as shown below.

Car up to 1000 cc	Rs.4.50 per km
Less than 1000 cc	Rs.3.60 per km
Scooter	Rs.2.00 per km
Moped	Rs.1.25 per km

Reimbursement of Medical Expenses: The bank provides medical facility through reimbursement of expenses in the following ways. Self – 100 per cent, family members and wholly dependents having income less than Rs.1,500/- per month is 75 per cent.

Allowances for clerks & sub-ordinate staff:

Halting Allowance:

EMPLOYEE	HIGHER CCA	LOWER CCA	NON CCA
Clerks	190	145	125
Subordinates	150	100	80

Medical Allowance: Medical expenses are reimbursed to clerks and subordinates subject to a fixed amount

Clerks for above 5 years of service Rs.1,200/- and for less than 5 years of service Rs.870/- (annually).

Subordinates for above 5 years of service Rs.1,200/- and for less than 5 years of service Rs.870/- (annually).

Conveyance Allowance: A fixed amount of Rs.65/- per month for both clerks and sub-ordinates.

Transfer Allowance (incidental): Actual expenditure incurred will be paid for both clerks and sub-ordinates.

Deputation Allowance: There is no fixed deputation allowance but usually conveyance is paid, if deputation period is more than 6 hours, halting allowance will also be paid in addition to conveyance.

8.5 EMPLOYMENT IN SBI

The employees of the SBI can be categorized into three groups. They are Officers, Clerks and Subordinate Staff. The share of the officers in the total employees varied from 25.50 per cent to 32.23 per cent during the study period. In other words, a little over ¼ of the total employees are officers.The Figure 8.1 reveals that, the number of officers which was 61,970 in the year 1999-00 increased to 2008-09 in the year 2008-09 recording an increase of 4.38 per cent.

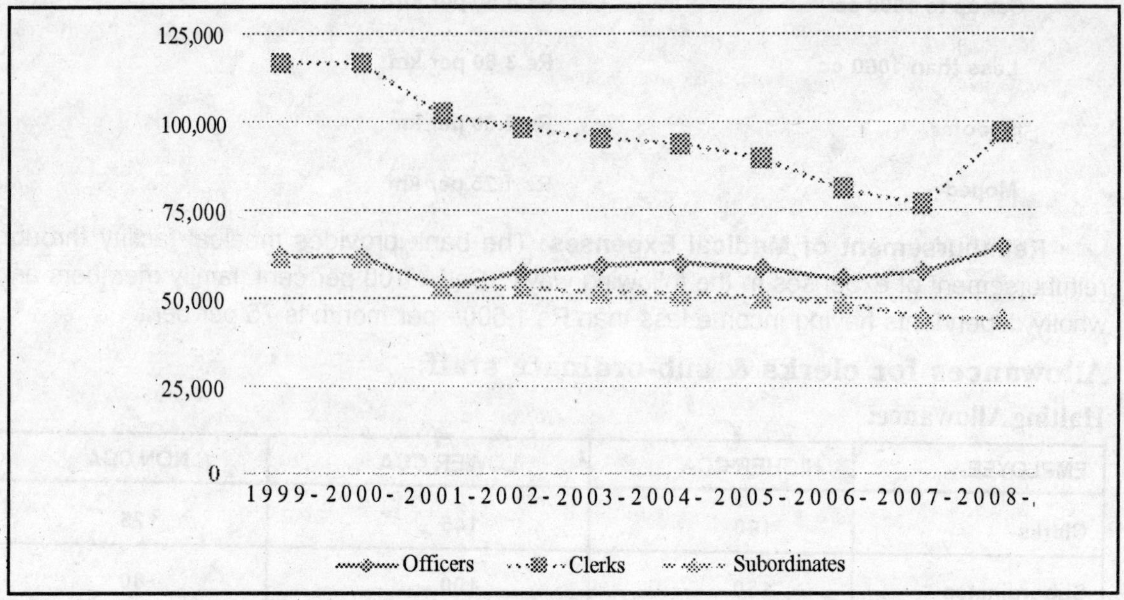

Fig 8.1: Number of Staff in State Bank of India during 1999-00 to 2008-09

Source: Annual Reports of SBI during 1999-00 to 2008-09.

The data relating to the total number of clerks working in SBI during 1999-00 to 2008-09, reveals that the total number of clerks which was 1.17 lakh in the year 1999-00 reduced to 0.97 lakh in the year 2008-09, recording a decrease of 17.09 per cent. The clerks constitute the largest group of employees in the bank. During the period under study, the share of clerks in the total employees varied from 42.87 per cent to 48.90 per cent.

The particulars relating to the number of sub-ordinate staff working in SBI, the number of sub-ordinate staff which was 60,060 in the year 1999-00, reduced to 44,237 in the year 2008-09 recording a decrease of 28.72 per cent. The share of sub-ordinate staff in the total employees which was 25.75 per cent in 1999-00, decreased to 21.49 per cent in 2008-09. It can be inferred that the size of the employees is reduced in all cadres in SBI during the period under study. It reflects the conscious efforts of the bank to develop a workforce of right size to deliver quality services to customers.

8.6 SUMMARY

The kind of effort service firms put in for designing a service product for the external market to respond, they have to make efforts for designing a product for internal market too. While customer satisfaction is the orientation for external market, employee satisfaction should be orientation for internal market. The needs and wants of the employees should be studied carefully along with their expectations, to design a package of benefits that are capable of satisfying them. Internal marketing is a philosophy of managing personnel and developing and enhancing a service culture systematically. The activities of internal marketing should promote service mindedness and customer orientation. Most of the internal marketing activities are part of human resource management and development. State Bank of India has a working force in different categories to serve the clientele and the society at large. The staff pattern of State Bank of India consists of officers, clerks, and sub-ordinates.

State Bank of India aims to enhance knowledge, develop skills and re-orient attitude of the employees to keep pace with the changing environment. The Bank's training net work consists of 4 apex level colleges viz. State Bank Staff College, Gurgaon; State Bank Staff College, Hyderabad; State Bank Institute of Rural Development and State Bank Institute of Information and Communication Management and over 50 learning centers located across the country.

The Bank has established the needed support systems to provide necessary information to the employees. For internal communication, the theme of SBI has been the customer is the king, he is not at mercy. The employees are also enlightened about various issues on contemporary developments in economy, the trends in the banking all over, and also the achievements of employees in the business.

8.7 REFERENCES

1. Christian Gronroos, 'The Internal Marketing Function – Strategic Management and Marketing in the Service Sector Report', *Marketing Science Institute,* Cambridge, (1983): 83-104.
2. Adrian Payne, *'The Essence of Services Marketing '*, Prentice Hall of India Pvt. Ltd., New Delhi, (1998): 167.
3. Tleonard A. Schiesinger and James I. Heskeltt,'The Service Driven Service Company', *Harvard Business Review*, (Sep.– Oct. 1991): 71-81.
4. Christopher Lovelock,*'Service Marketing'*, Addition Wesley Longman (Singapore) Pvt. Ltd., Delhi, (2001): 455.
5. Christopher Lovelock,*'Service Marketing '*, Addition Wesley Longman (Singapore) Pvt. Ltd., Delhi, (2001): 455.
6. Harsha, V. Varma,*'Marketing of Services'*, Global Business Press, New Delhi, (1993): 63.

□□□

Chapter 9

EXTERNAL MARKETING

Consumers are co–producers in the service business. The quality of services will not only depend upon the performance of the service provider but also on the performance of the service consumer. Therefore, it is the responsibility of service organisations to educate and, if necessary, train customers so as to make them prepared to use the services efficiently. A well designed external marketing program is of immense help to organizations to inform, persuade and train customers to better their experiences.

External marketing is concerned with effectively communicating the results of the marketing strategy to large audience. It is an active, explicit form of marketing program highlighting the marketing elements to persuade consumers and to make them committed to service.

External marketing takes place between company and customers. It is the interaction of the company with a service offer with the target market. There is a saying that 'nothing happens until somebody sells something in the market'. Unless and until a marketing organization comes with a proposal, there will not be any response from the market, either positive or negative. Marketing stimulus, therefore, is necessary to generate responses in the form of demand. External marketing includes all such kinds of communication campaigns by the service provider that inform, educate, persuade, train and influence the customers to purchase the services.[1]

Services are intangible. Therefore, the psychic costs of the customers would be high in services. As there will be nothing to see, touch and perfect measurements, consumers do entertain doubts, suspicious and look for proper evidence, in the absence of relevant and effective communication campaign.The campaign through appropriate media should provide evidence to the customers. Services quality depends to a large extent on the ability and effective participation of customers. Participation ability, skill, involvement, and mind tuning for experience depends upon, apart from consumer characteristics, the way the consumers were informed, educated, and trained through external marketing. Thus, the efforts on external marketing influence the customer perceived quality. Most customers cannot perceive value properly even after experiencing something, in the absence of proper communication.[2]

Often, service outlets are operated under certain limitations.The uncertainty over the time involved in handling a customer, demand uncertainties, employee, equipment and infrastructural problems cannot be eliminated totally. The problems of this kind certainly cause inconvenience to the customers and may lead to the creation of negative feelings against the service provider. Through external marketing, the service provider finds an opportunity to inform and convince the customer about possible problems and increase the zone of tolerance. Image building is one of the important goals of external marketing. Image acts as a guard against minor mistakes and provide an opportunity for recovery without much damage to the organisation. One of the major sources of image building is the communication campaign launched by the service provider.[3]

State Bank of India uses advertising and personal selling for communicating the marketing offers to the consumers.The major forms of media that carry State Bank advertising are newspapers, radio, television, magazines, outdoor and transit advertising. With the recent developments in technology, use of internet by creating websites which contain information about history of the bank, the products and services, the display of different loan schemes through which a customer gets direct access has increased. State Bank of India has opened websites like, www.statebankofindia.com, www.sbi.co.in, www.statebank.com and www.onlinesbi.com to facilitate customers to get the preliminary and basic information about the bank.

The external marketing programs of State Bank of India are taken at three levels; the Central Office, the Local Head Office and the Module.The Central Office conducts advertisement about various schemes directly in news papers and through hoardings at all important customer catchment areas. Certain advertisements like the introduction of new products are directly taken up by the central office and are published in all leading newspapers. The Central Office at Mumbai allocates funds to various local head offices for advertising. The LHOs at State level take up promotion programs through various schemes. Each LHO mainly concentrates on promotion activity at the capital city in which it is placed. It also gives directions to modules from time to time about the new directives in promotion policies. The third layer in the group which is allowed to undertake various measures to popularise the products and schemes is 'Module'. It gets advertisement material like brochures, pamphlets, calendars and other leaflets directly from the LHO and/or Central office. Besides, basing on the allocation of advertisement amount by the LHOs, a Module takes up advertisement in its jurisdiction mainly through the following four categories.

Hoardings	**Hoardings are placed at all important places in the catchy centres of the cities and towns. The various schemes with a special emphasis on personal loans, housing loans, education loans, loans for consumer durables, festival advances, rent plus advances are popularised through this mode of advertising.**
Newspapers	**The bank campaigns various schemes and their features through newspapers to the general public. This mode of advertisement is preferred whenever there is a change in interest rate structures, change in timings at the branches, shift of branch/branches from one premises to another premises, and auction notices about specific branches.**

	Statutory matters like RBI declaration for any holiday as working day are also published in all leading newspapers.
Brochures	**Promotion of various schemes and products is also taken up in the form of brochures, calendars, pocket calendars, leaflets which are freely distributed to customers at different branches. Captions like safety and security, bank for excellence, State Bank of India with you all the way, are printed in these materials in order to promote the bank's business.**
Electronic Media	**The bank's promotion methods also include electronic media. On occasions like, Pongal or any other important days (new year day) the bank promotes the schemes over the TV/Radio while expressing best wishes to the customers.**

The customer interacting personnel are used for personal selling purposes. The employees offer choices, guide and assist the customers in purchase decision process.

9.1 CUSTOMERS' FEEDBACK

State Bank of India follows a feedback system to know the opinion of the customers on the bank's product offer and services. At the end of every quarter, a feed back session will be conducted by the Bank. Besides this, the bank observes the 15th day of every month as a customer day. The head of the branch or head of the zone is deputed to redress the grievances.

State Bank of India has been taking measures towards ensuring customer satisfaction. By meeting or exceeding customer expectations and adding value through enhanced products and services, it is aiming at converting a satisfied customer to a loyal customer. The Bank regularly collects feedback from customers about the quality of the service, and identifies ways to serve the customers better. There are various formal structures available in the bank to improve customer service.The various formal programs organised for the purpose are discussed in the following paragraphs.

9.2 CUSTOMERS' DAY

As mentioned already, on the 15th of every month, various functionaries of the bank meet customers at their respective places of work. Depending on the size of the branch, the functionaries who meet the customers are:

Scale V branch	:	Branch Manager with AGM Cadre
Scale IV branch	:	Branch Manager with Chief Manager Cadre
Scale III, II & I	:	Branch Manager

9.3 CUSTOMER MEET

State Bank of India organises customer meet at various centres. The bank gives advance announcements in the press about such meetings. The top level executives of the bank meet customers in an open forum at various centres.

9.4 CUSTOMER RELATIONS PROGRAM

State Bank of India regularly asks customers about their needs and expectations. The bank regularly collects feedback from customers about the quality of service that they receive from the bank. All types of customers are invited to the branch at every quarter to give feedback on customer service.

9.5 CUSTOMER SERVICE COMMITTEE MEETING

The Bank branches conduct 'in house' meetings quite frequently depending on the size of the staff in the respective branches. The branches with staff strength of 100 and more will hold 'in house' meeting every month and the other branches with staff strength less than 100 will hold 'in house' meeting once in every quarter.

9.6 CUSTOMER COUNCILS

The bank organises interaction sessions at different branches depending on the size of the staff. In order to promote better interaction between staff and customers, a branch with a staff strength of 100 and more and specialised branches invite 3 to 6 customers who along with members of the customer service committee discuss various issues and steps needed to improve customer service.

9.7 DISPOSAL OF COMPLAINTS

Complaints Management System (CMS) is a comprehensive solution for managing customer complaints coming from multiple sources like phone, fax or email.CMS enables customer service representatives (CSRs) at contact centre, to initiate a complaint for a product or service. All crucial details and parameters about the customer, product, branch concerned as well as the incident are captured. The system guides the CSRs by dynamically enabling, disabling, mandating, or defaulting fields based on data being entered. Drop-down menus, logical validations, and auto-fill capabilities boost efficiency and ensure accuracy of information. Depending on the complaint parameter, the case is automatically routed for investigation, response, and reporting to the appropriate level in the bank. E-mail notifications are sent automatically to each level and escalation mechanism is triggered.

The real-time visibility provided by CMS enables the Bank to track each complaint through its lifecycle from recording and initiation to investigation, reporting, and closure – following the appropriate process to ensure that nothing slips through the cracks.

The powerful analytic and reporting capability of the Complaints Management System, helps complaint managers to perform trend analysis and spot recurring problems to drive root cause analysis in a timely manner.

The bank has set certain norms to settle the disputes of the customers. The following are the details of such norms.

- All complaints should ordinarily be disposed of within 3 weeks. However, for complaints received through Director of Public Grievances, Government of India, a fixed time frame of 6 weeks from the date of receipt of complaints is set for the disposal of complaint.

- The customer grievance cell at Local Head Offices (LHOs) monitors complaints pending for three weeks and above and put up the position to the respective GMs. All complaints pending for over one month are put up to Central Management Committee (CMC) for necessary action.
- In addition to the above, there is also a customer grievances cell in Prime Minister's Office (PMO), Ministry of Finance, Government of India and RBI. Any grievance registered at the above places is to be redressed within two days. Any type of grievance can be registered in the above mentioned offices, if the customer intends to air any grievance. Regarding any type of complaint, a written communication has to be invariably sent to the customer, besides a copy to the Reserve Bank of India.

To ensure efficient customer service, the bank collects feedback on a regular basis through visits of senior officials from controlling offices to branches – the ultimate service delivery points.The system of holding customer meets at regular intervals at branches is another mechanism evolved by the bank to elicit customer reactions about the quality of service rendered. More than 10,000 of such meets were organised by the bank, which were attended by more than 1,00,000 customers, including about 400 meets at rural centres attended by more than 10,000 customers during 1990s.

9.8 CUSTOMER SERVICE COMMITTEES

The State Bank of India has introduced the system of customer service committees in which a few customers of the bank are also the members. This council provides a forum to the representatives of the customers to participate in the bank's efforts. About 500 branches have such customer councils.

9.9 COMMUNITY SERVICES BANKING

The bank undertakes non-loaning activities or programs with a high social content involving voluntary efforts of staff members of branches and other offices throughout the country. The following are some of the main non-banking activities; blood donation camps, medical/health/eye camps for poor persons/children/pensioners, medicine banks, family welfare camps, veterinary camps, literary classes, special program like award for meritorious students, tree plantation and other environmental protection program.

The data presented in Table 9.1, reveals the expenditure on advertising and publicity by State Bank of India. It can be seen from the table that the expenditure on advertisement which was Rs.18 crore in 1999-00, increased to Rs.251 crore in 2008-09. In other words, the expenditure on advertising has increased by 1295 per cent during the period. As a percentage of the total expenditure, the expenditure on advertisement was less than 1 per cent in all the years except last two financial years of the decade. In the light of the competitive environment from private sector banks and foreign banks, the amount being spent on advertising is far less than what is desirable. The bank, therefore, should increase the advertising budget and focus on persuasive communication to promote the business to the new prospects and also to retain the existing customers.

Table 9.1: SBI's Expenditure on Advertisements and Publicity during 1999-00 to 2008-09

(Rs. in Crore)

Year	Advertisement Expenditure	Total Operating Expenditure	As a % of Total Operating Expenditure
1999-00	18	5,380	0.33
2000-01	30	5,617	0.53
2001-02	24	7,210	0.33
2002-03	34	7,942	0.43
2003-04	67	9,245	0.72
2004-05	67	10,074	0.67
2005-06	109	11,725	0.93
2006-07	88	11,824	0.74
2007-08	173	12,608	1.37
2008-09	251	15,648	1.60

Source: Annual Reports of SBI during 1999-00 to 2008-09.

9.10 COMPLAINT HANDLING SYSTEM

The complaints against banks are handled at two levels in the Reserve Bank. Fifteen Banking Ombudsman Offices handle the complaints maintainable in terms of the provisions of the Banking Ombudsman Scheme. Regulatory departments in the Reserve Bank handle complaints that are not maintainable under the provisions of the Banking Ombudsman Scheme. The complaints have been categorised into deposit accounts, loans and advances, credit cards, activities of direct selling agents, harassment in recovery of loans and general/others.

The Banking Ombudsman Scheme was first notified by the Reserve Bank on 14th June, 1995 under Section 35A of the Banking Regulation Act, 1949 to provide for a system of redressal of grievances against banks. The scheme sought to establish a system of expeditious and inexpensive resolution of customer complaints. The scheme was revised twice, first in 2002 and then in 2006. At present, the scheme is being executed by Banking Ombudsman (BO) appointed by the Reserve Bank at 15 centres covering the entire country. The BO scheme covers all commercial banks and scheduled primary cooperative banks.

The revised scheme came into effect from January 1, 2006. It incorporated new grounds of complaints such as credit card issues, failure in providing the promised facilities, non-adherence to the Fair Practices Code and levying of excessive charges without prior notice. It relaxed the mandatory requirement of filing of complaint to facilitate registering of complaints on-line or through e-mail. Further, the complainants can also appeal against the award of

BO. The scheme provided for appointment of only serving senior officers of the Reserve Bank as BO and the secretariat of BO would consist of only Reserve Bank officers. However, banks are required to appoint nodal officers in their Zonal Offices/Regional Offices for the Scheme. Also, the cost of the scheme is borne entirely by the Reserve Bank. Furthermore, in order to enable the BO to concentrate on the complaints, rather than on arbitration of inter-bank disputes, the arbitration option rested with the BO was removed. The revised scheme has witnessed an unprecedented surge in the inflow of complaints mainly due to the inclusion of credit card related issues within the ambit of the scheme, the wide publicity given and the facility of on-line complaint filing.

In July 2006, banks were advised to place service charges and fees on the homepage of their websites at a prominent place to facilitate easy access to the bank customers. A complaint form, along with the name of the nodal officer for complaint redressal, could also be provided on the homepage itself to facilitate complaint submission by the customers. The complaint form is required to indicate that the first point for redressal of complaints is the bank itself and that complainants may approach the BO only if the complaint is not resolved at the bank level within a month.

Banks were advised to constitute grievance redressal machinery within the bank for redressing complaints about services rendered by business facilitators and correspondents and give wide publicity about it through electronic and print media. The name and contact number of the designated grievance redressal officer of the bank were required to be made known and widely publicised. Banks were also required to place on their websites the grievance redressal procedure and the timeframe for responding to the complaints. If a complainant does not get satisfactory response from the bank within the stipulated time from the date of lodging the complaint, the complainant has the option of approaching the Banking Ombudsman concerned for the redressal of grievances.

To improve grievance and complaints redressal mechanism, the Banking Ombudsman Scheme (BO) was revamped in January 2006, enlarging its scope and authority. It incorporated new grounds of complaints such as credit card issues, failure in providing the promised facilities, non-adherence to the Fair Practices Code and levying of excessive charges without prior notice. It relaxed the mandatory requirement of filing of complaints to facilitate registering of complaints through on-line or through e-mail. Further, the complainants can also appeal against the award of BO.

State Bank of India became a member of the Banking Codes and Standards Board of India (BCSBI) in September 2006. The Bank has thereby adopted the BCSBI's Code of Bank's Commitments to Customers as the Fair Practice Code for implementation at all its branches. The Bank has also appointed Code Compliance Officers at all its Local Head Offices. The Bank places importance not only to redress customer grievances but also in identifying systemic/attitudinal issues, if any, that lead to a high frequency of complaints in particular areas and in rectifying them.

9.11 SUMMARY

State Bank of India uses advertising and personal selling for communicating the marketing offers to the consumers.The major forms of media that carry State Bank advertising are newspapers, radio, television, magazines and outdoor and transit advertising. With the recent developments in technology, use of internet by creating websites which contain information about history of the bank, the products and services, the display of different loan schemes through which a customer gets direct access.

State Bank of India follows a feedback system to know the opinion of the customers on the bank's product offer and services. At the end of every quarter, a feed back session will be conducted by the bank. Besides this, the bank observes the 15th day of every month as a customer day. The head of the branch or head of the zone is deputed to redress the grievances.

State Bank of India has been taking measures towards ensuring customer satisfaction. By meeting or exceeding customer expectations and adding value through enhanced products and services, it is aiming at converting a satisfied customer to a loyal customer. The Bank regularly collects feedback from customers about the quality of the service, and identifies ways to serve the customers better. There are various formal structures available in the bank to improve customer service. The bank organizes the various programs to obtain feedback from customers.The programs are Customers' day, Customer meet, Customer relations program, Customer service committee meeting, and Customer councils.

9.12 REFERENCES

1. Rama Mohana Rao, K.,*'Services Marketing '*, Pearson Education, New Delhi, (2005).
2. Frank Jefkins, *'Advertising '*, McMillan, New Delhi, (1999): 5.
3. Ronalt T. Markes. B.,*'Personal Selling an Interactive Approach '*, Allyn and Bacon Inc. Boston, (1981): 8.

❑❑❑

Chapter 10 EMPLOYEES' OPINION ON INTERACTIONS

Employees play a vital role in the performance of every service organization. Banking is a high customer interaction business in India. The performance of the employees in a banking organisation will influence significantly by the achievement of company objectives.The strategies adopted in the internal marketing are to ensure positive and efficient performance of the employee in interactions. In the process of service production and delivery in banking sector, the employee needs to perform major part of the process by involving customers and making them participated well. The quality perceptions of the customers are influenced by the way employees perform and support the customers in the process of service production.The interactive performance of the employees depend upon many factors such as training, compensation, communication, physical environment, systems and procedures, interaction with superiors and co-employees, and the kind of customers they interact.The management of a bank should not only provide better conditions for employee-customer interactions, but also collect feedback from employees periodically, so as to make improvements in the process. Keeping this in view an attempt is made to study the opinion of the employees on interaction experiences.The following are the findings of the study.

10.1 DEMOGRAPHIC PROFILE

The age of the respondents varied between 24 years and 56 years. The majority of the respondents (54.7 per cent) are in the age group of 41 – 50 years. The mean age of the respondents is 43.97. The standard deviation of the age of the respondents in the five zones is 0.774. The mean value of the respondents is 2.94. The majority of the respondents (50.7 per cent) are graduates. Out of the total, 18.7 per cent are qualified graduates with CAIIB. There are 17.3 per cent of the respondents who are post graduates and 13.3 per cent are qualified post graduates with CAIIB.

The data relating to the designation of the respondents reveals that out of the total, Senior Assistants are large in number followed by Assistant Managers, Special Assistants and Deputy Managers. The other positions that are part in the sample include Assistants, Trainee Officers, Officers, Managers, Chief Manager and Assistant General Manager.

The annual income of the respondents varied between Rs.1 lakh and above Rs.3 lakh. The mean of the annual income of the respondents is Rs.2,53,333. The standard deviation of the annual income of the respondents among the five zones is 1.05.

An attempt is made in the study to know whether the respondents had previous bank service experience or any other experience prior to be joining of the bank service. The data shown in Figure 10.1 reveals, only 3.3 per cent of the respondents had bank service experience prior to joining State Bank of India. The respondents who had work experience other than banking constitute 16.67 per cent of the total. The vast majority of the respondents (80 per cent) did not have any previous work experience.

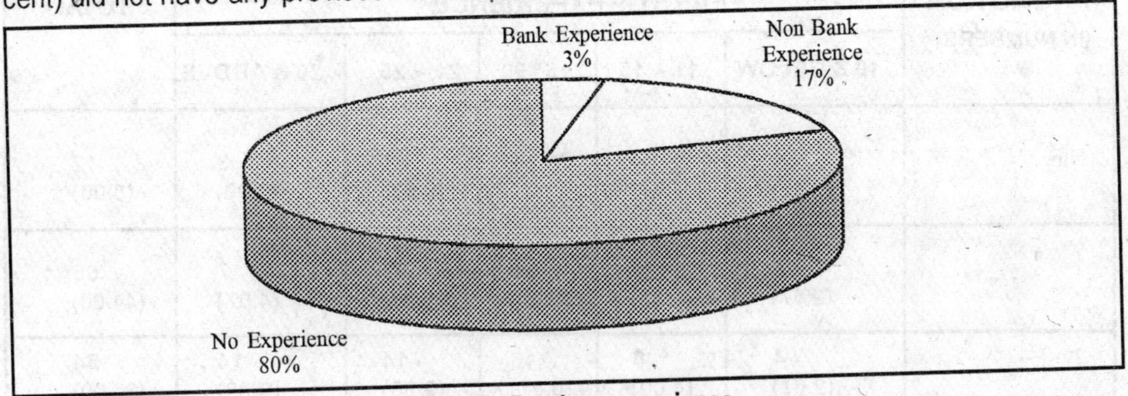

Fig 10.1: Previous experience

The motivating factors for choosing bank service as a career were ascertained and presented in Table 10.1. 'The first job I got' secured low mean rank of the respondents followed by 'prestigious job'. Therefore, the first opportunity in the career and the status associated with the job in the society are the chief motivating factors for the respondents to join in banking services. The other motivating factors are 'career growth opportunities' (mean rank 3.23), 'special interest in banking services' (mean rank 3.27), 'suitable to the respondents abilities' (mean rank 3.36), 'convenient job' (mean rank 3.37), and the 'best among available' (mean rank 3.39).

Table 10.1: What motivated you to join banking services?

REASONS FOR MOTIVATION	N	MEAN RANK
Prestigious job	76	2.51
Convenient job	57	3.37
Career growth opportunities	65	3.23
I have special interest in banking services	59	3.27
Suitable to my abilities	58	3.36
The first job I got	100	1.75
The best among available	66	3.39

There are eight per cent of respondents who are not promoted even one time in their career (Table 10.2). Though, they have put up experience of below 10 years and above 26 years in the bank. As many as 44 per cent of the respondents got one promotion and 36 per cent of the respondents got two promotions in their service with the bank. There were 10 per cent of the respondents who were promoted thrice while, two per cent got promotion four times.

Table 10.2: Promotion vs. Experience

PROMOTION (IN NUMBERS)	YEARS OF EXPERIENCE					TOTAL
	10 & BELOW	11 – 15	16 -20	21 – 25	26 & ABOVE	
Nil	4 (2.67)	4 (2.67)	-	1 (0.67)	3 (2.00)	12 (8.00)
1	4 (2.67)	14 (9.33)	18 (12.00)	23 (15.33)	7 (4.67)	66 (44.00)
2	4 (2.67)	6 (4.00)	16 (10.67)	14 (9.33)	14 (9.33)	54 (36.00)
3	-	2 (2.00)	2 (2.00)	4 (4.67)	7 (4.67)	15 (10.00)
4	-	-	-	1 (0.67)	2 (1.33)	3 (2.00)
Total	6 (10.67)	36 (17.33)	43 (24.00)	33 (28.67)	(22.00)	150 (100.00)

Figures in parenthesis indicate percentage to the total.

An attempt is further made to study the number of transfers, the respondents experienced during their service in the bank. The number of transfers varied between one and six and above. Out of the total, 25.33 per cent of the respondents were transferred 6 times and above. As many as 19.33 per cent were transferred 5 times, while an equal number of respondents revealed that they were transferred 4 times. Out of the total, 21.33 per cent of the respondents were transferred 3 times, 11.33 per cent of the respondents were transferred 2 times and 2.67 per cent of the respondents were transferred only once.

The average working period between transfers were calculated and shown in Figure 10.2. It can be seen from the figure, the average working period between joining and first transfer was 4.85 years, between first and second was 4.72 years, between 2nd and 3rd was 5.33 years, between 3rd and 4th was 6.10 years and between 4th to 5th it was 5.6 years.It indicates that form second transfer, the study period was lower.

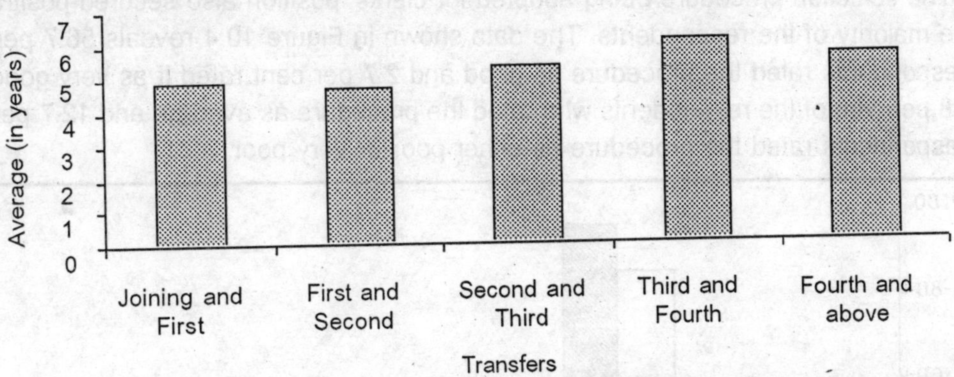

Fig 10.2: Average working period between Transfers

10.2 RECRUITMENT, SELECTION AND TRAINING

The respondents were asked to express their opinion on recruitment policy of the State Bank of India. The data shown in the Figure 10.3 reveals that the majority of the respondents representing 66 per cent of the total opine that the recruitment policy of the bank is good. There are 16.7 per cent respondents who opine that the bank should go for recruitment drive every year, so that new generation employees will join the bank and energize the banking operations. A few respondents are of the opinion that the bank should conduct campus interviews in reputed educational institutions. Only 4 per cent of the respondents felt that the existing recruitment policy of the bank is not capable of attracting right people to the banking services. However, there are 10 per cent of the respondents who are unwilling to give their opinion on recruitment policy.

Fig 10.3: Opinion on the recruitment

Figure 10.4 depicts the opinion of the respondents on the selection procedure for officer positions. Out of the total, 64 per cent rated the existing procedure being followed for the selection of officers as good. A little over 10 per cent rated the procedure as either poor or very poor.

The selection procedure being adopted for clerks' position also secured positive rating by the majority of the respondents. The data shown in Figure 10.4 reveals 56.7 per cent of the respondents rated the procedure as good and 2.7 per cent rated it as very good. There are 28 per cent of the respondents who rated the procedure as average and 12.7 per cent of the respondents rated the procedure as either poor or very poor.

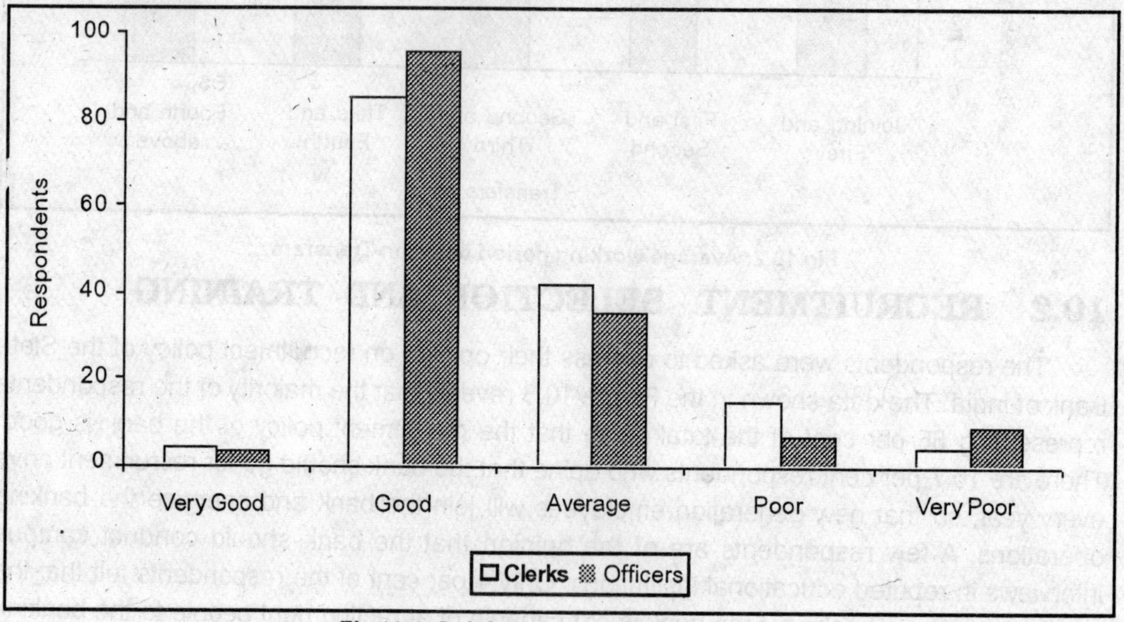

Fig 10.4: Opinion on selection procedure

Out of the total, 77 per cent have taken training during their service period (Figure 10.5). The respondents revealed that the areas in which training was given includes General Banking, Marketing, Cash and Advances, Customer Service, Foreign Exchange, Systems, Managerial skills, Agricultural Banking, HRD, Credit, Govt. Business, Work area problems, Deposits, Cross Selling, Personal banking, Audit, Leadership skills, Accounts, Relationship Management, NRI Service, Behavioral Aspects and Hindi. It can be seen from the Figure 10.6, the training modules are mostly focusing upon General Banking, Customer Service, Credit, Foreign Exchange and Systems.

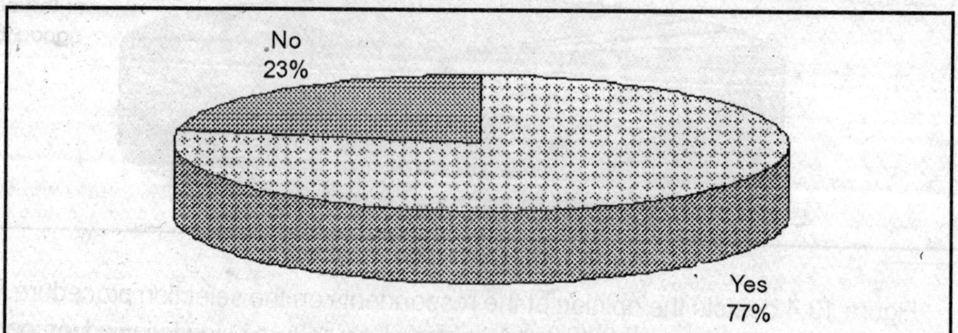

Fig 10.5: Are you given training for performing your task effectively?

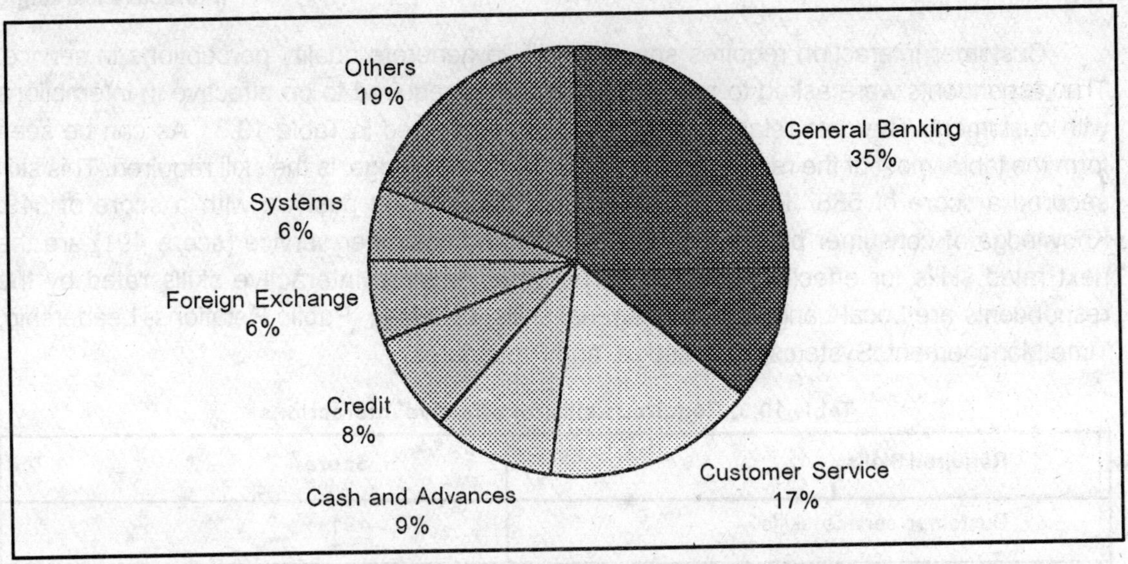

Fig 10.6: What are the areas in which you're trained?

The employees opined that there is a need of periodic training on the issues like emerging changes in banking sector, interactive skills, job related aspects, computer skills, new technology, customer satisfaction, motivation, behavioural science, new product selling, practical training on job area, systems and procedures, human resource management, etc. The data presented in Figure 10.7 reveals that a little over 74.6 per cent wanted periodic training on emerging changes in banking sector. As many as 46 per cent identified the need for training on interactive skills and they wanted periodic training be given to all the employees who interact with customers regularly. Out of the total, 28 per cent wanted training on specific aspects relating to the job, 24 per cent expressed the need for periodic training in new technology, 20 per cent wanted training on customer satisfaction and 10.7 per cent expressed the need for periodic training on computer skills.

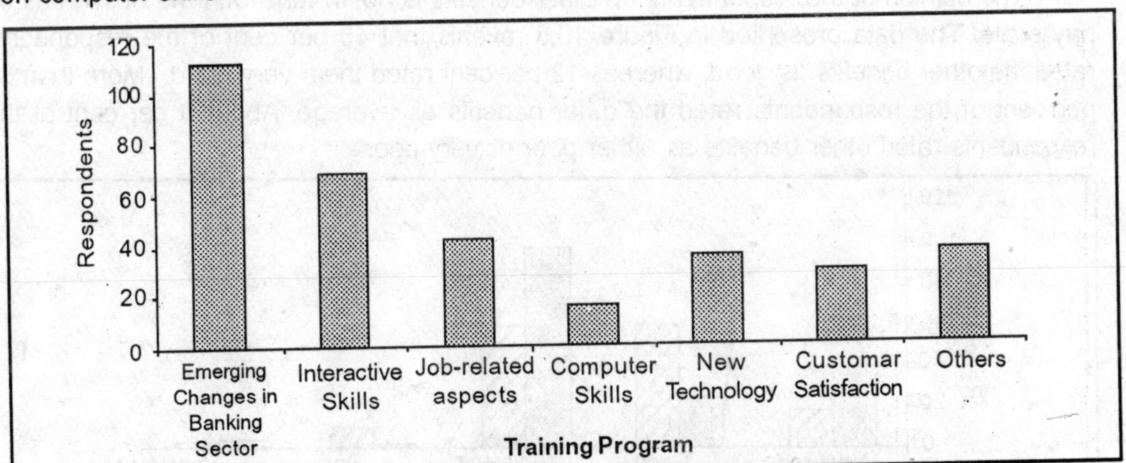

Fig 10.7: What type of periodical training program do you suggest?

Customer interaction requires specific skills to generate quality perceptions in service. The respondents were asked to reveal the skill that is required to be effective in interactions with customers. The data relating to the above is presented in Table 10.3. As can be seen form the table, most of the respondents revealed 'job knowledge' is the skill required. This skill secured a score of 588. 'Marketing skills' occupied second position with a score of 549. Knowledge of consumer psychology (score 519) and customer service (score 491) are the next rated skills for effective interaction.The other required interactive skills rated by the respondents are Local Language, Managerial skills, Listening, Public Relations, Leadership, Time Management, Systems, Knowledge, and Procedures.

Table 10.3: Required skills for effective interactions

Required Skills	Score
Customer service skills	491
Job knowledge	588
Knowledge of Consumer Psychology	519
Marketing skills	549
Others*	449

* The others are Local Language, Managerial Skills, Listening, Public Relations, Leadership, Time Management, Systems Knowledge and Procedures.

The data presented in Figure 10.8 reveals the opinion of the employees on pay scale. Out of the total, 64 per cent rated the present pay scale as average and 15.3 per cent rated it as good. Only 4 per cent rated the present pay scale as either poor or very poor.

The opinion of the respondents on other benefits is not in tune with the opinion as on pay scale. The data presented in Figure 10.8 reveals that 40 per cent of the respondents rated the other benefits as good, whereas 12 per cent rated them very good. More than 39 per cent of the respondents rated the other benefits as average. About 9 per cent of the respondents rated other benefits as either poor or very poor.

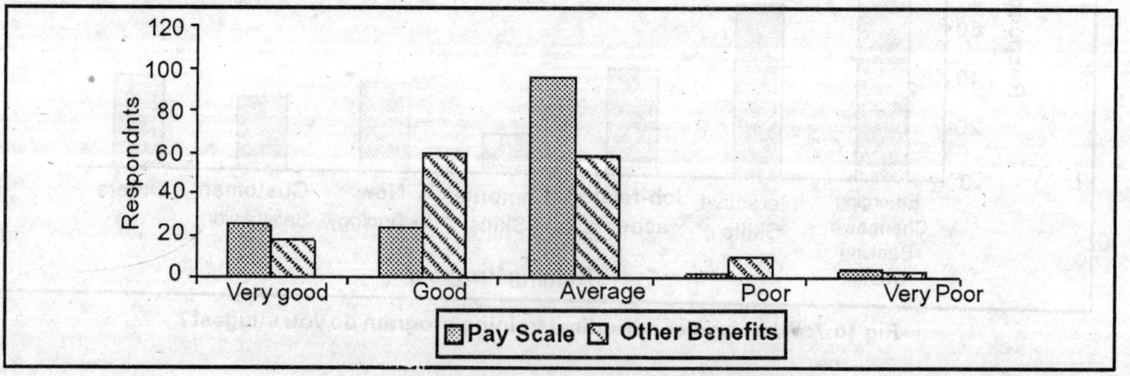

Fig 10.8: Opinion on Pay Scale and Other Benefits

The employees were asked to reveal whether employee merit is recognized in the bank. The data presented in Figure 10.9 reveals that a little over 59 per cent opined that the merit is recognized in the bank while the others gave a negative response.

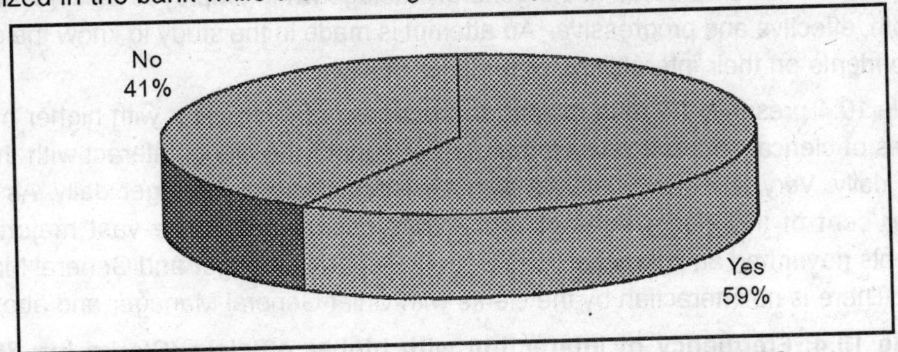

Fig 10.9: Whether employee merit is recognized in the bank?

Upward communication system is considered to be one of the vital parts of the organization system in the light of dynamic changes in the business environment. Its important is much more in a service organization where the quality generates in employee-customer interaction and each and every interactive point is a vital source for customer feedback. Well designed and executed upward communication system provides valuable information to the policy makers to make the service more customer oriented and to develop a realistic path for the future. The respondents were asked to rate the upward communication system of the State Bank of India. As can be seen from Figure 10.10, more than 71 per cent of the respondents rated the present upward communication system as either good or very good.

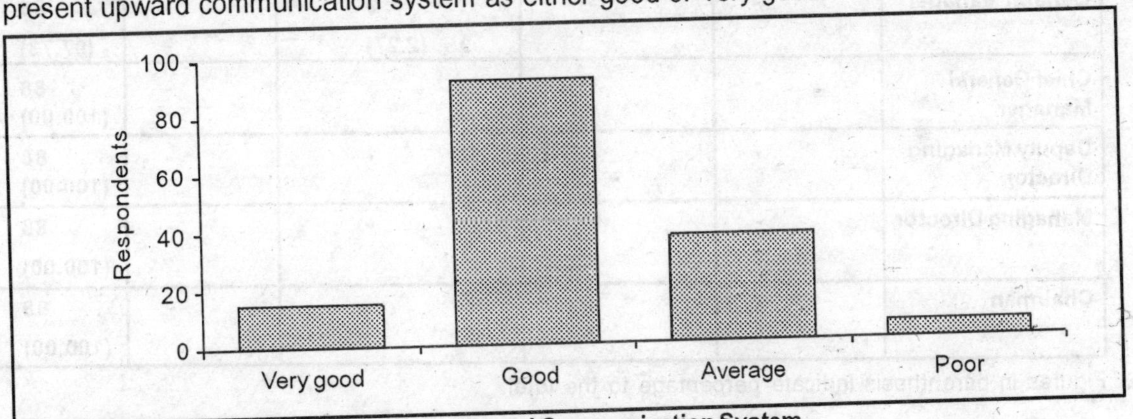

Fig 10.10: Upward Communication System

10.3 EMPLOYEE – MANAGEMENT INTERACTIONS

Interaction between the decision makers and job performers is important in service organization due to several reasons. Employees whether the front line or supporters face heterogeneous customer problems day in and day out. Many a time employees make minor changes in the system to suit to the needs of the customers while executing the system to solve customer problems. The employees are generally in a position to assess the limitations and short comings in the design. They will be in a position to analyse the problems of the system both from the management and customers' point of view. The employees' interactions with higher officials will help to make the system more customer centric. Many problems can be prevented or can be uprooted at the generation stage when employee-officers interactions are smooth, effective and progressive. An attempt is made in the study to know the opinion of the respondents on their interactions with higher officials.

Table 10.4 presents the data relating to frequency of interaction with higher officials by employees of clerical cadre. It reveals that 92 per cent of the clerks interact with the branch manager daily. Very few clerks interact with Assistant General Manager daily. As many as 36.35 per cent of the clerks interact with AGMs occasionally. The vast majority of the respondents never had an interaction with Deputy General Manager and General Manager of the bank. There is no interaction by the clerks with Chief General Manager and above cadre.

Table 10.4: Frequency of interaction with higher officials (Clerks (n= 88))

HIGHER OFFICIAL	DAILY	WEEKLY	OCCASIONALLY	RARELY	NEVER
Branch Manager	81 (92.05)	-	7 (7.95)	-	-
Assistant General Manager	7 (7.95)	-	32 (36.35)	-	49 (55.70)
Deputy General Manager		1 (1.14)	6 (6.82)	1 (1.14)	80 (90.91)
General Manager	-	-	2 (2.27)	-	86 (97.73)
Chief General Manager	-	-	-	-	88 (100.00)
Deputy Managing Director	-	-	-	-	88 (100.00)
Managing Director	-	-	-	-	88 (100.00)
Chairman	-	-	-	-	88 (100.00)

Figures in parenthesis indicate percentage to the total.

The vast majority of the officers interact daily with branch managers. Only 28.8 per cent of the officers interact with AGMs daily (Table 10.5). As many as 53.23 per cent of the officers revealed that they interact with AGMs occasionally. Out of the total, 22.58 per cent revealed that they never had interaction with AGM of the bank. The officers' interaction with DGM is occasional as 38.71 per cent revealed the same. Only one respondent is having daily interaction with DGM and four respondents interact with DGM weekly. Out of the total, 35.48 per cent of the respondents never had interaction with DGM, while 17.4 per cent revealed that their interaction with DGM is rare. The table further reveals that only few respondents had occasional interaction with the General Manager and above cadres.

Table 10.5: Frequency of interaction with higher officials (Officers (n= 62*))

Higher Official	Daily	Weekly	Occasionally	Rarely	Never
Branch Manager	42 (93.33)	-	3 (6.67)	-	
Assistant General Manager	15 (24.19)	-	33 (53.23)	-	14 (22.58)
Deputy General Manager	1 (1.61)	4 (6.45)	24 (38.71)	11 (17.4)	22 (35.48)
General Manager	-	-	10 (16.13)	2 (3.23)	50 (80.64)
Chief General Manager	-	-	5 (8.06)	2 (3.23)	55 (88.71)
Deputy Managing Director	-	-	3 (4.84)	-	59 (95.16)
Managing Director	-	-	2 (3.23)	-	60 (96.77)
Chairman	-	-	1 (1.61)	-	61 (98.39)

* Out of the total 17 respondents are Branch Managers. Figures in parenthesis indicate percentage to the total.

The mode of interaction with branch manager is largely face to face in case of both officers and clerks (Table 10.6). The mode of interaction with AGM and above cadres has been telephone in the case of majority of clerks, while it is face to face for officers.

Table 10.6: Mode of interaction with higher officials (Clerks (n= 88))

HIGHER OFFICIAL	FACE TO FACE	PHONE	NEVER
Branch Manager	86 (97.73)	2 (2.27)	-
Assistant General Manager	22 (25.00)	17 (19.31)	49 (55.69)
Deputy General Manager	13 (14.76)	19 (21.60)	56 (63.64)
General Manager	-	3 (3.41)	85 (96.59)
Chief General Manager		-	88 (100.00)
Deputy Managing Director	-	-	88 (100.00)
Managing Director	-	-	88 (100.00)
Chairman	-	-	88 (100.00)

Figures in parenthesis indicate percentage to the total.

Table 10.7 depicts the data on mode of interactions with higher officials. As many as 97.78 per cent of the respondents reveal that they were having face to face interaction with Branch Manager. In the case of interaction with Assistant General Manager 48.38 per cent of the respondents reveal that they have face to face interaction and 29.03 per cent respondents reveal that they interact over phone.There are 22.59 per cent of respondents who reveals that they never interact with Assistant General Manger. With respect to Deputy General Manager 37.10 per cent having face to face interaction, 27.42 per cent having interaction over phone, while 35.48 per cent are not having any interaction. A little over 80 per cent of the respondents reveal that they are not any interaction with General Manager. As may as 88.71 per cent reveals that they do not interact with Chief General Manager. The respondents who are having interacted with Deputy Managing Director, Managing Director and Chairman constitute less than 5 per cent of the total.

Table 10.7: Mode of interaction with higher officials (Officers (n= 62*))

HIGHER OFFICIAL	FACE TO FACE	PHONE	NEVER
Branch Manager	**44** (97.78)	**1** (2.22)	**-**
Assistant General Manager	**30** (48.38)	**18** (29.03)	**14** (22.59)
Deputy General Manager	**23** (37.10)	**17** (27.42)	**22** (35.48)
General Manager	**5** (8.06)	**7** (11.29)	**50** (80.65)
Chief General Manager	**4** (6.45)	**3** (4.84)	**55** (88.71)
Deputy Managing Director	**2** (3.23)	**1** (1.61)	**59** (95.17)
Managing Director	**1** (1.61)	**1** (1.61)	**60** (96.78)
Chairman	**1** (1.61)	**-**	**61** (98.39)

* Out of the Total 17 respondents are Branch Managers. Figures in parenthesis indicate percentage to the total.

An attempt is further made to study the opinion of the respondents on the interaction with higher officials. The respondents were asked to give their rating varying from strongly agree and strongly disagree on six parameters such as courteous, empathetic, responsive, objective, action oriented and friendly. The data presented in Table 10.8 reveals that all the parameters secured high positive score both in the case of clerks and officers. The clerks rated high for courteousness, responsiveness and friendliness, where as the officers rated for action orientation, friendliness and courteousness in the order.

Table 10.8: What is your rating on the interactions of higher officials?

PARTICULARS	SCORE	
	CLERKS	OFFICERS
Courteous	370	227
Empathetic	347	218
Responsive	369	217
Objective	350	220
Active	347	231
Friendly	365	228

An attempt is made to know the superior with whom the respondents belonging to clerical cadre like to interact most. Figure 10.11 presents the details. As may as 40 per cent of the respondents like to interact with Accountant of the branch and 39 per cent of the respondents like to interact with Branch Manager. There are 6 per cent of respondents who like to interact with all superiors while, 3 per cent of the respondents do not like to interact with superiors.

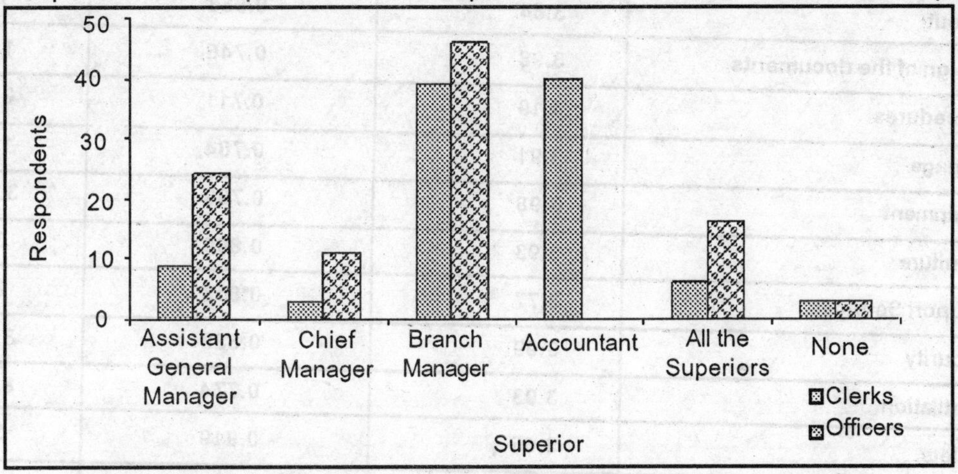

Fig 10.11: With whom do you like to interact most among your superiors

The respondents belonging to officer cadre were asked to reveal with whom they like to interact most among their superiors. Figure10.11 reveals, 46 per cent of the officers like to interact with Branch Manager. As many as 24 per cent of the respondents like to interact with Assistant General Manager and 11 per cent like to interact with Chief Manager. There are 16 per cent of the respondents who like to interact with all superiors where as 3 per cent of the respondents do not like to interact with superiors.

Table 10.9 shows the employees' opinion on Physical environment, Systems and Procedures. The issues identified are Exterior of the bank, Interior of the bank, Ambiance, Layout, Design of the documents, Procedures, Signage ,Equipment, Furniture, Support Services, Security, Ventilation, Toilets, Drinking Water, Canteen, Other physical facilities, Bank timings, Promotion system, Punishment system, Quality Assurance System, and Overall rating on Physical environment. It can be seen from the table that employees from Hyderabad and Secunderabad zones were reported significantly indifferent opinion on most of the aspects measured. Employees from Hyderabad zone were happy with regard to the exterior of the bank (F=4.38, p<.01), interior of the bank (F=5.07, p<.01), ambiance (F=5.85, p<.01), layout (F=7.91, p<.01), quality assurance system (F=4.58, p<.01) and other physical facilities (F=2.56, p<.05) comparing with the opinion of respondents from other zones. The employees from Secunderabad zone do not have positive opinion on equipment (F=3.87, p<.01), furniture (F=3.90, p<.01), support services (F=2.98, p<.05), security (F=8.34, p<.01), ventilation (F=8.64, p<.01), toilets (F=3.36, p<.05), drinking water (F=4.96, p<.01), canteen (F=5.52, p<.01), bank timings (F=4.63, p<.01) and overall rating of the bank (F=7.46, p<.01) when compared with the employees of other above zones. On most of the aspects, employees' from Visakhapatnam zone shows positive opinion.

Table 10.9: Rating on Physical Environment, Systems and Procedures

PARTICULARS	MEAN	SD	F
Exterior of the bank	3.91	0.889	4.38**
Interior of the bank	4.07	0.887	5.07**
Ambience	3.97	0.953	5.85**
Layout	3.84	0.883	7.9**
Design of the documents	3.98	0.746	1.985
Procedures	4.19	0.711	2.081
Signage	3.91	0.704	1.134
Equipment	3.98	0.709	3.87**
Furniture	3.93	0.800	3.9**
Support Services	3.77	0.853	2.98*
Security	3.99	0.823	8.34**
Ventilation	3.93	0.774	8.64**
Toilets	3.65	0.919	3.36*
Drinking Water	4.03	0.732	4.96**
Canteen	3.43	0.937	5.52**
Other physical facilities	3.63	0.805	2.55*
Bank timings	4.21	0.594	4.63**
Promotion system	3.76	0.817	1.77
Punishment system	3.69	0.868	2.327
Quality Assurance System	3.9	0.740	4.57**

**p<.01 and *p<.05

The respondents were asked to suggest changes for the improvement of the physical environment, systems and procedures. The data presented in Figure 10.12 reveals 39.3 per cent of the total opined that the physical environment of the bank should be maintained properly. A little over 29 per cent opined that there is a need for further improvements in physical environment. About 21 per cent of the respondents opined that there is no change required in the existing physical environment. The few respondents suggested improvements in customer convenience, uniqueness in physical environment, improvement of bank ambience, modernizing bank premises and display of product information.

The vast majority of the respondents representing 88.7 per cent opined that the systems of the bank need to be simplified. Only 11.3 per cent preferred *status quo* the position. As many as 44 per cent of the respondents opined that the procedures of the bank need to be simplified. A little over 26 per cent of the respondents opined that the procedures need improvement while the remaining 18.7 per cent preferred *status quo* position on procedures.

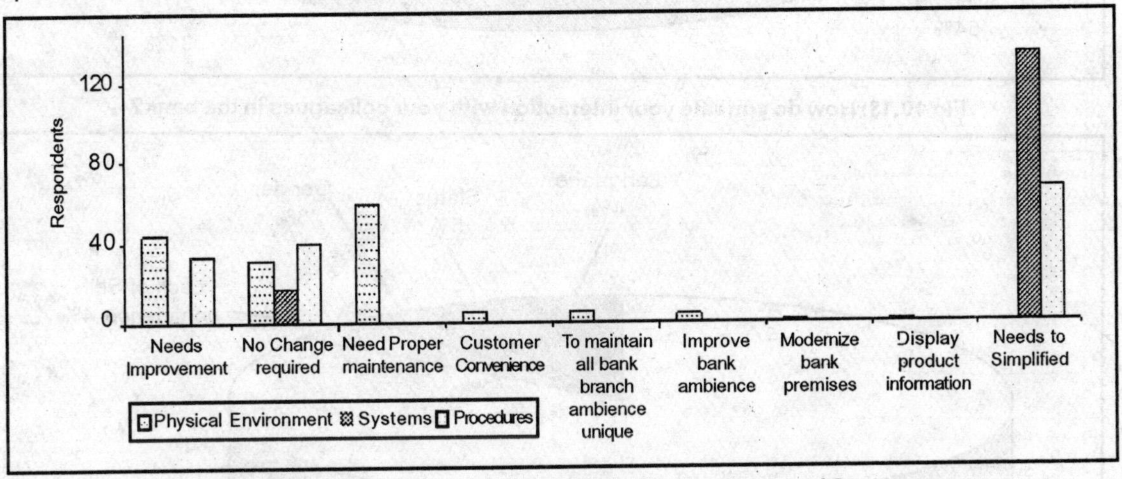

Fig 10.12: Opinion on Physical Environment, Procedures and Systems

10.4 INTERACTION WITH COLLEAGUES

Interactions with co-workers influence significantly the performance of an employee particularly in a service organization. The interactions may be work related or social. The service processes are effective only when the interactions are timely, positive and cooperative. The psychological state of the employee particularly in relation to mood, emotion, perceived ability to perform the task and the willingness to perform the task are greatly influenced by interactions with co-workers. Keeping this in view, the respondents were asked to rate their interactions with colleagues in the bank.

The data presented in Figure 10.13 reveals that 54 per cent rated interactions with their colleagues as average and 42 per cent rated the interactions are either good or very good. Further, about 85 per cent of the respondents rated that they have no problem in interacting with their colleagues (Figure 10.14). Very few respondents revealed problem like language, status, gender and lack of self confidence in interactions with colleagues.

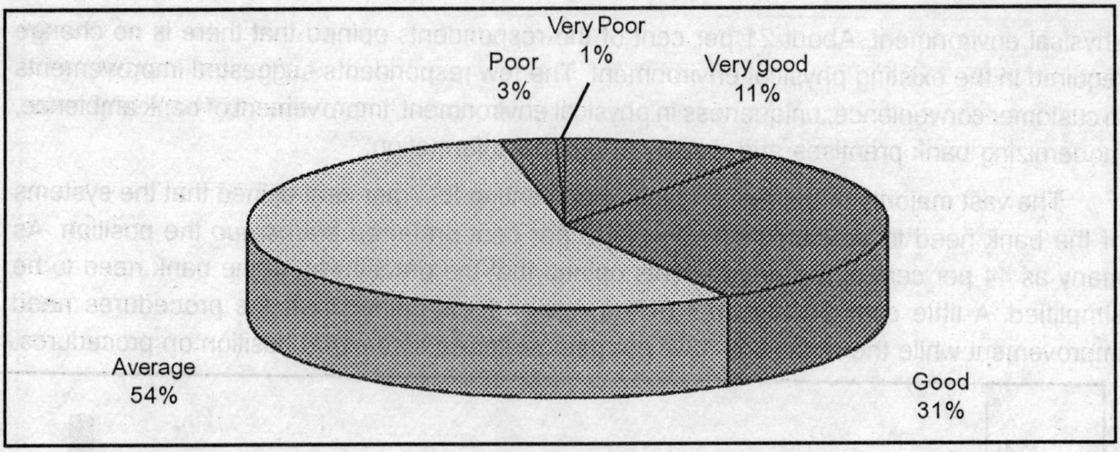

Fig 10.13: How do you rate your interaction with your colleagues in the bank?

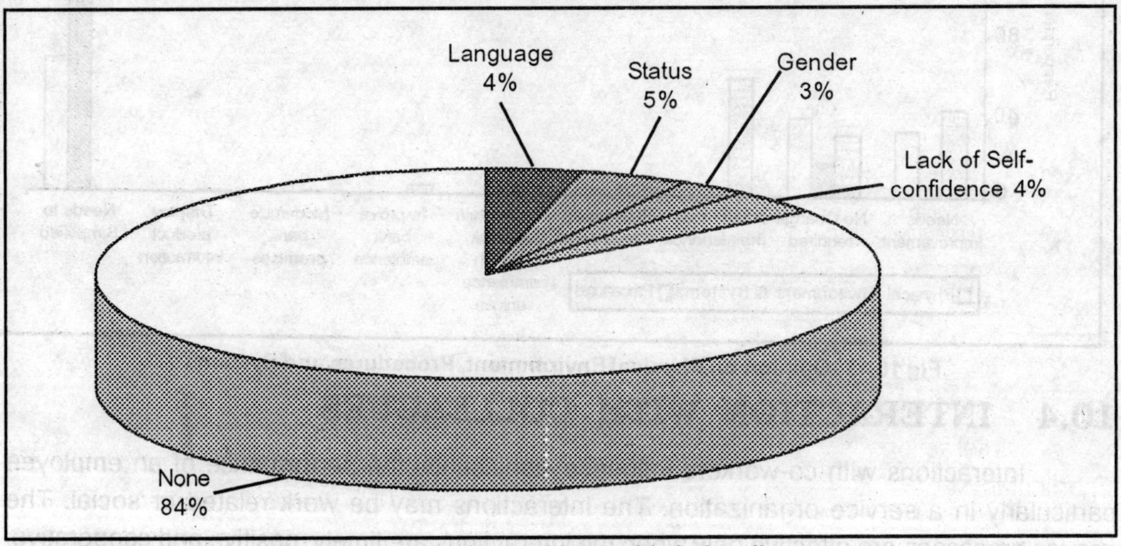

Fig 10.14: Interaction problems with their colleagues

The respondents were asked to reveal their opinion on the 'interaction with colleagues'. The data presented in Figure 10.15 shows that the majority of the respondents representing 43.33 per cent rated 'neutral' to the statement 'colleagues are cooperative'. As many as 41.33 per cent of the respondents were rated 'agree' to the statement. The response is similar for the statement 'colleagues are helpful' where in 49.33 per cent rated 'neutral' and 37.33 per cent rated 'agree'. The statement 'colleagues are understanding' was rated disagree by 39.33 per cent and 'neutral' by 31.33 per cent, 'colleagues are courteous' is rated 'agree' by 52.00 per cent and 'neutral' by 28.00 per cent, 'colleagues are righteous' is rated 'agree' by 43.33 per cent and 26.00 per cent rated 'strongly agree'. It can be inferred from the above, that the employee to employee interactions in the bank are either positive or neutral. Further, the mean and standard deviation calculated on the opinion of the respondents belonging to different zones also indicate that there is no significant difference in opinion among different zones.

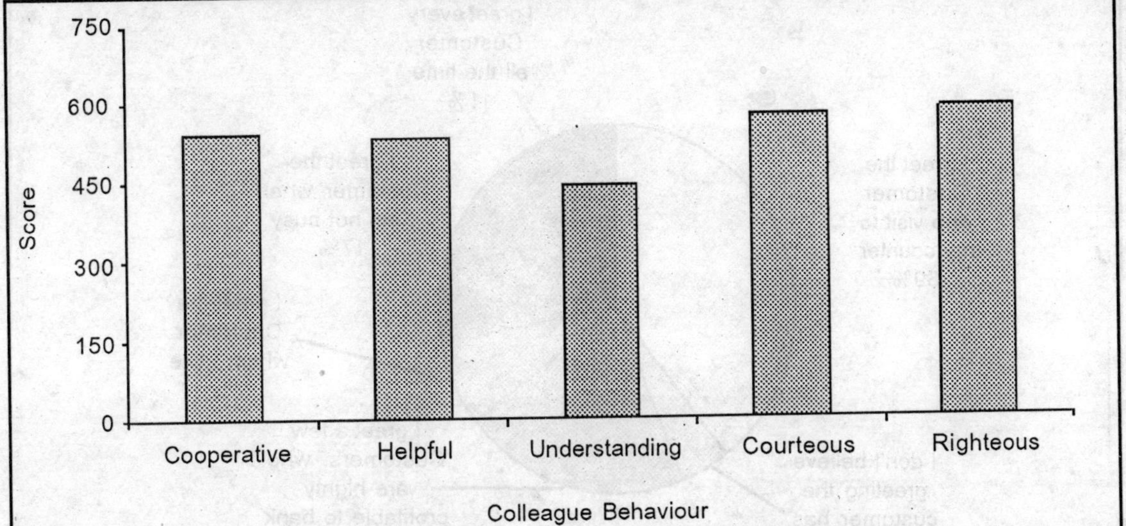

Fig 10.15: Interactive behaviour of colleagues

10.5 EMPLOYEE—CUSTOMER INTERACTIONS

The service production and consumption process begins with employee-interaction with customers at the branch net work of the bank. The employee-customer interaction is called 'service encounter'. Customer perceived quality is influenced greatly by the way the customer interactions are managed. An attempt is made in the study to know the interactive experiences of the employees of the bank.

The data presented in Figure 10.16 reveals how the employees behave at first contact with customer. As many as 39.3 per cent of the respondents revealed that they greet such customers who visit to their counters. Out of the total, 32.67 per cent revealed that they greet a few customers, who are highly profitable to the bank. There are 10.67 per cent of the respondents who revealed that they greet every customer all the time. It is significant to note that only less than 5 per cent of the respondents who discriminate in greeting customers. It can be inferred from the above, that the majority of the employees are positively inclined to greet the customers at the first contact to make a positive beginning to the service production process.

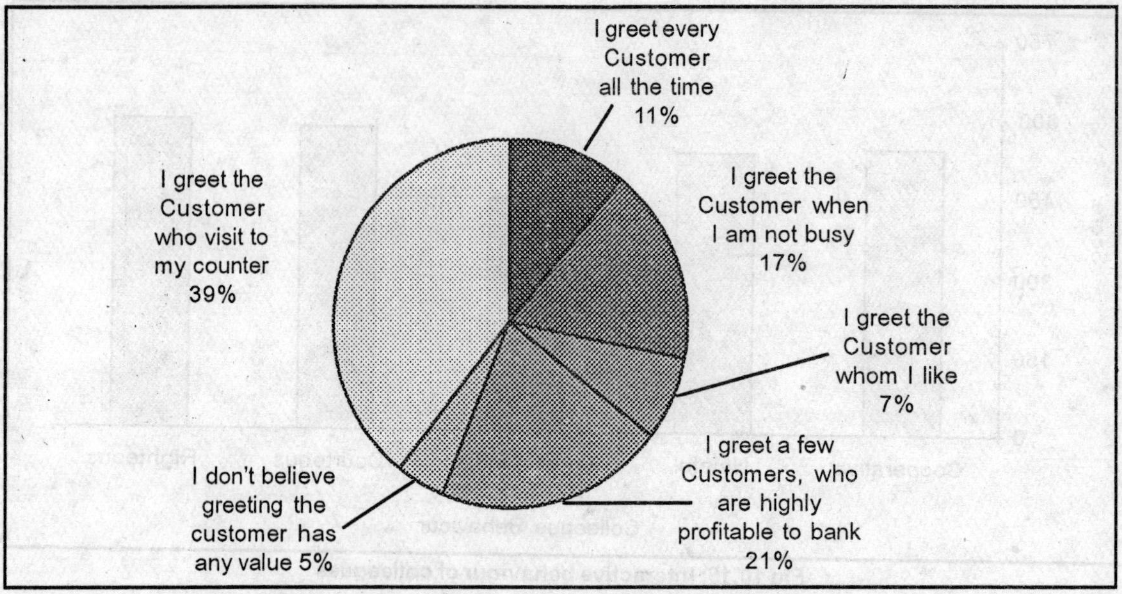

Fig 10.16: First contact with customer

The respondents are further asked whether they are agreeable to the concept of 'customer is always right'. The data presented in Figure 10.17 reveals that a little over 40 per cent of the respondents disagree to the statement. As many as 32.67 per cent took neutral stand in giving response to the statement and 10.67 per cent rated strongly agree to the statement. However, about 14.67 per cent of the respondents expressed their agreement to the statement.

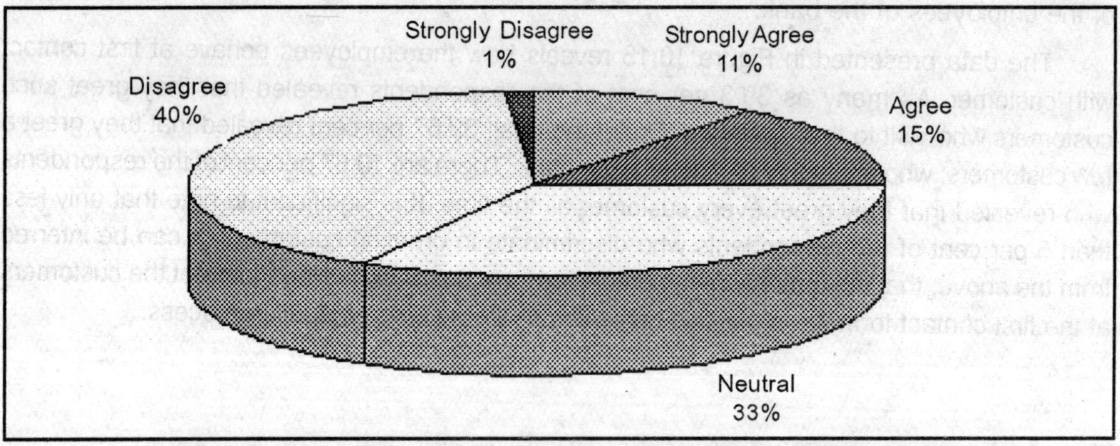

Fig 10.17: Do you agree the concept called "Customer is always right?"

The data presented in Table 10.10 reveals the type of customers the employees prefer to interact. The first preference was given to the 'privileged customers (mean rank 1.68). The second preference to the 'regular customers' (mean rank 1.93).

Table 10.10: What type of customers do you prefer to interact? (n=150)

Particulars	N	MEAN RANK
Regular customers	108	1.93
Privileged customers	114	1.68
New customers	85	3.22
Old customers	85	3.31
Young customers	69	4.57
All customers	83	3.19

The data presented in Table 10.11 reveals the reaction of employees when customers pickup an argument. It can be seen from the table 'try to convince the customer' secured (mean rank 1.14) first position followed by 'direct the customer to the superior' (mean rank 2.40). The other reactions are 'seek the help of the colleagues' (mean rank 3.04), 'seek the help of the customers' (mean rank 3.20), 'Neck out the customer' (mean rank 5.33) and 'direct the security to handle the customer (mean rank 5.38).

The customer argues with the employees out of frustration because of different causes. The employee should help the customers with smiling face even though the customers pose irrelevant questions as banking is a service motto.

Table 10.11: When a customer pick up an argument with you, how do you react?

Particulars	N	MEAN RANK
Try to convince the customer	150	1.14
Seek the help of the colleagues	103	3.04
Seek the help of the co-customers	80	3.20
Direct the customers to the superior	96	2.40
Neck out the customer	21	5.33
Direct the Security to handle the customer	24	5.38

The rating of the respondents on the interactive experiences with the customers throughout their service is elicited and the data was presented in Figure 10.18. It reveals from the data that 59.3 per cent rated their experience with customers as good, 29.3 per cent rated their experience as very good, and 11.4 per cent rated their interactive experience as average. None of the respondents rated their interactive experience with customers as either poor or very poor.

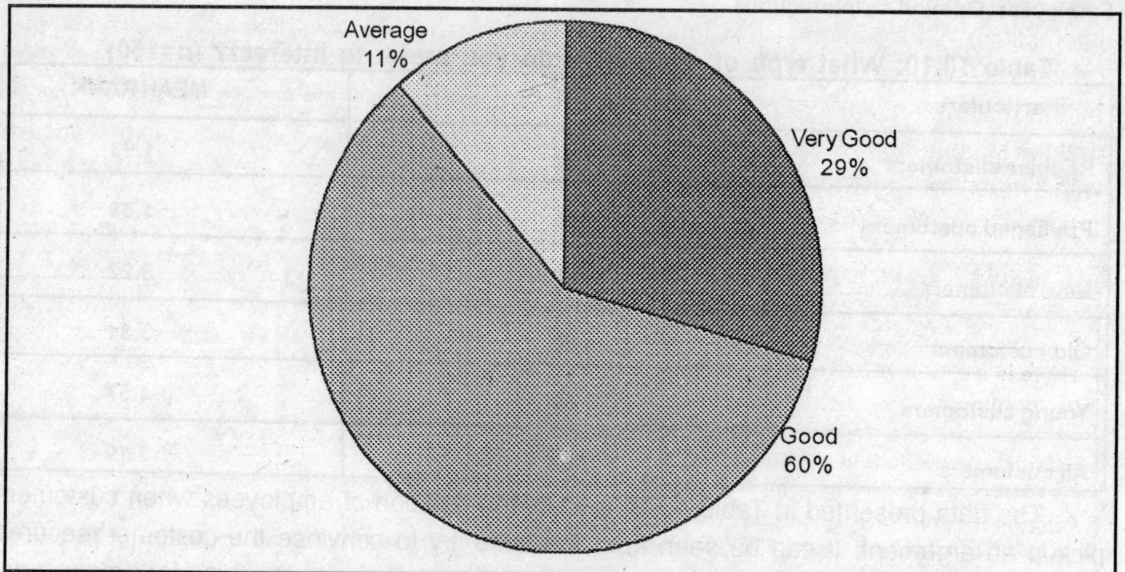

Fig 10.18: What is your experience so far with the Interaction of the customers?

Out of the total, 55.33 per cent revealed that they have not experienced any problems in interacting with the customers and at the same time 44.67 per cent of the respondents said that they faced problems in interaction with customers (Figure 10.19). The respondents who have encountered some problems revealed that the problems are comparatively low and they could resolve them on the spot, some times by themselves and some times with the help of their colleagues.

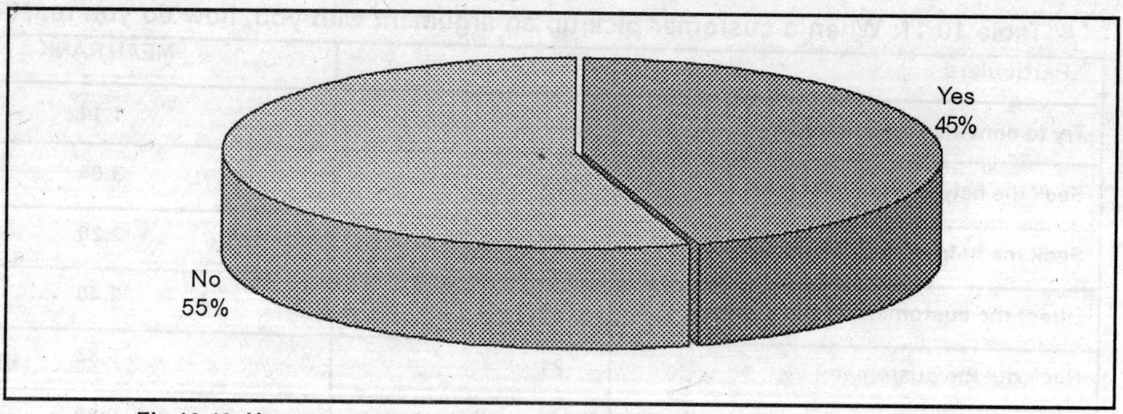

Fig 10.19: Have you experienced any problems in interacting with customers?

An attempt is made in the study to know the opinion of the respondents on customer interactive behavior. The data presented in Table 10.12 shows that the vast majority of the respondents gave positive rating to the statements 'there is a visible change in the attitude of customers', 'customers are quality conscious', 'customers are time conscious', 'customers are demanding' and 'customers are experienced with the services of other banks'. Most of the respondents gave their disagreement to the statements 'customers are well informed', 'customers show respect to system designed' and 'customers like to share pleasantries in interactions'. 'Customers are less tolerant of the system deviations', 'customers are less tolerant on indiscipline', and 'customers are less tolerant on system failures' these statements rated by the respondents as neutral. A comparative analysis of the rating of the statement reveals that the statements 'There is a visible change in the attitude of customers' secured first position with a mean rank of 1.58 followed by 'customers are demanding' (mean rank 1.66), 'customers are time conscious' (mean rank 1.67) and 'customers are quality conscious' (mean rank 1.67).

Table 10.12: Respondents' opinion on Customer interaction behavior

PARTICULARS	SCORE	MEAN RANK
There is a visible change in the attitude of customers	663	1.58
Customers are quality conscious	639	1.67
Customers are time conscious	642	1.67
Customers are demanding	651	1.66
Customers are experienced with the services of other banks	612	1.92
Customers are well informed	436	3.09
Customers show respect to system designed	440	3.07
Customers are less tolerant of the system deviations	542	2.33
Customers are less tolerant on indiscipline	555	2.33
Customers are less tolerant on system failures	550	2.33
Customers like to share pleasantries in interactions	404	3.33

Figure 10.20 reveal that 6.67 per cent of respondents evaluate their interaction with superiors every day, 48 per cent occasionally, 43.33 per cent only when something goes wrong and 2 per cent when pleasant things happen in their professional life. This shows that interaction with superiors at regular intervals provides fruitful results in the professional life of the employees.

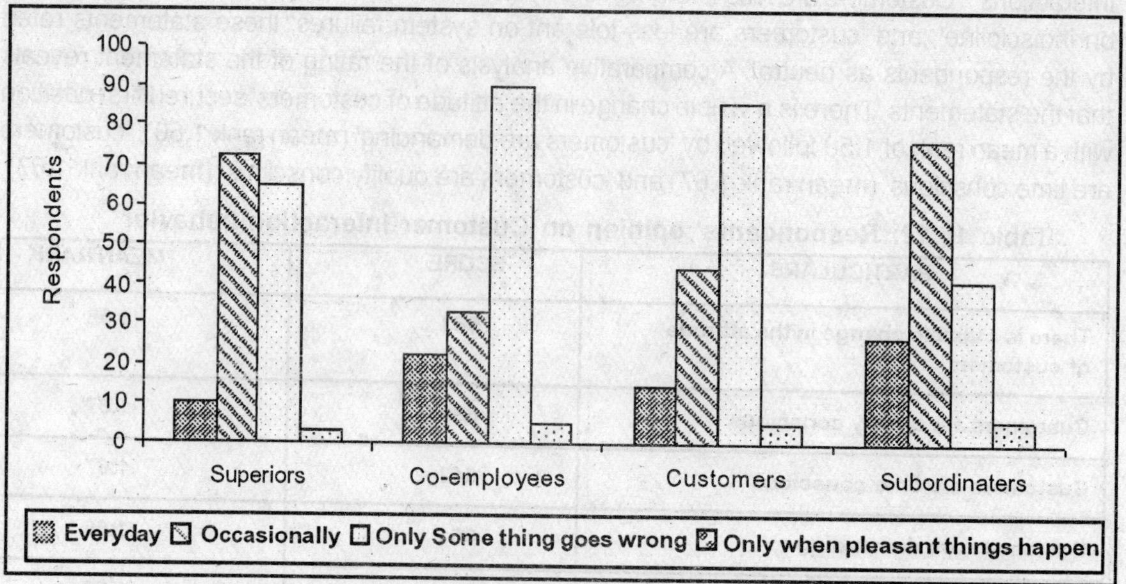

Figure10.20: Do you evaluate yourself the way your interactions take place with superiors?

The data relating to the self-evaluation of respondents on their interaction with co-employees is shown in Figure 10.20. The figure reveals that, 14.67 per cent interact regularly, 22 per cent occasionally, 60 per cent only when something goes wrong, and a meager 3.33 per cent interact only when pleasant things happen. This shows that the interaction of employees with their co-employees is higher only when some thing goes wrong while performing their duties. The data relating to the self-evaluation of respondents on their interaction with subordinates reveals that 18 per cent of the employees evaluate regularly, 50.67 per cent occasionally, 27.33 per cent only when something goes wrong, and only 4 per cent when pleasant things happen.

The data relating to the self-evaluation of respondents on their interaction with customers is also shown in Figure 10.20. The figure shows that 10 per cent of the respondents evaluate on regular basis, 29.33 per cent evaluate occasionally, 57.33 per cent evaluate only when some thing goes wrong with them while performing their duties and 3.33 per cent evaluate their interaction with customers only when pleasant things happen for them in their duties.

The study revealed, out of the total, 61.33 per cent do not observe the reactions of the opposite party while interactive process is going on (Figure 10.21). As many as 49.33 per cent of the respondents opined that the interaction with the people in the bank is a learning experience form them (Figure 10.22). Further, the respondents expressed that they do not believe in transfers to various places helped them to become better in interacting with superiors, colleagues, subordinates and customers (Figure 10.23).

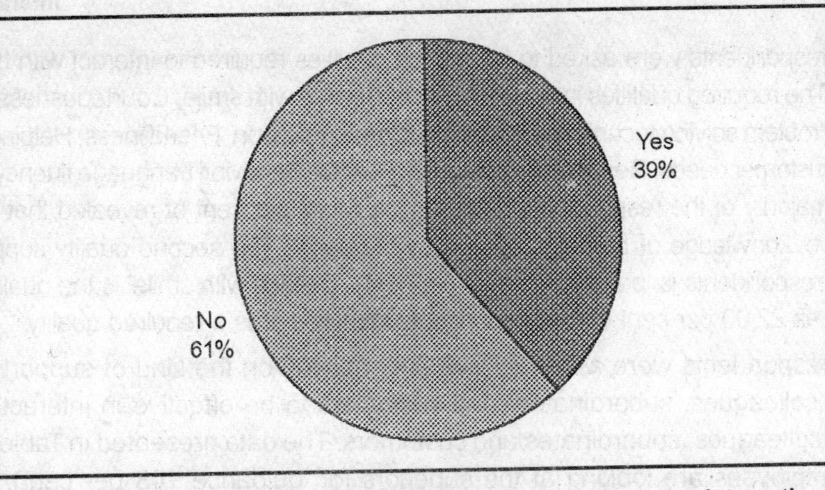

Fig 10.21: Do you observe the reactions of the opposite party during interactions?

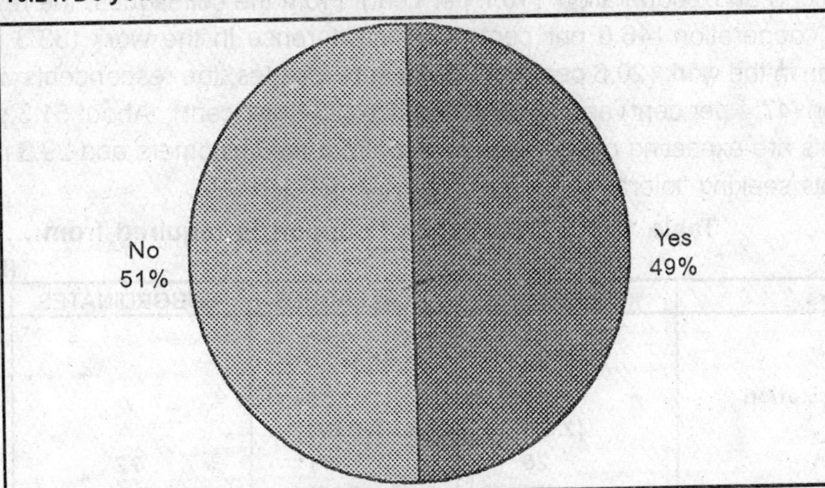

Fig 10.22: Do you think that you had learning experience in interaction with people?

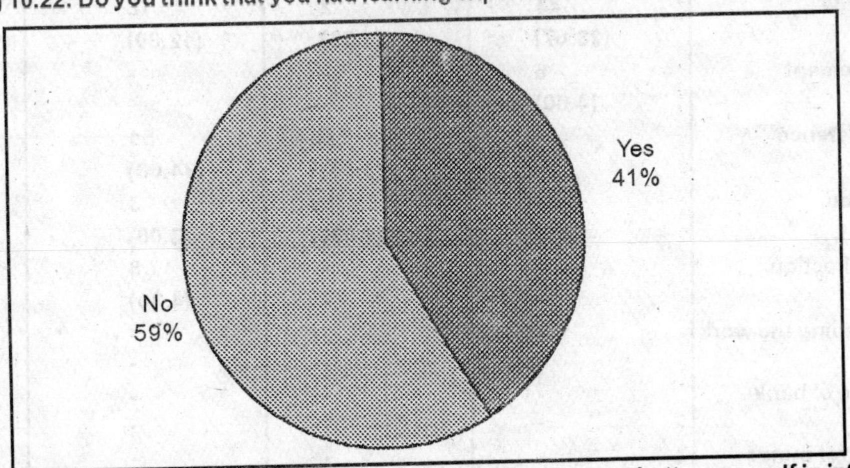

Fig 10.23: Do you believe that transfers to various places helped you to better yourself in interactions?

The respondents were asked to list out the qualities required to interact with bank customers effectively.The required qualities include Patience, Service with smile, Courteousness, Knowledge of products, Problem solving techniques, Listening, Communication, Friendliness, Helping Nature, Ability to identify customer needs, Respect the customer, Positive Behavior, Language fluency and Marketing skills.The majority of the respondents representing 54.67 per cent of revealed that the employees should have 'knowledge of products offered by the bank'. The second quality supported by large number of respondents is 'patience' (34.67 per cent). 'Service with smile' is the quality that secured third place as 22.00 per cent of the respondents identified it as a required quality.

The respondents were asked to give their opinion on the kind of support required from superiors, colleagues, subordinators and customers to be effective in interactions with their superiors, colleagues, subordinates and customers. The data presented in Table 10.13 reveals that the employees are looking at the superiors for 'guidance' (48 per cent), 'help attitude' (28.7 per cent) and 'cooperation' (16.7 per cent). From the colleagues, the respondents are expecting cooperation (46.6 per cent), non interference in the work (33.3 per cent) and participation in the work (20.6 per cent). From subordinates, the respondents were expecting cooperation (47.4 per cent) and non interference (33.6 per cent). About 51.3 per cent of the respondents are expecting cooperation in work from the customers and 29.3 per cent of the respondents seeking 'tolerance for minor service deficiencies.'

Table 10.13: What type of support is required from ...

(N=150)

Particulars	SUPERIORS	COLLEAGUES	SUBORDINATES	CUSTOMERS
Guidance	72	-	-	-
	(48.00)	-	-	-
Work participation	4	31	-	-
	(2.67)	(20.67)	-	-
Cooperation	25	61	72	77
	(16.67)	(40.67)	(48.00)	(51.33)
Help attitude	43	2	18	-
	(28.67)	(1.33)	(12.00)	-
Encouragement	6	-	-	-
	(4.00)	-	-	-
Non Interference	-	50	51	-
	-	(33.33)	(34.00)	-
Duty Minded	-	6	3	-
	-	(4.00)	(2.00)	-
Obeying direction	-	-	6	-
	-	-	(4.00)	-
Understanding the work	-	-	-	14
situation	-	-	-	(9.33)
Knowledge of bank	-	-	-	15
services	-	-	-	(10.00)
Tolerance for minor	-	-	-	44
service deficiencies	-	-	-	(29.33)
Total	150	150	150	150
	(100.00)	(100.00)	(100.00)	(100.00)

Employees' Opinion on Interactions

An attempt is further made to know the opinion of the respondents on various issues of the bank. The opinion is collected on a five point scale varied from strongly agree to strongly disagree. The data relating to the above is presented in Table 10.14. For the statement 'State Bank of India continues to be the leader in the Indian banking system', 58 per cent rated 'strongly agree' and 38.7 per cent rated agree. This opinion reflects the strong belief of the employees on the future performance of the bank. For the statement 'State Bank of India is the best bank to serve', 35.33 per cent rated agree, 8 per cent rated 'strongly agree' and 53.33 per cent rated 'neutral'. The opinion leads to the inference that the majority of the employees of the bank are not enjoying the pride for being in service of the bank. The statement 'The bank is pursuing customer centric policies' was rated 'agree' by 27.33 per cent 'strongly agree' by 6.00 per cent and neutral by 54.67 per cent, which shows that the employees are not convinced with the bank policy towards customers. The vast majority of the respondents representing 86 per cent expressed their agreement of the statement 'The bank offers better quality of service to the customers compared to other public sector banks'. Comparing private sector banks, 7.33 per cent rated 'strongly agree' and 22 per cent rated 'agree' to the statement. Comparing foreign banks, only 7.33 per cent rated either 'agree' or 'strongly agree'. It can be inferred form the above that employees are convinced that the bank services are not of superior quality compared to private banks and the foreign banks are providing superior services then SBI. As many as 74 per cent of the respondents either 'strongly agree' or 'agree' to the statement 'customer loyalty is very high in State Bank of India'. However, 22.67 per cent took a neutral stand and 3.33 per cent disagreed to the statement. About 87 per cent of the respondents either 'agree' or 'strongly agree' to the statement 'The employees of the bank are respected, because of their expertise in banking operations'. There are 57.33 per cent of the respondents disagree that the interactive skills of the employees is a reason for being respected. As many as 50 per cent of the respondents took neutral stand on the statement 'employees are respected because of quality consciousness'. About 62 per cent of the respondents strongly agree or agree and 34.67 per cent rated neutral to the statement 'State Bank of India is highly adaptable to the changing market requirements'. The study reveals that out of the total, 42 per cent of the respondents 'agree' to the statement 'Competitors could not attack the State Bank of India from any quarter'. There are 16 per cent of the respondents who took 'neutral' stand and 24.67 per cent rated either 'disagree' or 'strongly disagree' to the statement. As many as 57.34 per cent of the respondents rated either 'agree' or 'strongly agree' to the statement 'the employees of State Bank of India feel proud of the performance of the bank'. For the statement 'the employees of the State Bank of India are highly motivated', 47.33 per cent of the respondents rated 'neutral', 23.3 per cent 'disagree', and 28.67 per cent rated either 'agree' or 'strongly agree'. As many as 53.33 per cent of the respondents rated 'neutral' to the statement 'employee morale is high in the bank'. Out of the total, 28 per cent of the respondents rated either 'disagree' or 'strongly disagree' to the statement. As many as 57.33 per cent of the respondents rated 'neutral' to the statement 'very strong service culture has been established throughout the organisation'. About 71.33 per cent of the respondents rated either 'strongly agree' or 'agree' to the statement 'all the employees are involved in the process of development of the bank'. There are 21.33 per cent of the respondents who rated 'neutral' to the statement. A little over 33.33 per cent of the respondents rated either 'disagree' or 'strongly disagree' to the statement 'internal disturbances are almost absent in the bank'. The majority (51.33 per cent) of the respondents rated either 'disagree' or 'strongly disagree' to the statement 'the employees are well compensated'. The statement 'the interests of the employees are taken care of by management' secured positive rating from 26.67 per cent of the respondents. As many as 78.67 per cent of the respondents rated either 'agree' or 'strongly agree' to the statement 'State Bank of India should be given total autonomy'.

Table 10.14: Opinion on various issues of the bank (n=150)

PARTICULARS	SCORE
State Bank of India continues to be the leader in the Indian banking system	679
SBI is the best bank to serve	522
The bank is pursuing customer centric policies	491
The bank offer better quality of service to the customers compared to:	
Other public sector banks	647
Private sector banks	459
Foreign banks	335
Customer loyalty is very high in SBI	593
The employees of the bank are respected, because of their:	
Expertise in banking operations	621
Interactive skills	402
Quality consciousness	469
SBI is highly adaptable to the changing market requirements	558
Competitors could not attack the SBI from any quarter	484
The employees of SBI feel proud of the performance of the bank	540
The employees of the SBI are highly motivated	468
The employee morale is high	443
Very strong service culture has been established throughout the organization	449
All the employees are involved in the process of development of the bank	574
Internal disturbances are almost absent in the bank	459
The employees are well compensated	418
The interests of the employees are taken care of by management	465
SBI should be given total autonomy	605

Positive attitude of the employees and willingness of the employees paves the way for effective interactive marketing. As per the findings of the study, the State Bank of India needs to improve the physical environment, simplify the systems, procedures and documents and reduce customer interactive time significantly.Though the consumers are not seriously grievous, they really unhappy with the kind of interactions with the bank. Their opinion on various interactive factors clearly indicates their dissatisfaction. The bank should focus on the employee-customer interactions, the customer-ATM interactions and interactions though internet. The branch reengineering process and the creation of a new position called 'Grahak Mitra' are the steps in the right direction for effective interaction processes. However, there are many areas particularly at the joining phase, at the service production and consumption phase, and the detachment phase that requires serious attention by the bank. All changes shall be oriented to provide customer convenience and create quality perceptions to consumers.

10.6 SUMMARY

The findings of the employees' opinion survey brought to focus many critical issues: According to them employee training is focused on general banking, customer service, credit, core banking, foreign exchange and systems. The majority of the respondents want periodic training on emerging changes. As many as 46 per cent of the respondents have identified the need for training on interactive skills. Out of the total, 41 per cent of the respondents opined that their merit is not recognized by the bank. Employee interaction with higher officials of above the branch manager cadre is low. The vast majority of the employees opined that the systems need to be simplified. As many as 44 per cent of the respondents opined that the procedures need to focus on customer convenience. The opinion on co-employees indicates that the employee-employee interactions are not at the desired level. The majority of the employee respondents are not accepting the statement 'customer is always right'. About 45 per cent of the respondents are facing problems while interacting with customers. Self evaluation of interactions is done by majority of the employees only when 'something goes wrong'. The majority of the employee respondents do not observe reactions of thc opposite party while interacting. The employees seek support from superiors in the form of guidance, help attitude and cooperation; from colleagues and subordinates cooperation and non-interference in work; and from customers they expect cooperation. The majority of the employees do not rate SBI as the best bank to serve. The majority of the employees are not convinced that the bank is pursuing customer centric policies. The employees of the bank agree that the private sector banks are providing better services compared to the SBI. The vast majority of the employees opined that foreign banks offer superior services compared to SBI. The vast majority of the employees revealed that the morale of SBI employees is not high. The majority of the respondents are not in favour of the statement 'very strong service culture established throughout the organisation'. The majority of the respondents are not satisfied with compensation and the care of the management.

□□□

Chapter 11

CUSTOMERS' OPINION ON INTERACTIONS

The interactive process that takes place between service provider and service consumer contributes significantly to generate quality perceptions.The customer perceived quality is the ultimate result of any service company. The service providers should try through all possible means to collect feedback from the customers. A periodic research on quality perceptions of consumers during their interactions with service provider is of immense help to the organization to better its performance.It helps in improving the processes, in identifying the process deficiencies, disorders and in efficiencies. It further helps the service providers to better the processes, process performances and customer interactions.The positive feedback from customers will motivate the employees to participate in the interactive process confidently and with positive attitude. Against this background, an attempt is made in the study collect the opinion of the respondents on their interactive experiences with State Bank of India.The findings of the study are presented in this chapter.

11.1 DEMOGRAPHIC PROFILE

The age of the respondents varied between 21 years and above 50 years. More than 41 per cent of the respondents are in the age group of 31 – 40 years, while about 30 per cent of the respondents are in the age group of 41 – 50 years.Thus, 70 per cent of the respondents are between 31 and 50 years. The average age of the respondents is 38.37 and it is varied between 36 and 40.5 among the five zones under the study.

The educational background of the respondents reveals that a little over 34 per cent of the respondents studied professional education, where as about 24 per cent of the respondents are graduates. There are 18 per cent of the respondents studied primary education or under graduate courses.

The annual income of the respondents varied between below Rs.1,00,000 and above Rs.5,00,000. The majority of the respondents (55.6 per cent) earned in between Rs.2,00,001 and Rs.4,00,000 per annum.The annual income of 58 respondents representing 19.3 per cent is more than Rs.5,00,000 per annum.The average annual income of the respondents is Rs.3,63,667. The respondents from Hyderabad zone earned on an average Rs.3.37 lakh per annum, while Secunderabad zone and Visakhapatnam zone earned Rs.3.53 lakh and Rs.3.67 lakh per annum respectively. The average annual income of respondents from Vijayawada zone and Tirupati zone is Rs.3.68 lakh and Rs.3.93 lakh respectively.

11.2 RELATIONSHIP WITH BANK

The respondents' experience or relation with the bank varied between 3 years and more than 20 years (Figure 11.1). As many as 113 respondents representing 37.7 per cent had experience with the bank between 6 and 10 years. About 29 per cent of the respondents experience with the bank varied between 3 and 5 years.The experience of 20 per cent of the respondents varied between 11 and 15 years, while the experience of 12.3per cent of the respondents is in between 16 and 20 years. On an average the respondents had an experience of 9.3 years with the bank.

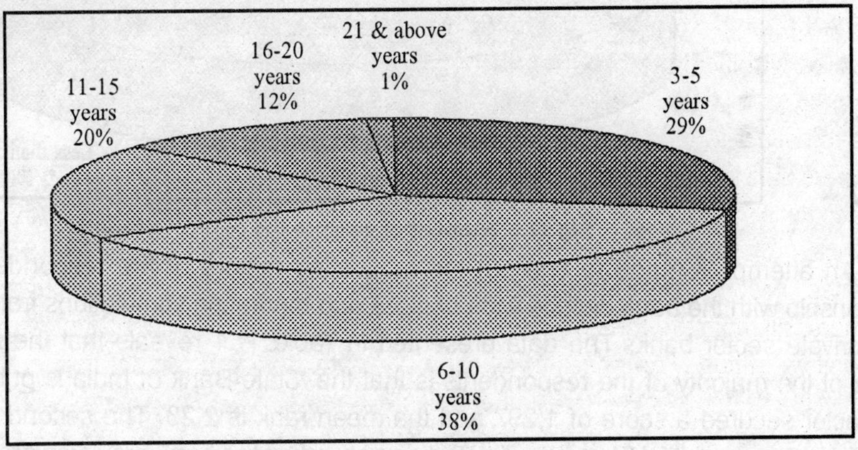

Fig 11.1: Customer relationship with the bank

The data relating to the type of bank accounts, the respondents are having with the State Bank of India, is presented in Figure 11.2.The vast majority of the respondents representing about 97 per cent of the total are having savings account with the bank. About 38 per cent of the respondents are operating current account. A little over 38 per cent of the respondents are having term deposits, while 52 per cent of the respondents are having loan account with the bank.

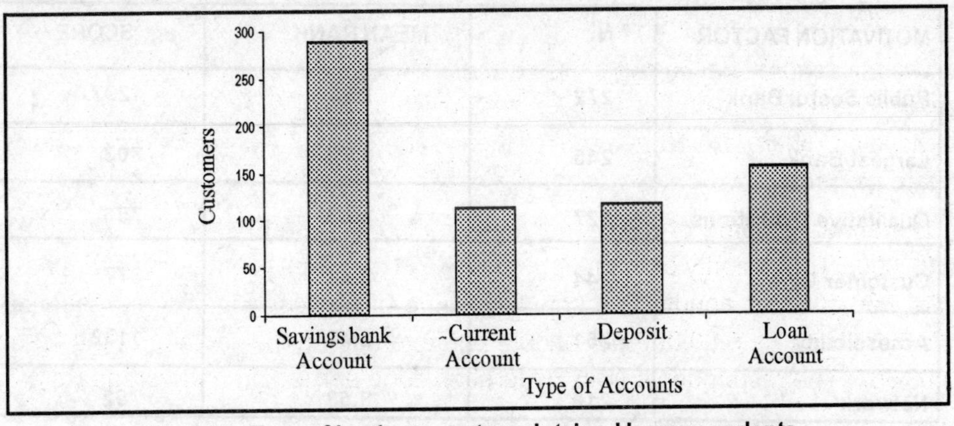

Fig 11.2: Type of bank accounts maintained by respondents

The respondents monthly visits to the bank varied between less than 5 and more than 15 times in a month (Figure 11.3). A little over 78 per cent of the respondents are confining visits to the bank to less than 5 in number and 15 per cent of the respondents make 5 to10 visits in a month.The average number of monthly visits to the bank by the respondents is 4.53. The zone wise analysis of average monthly visits reveals that the respondents from Hyderabad zone make 4 visits, Secunderabad zone 4.25, Viskhapatnam zone 4.08, Vijayawada zone 4.75 and Tirupati zone 5.58.

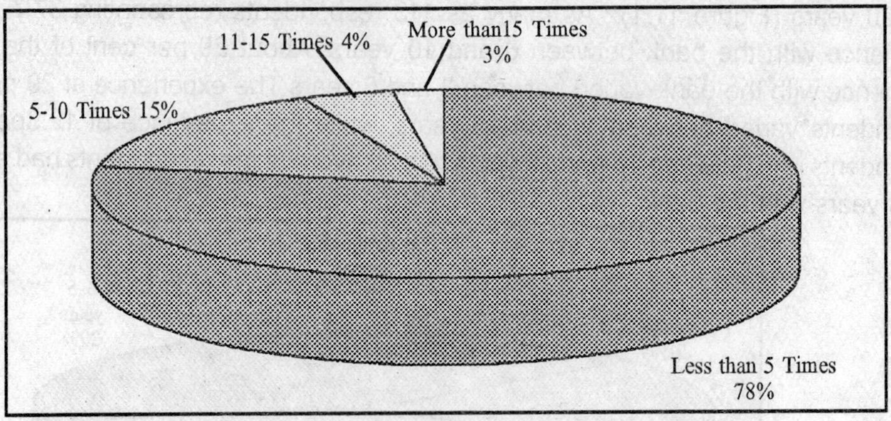

Fig 11.3: Number of visits to the bank in a month

An attempt is made to find out the motivating factors of the respondents to establish relationship with the bank despite wide choices and marketing stimulations from different public and private sector banks.The data presented in Table 11.1 reveals that the major motivating factor of the majority of the respondents is that the 'State Bank of India is public sector bank', this factor secured a score of 1,297 and the mean rank is 2.23. The second most influencing factor was 'accessibility'.The wide distribution network of the bank providing greater accessibility to the customers and this factor secured a score of 1,132 and the mean rank is 2.49. 'Customer care' is the third motivating factor with a score of 877 and the mean rank is 3.41 followed by 'largest bank' (score 803, mean rank 3.72). 'Qualitative operations' and 'network' are the other two motivating factors secured the scores of 756 and 752 respectively.

Table 11.1: What factors motivated you to establish relationship with the bank?

MOTIVATION FACTOR	N	MEAN RANK	SCORE
Public Sector Bank	272	2.23	1297
Largest Bank	245	3.72	803
Qualitative Operations	227	3.67	756
Customer Care	244	3.41	877
Accessibility	251	2.49	1132
Network	218	3.53	752

The criteria followed for selecting a bank to open an account by respondents is studied and the data presented in Table 11.2.The criteria used by the respondents include security, credibility, accessibility, customer service and package of services.Security is the major consideration for choosing a bank to open an account as the mean rank of the factor was 1.26. Accessibility is the second major criteria which got a mean rank of 2.58, credibility is the third criteria that secured a mean rank of 3.0 and 'package of service' got a high mean value of 4.07.

Table 11.2: What are the criteria for choosing a bank to open an account?

CRITERIA	N	MEAN RANK
Security	298	1.26
Credibility	242	3.00
Accessibility	240	2.58
Customer Service	263	3.13
Package of Service	203	4.07

Banks of-late are providing number of ways to the customer to interact with the bank. Besides the traditional contact approaches the customers interact with the bank through Telephone, ATMs and Internet.Table 11.3 reveals the respondents preference to interact with the bank. 'Personal visit to the bank', 'ATM', 'Phone', and 'Internet' are the options available to the customers. As can be seen from the table, most of the respondents prefer 'personal visit to the bank, this option secured a score of 674 and the mean rank is 1.75. ATM is the second preference to interact.This option got a score of 577 and the mean rank is 2.08. The other two interaction options such as phone and internet secured scores of 381 and 167 respectively.

Table 11.3: Preference of the respondents to interact with the bank

PARTICULARS	MEAN RANK	SCORE
Personal visit to the Bank	1.75	674
ATM	2.08	577
Phone	2.73	381
Internet	3.44	167

The interaction of the customers with the bank may be personal or through machines. The bank has promoted extensively the interactions through ATM, Telephone and Internet to increase customer accessibility and also to reduce the interaction costs significantly.The respondents were asked to reveal whether they are using means other than personal visit to interact with the bank.The data shown in Table 11.4 reveals 85 per cent of the respondents are using other means also to interact with the bank. There are 15 per cent of the respondents who confine only to personal visits for interactions.The table reveals all the respondents are making personal visits to the bank.Out of the total, 84.67 per cent are using ATMs, 37 per cent are using Telephone and 12.33 per cent are using Internet for bank interaction. The share of ATM in the total interactions is varied between 10 to 80 per cent, while it was a maximum of 30 per cent in the case of phone and 40 per cent in the case of Internet.

Table 11.4: Interaction Modes(n=300)

PERCENTAGE	PERSONAL VISIT	ATM	PHONE	INTERNET
100	45 (15.00)	-	-	-
90	26 (8.67)	-	-	-
80	25 (8.33)	2 (0.67)	-	-
70	28 (9.33)	6 (2.00)	-	-
60	72 (24.00)	25 (8.33)	-	-
50	23 (7.67)	26 (8.67)	-	-
40	36 (12.00)	74 (24.67)	-	3 (1.00)
30	19 (6.33)	49 (16.33)	7 (2.33)	8 (2.67)
20	21 (7.00)	45 (15.00)	34 (11.33)	11 (3.67)
10	5 (1.67)	27 (9.00)	70 (23.33)	15 (5.00)
0	-	46 (15.33)	189 (63.00)	263 (87.67)

Figures in parenthesis indicate percentage to the total.

11.3 INTERACTIONS

An attempt is made to know the bank employees with whom the respondents are interacting. The data presented in Figure 11.4 reveals 90.3 per cent of the respondents are mostly and 9.7 per cent of the respondents are occasionally interacting with frontline employees available at various bank counters. As many as 25 per cent of the respondents interact with branch manager mostly and 43 per cent occasionally. Only 10 per cent of the respondents mostly and 50 per cent occasionally interact with back office employees on the line of visibility. Grahak Mitra is the counter interacted by 20 per cent of the respondents mostly and 39 per cent occasionally. Out of the total, 26 per cent mostly and 74 per cent occasionally interact with co-customers.

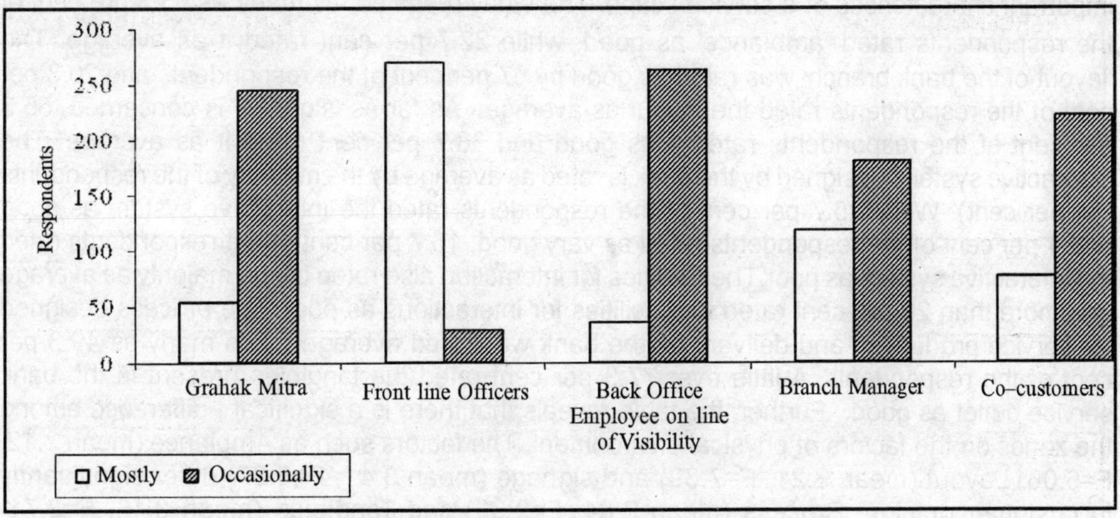

Fig 11.4: Whom do you interact in the bank?

11.3.1 Opinion on Physical Environment and Process

Physical environment plays a vital role in influencing the behaviour of customers as well as employees of any service organization including banking organization.The design of the service scape should facilitate comfortable and efficient participation of customers and employees in the service production and consumption process. The quality of the service will be influenced greatly in the way the process is facilitated. There are many dimensions, which can be exploited in the physical environment to create quality perceptions to the customers. Competition considerations cannot be overlooked in the design of physical environment. Whatever efforts the service provider makes in shaping the physical environment, it should suit to the needs and desires of the target customers.They should remember that customer is the ultimate judge of the performance of the service provider. In fact, service organization should focus on exploring new ways of presenting a service outlet by encouraging customer participation in introducing refinements and modifications in the physical environment.The beginning is definitely to know the opinion of the customers on the physical environment. Since the customer interaction with the physical environment is a vital input in shaping the first impression on the bank and also the quality perception of customers, an attempt is made in the study to know the opinions of the respondents on the physical environment of the bank.

The opinion of the respondents is elicited physical environment of the bank using ET Scale (varied from Excellent to Terrible).The data presented in the Table 11.5 shows that 83.7 per cent of the respondents rated the exterior of the bank as good, 10.3 per cent of the respondents rated the exterior either very good or excellent. Ambience represents the surroundings of service outlet and an atmosphere in the service outlet that persuades the employees as well as customers to get involved pleasantly and comfortably in the service production and consumption process.This is the reason why ambience is considered as an important characteristic of a service scape. The study revealed, as many as 63.3 pre cent of the respondents rated 'ambiance' as good, while 22.7 per cent rated it as average. The 'layout of the bank branch' was rated as good by 67 per cent of the respondents and 20.3 per cent of the respondents rated the layout as average. As far as 'signage' is concerned, 55.3 per cent of the respondents rated it as good and 38.7 per cent rated it as average. The 'interactive system' designed by the bank is rated as average by the majority of the respondents (54 per cent). While 25.7 per cent of the respondents rated the interactive system as good and 4 per cent of the respondents rated as very good, 15.7 per cent of the respondents rated the interactive system as poor.The facilities for interaction also rated by the majority as average and more than 20 per cent rated the facilities for interactions as poor. The process designed for service production and delivery by the bank was rated average by as many as 49.3 per cent of the respondents. A little over 77.3 per cent rated the tangibles present in the bank service outlet as good. Further, the table reveals that there is a significant difference among the zones on the factors of physical environment. The factors such as Ambiance (mean 3.12, F=6.06) Layout (mean 3.21, F=7.39) and signage (mean 3.41, F=5.87) differ significantly in customer opinion. Process (mean 3.84, F=2.39) and Tangibles (mean 3.16, F=2.71) are the other factors got significant differences in the zones. It can be inferred from the table, that the exterior of the bank, secured positive rating as the mean value of the factor was 2.95.The other factors though were not rated negatively, but failed to secure positive rating as the mean value of the factors varied between >3 and <4.

Table 11.5: Opinion on Physical Environment of the Bank (n=300)

PARTICULARS	MEAN/SD	F	SCORE
Exterior of the bank	2.95	2.23	1360
	0.437		
Ambience	3.12	6.06**	1465
	0.569		
Layout	3.21	7.39**	531
	0.579		
Signage	3.41	5.87**	1376
	0.614		
Interactive System	3.84	0.65	1249
	0.769		
Facilities for interaction	3.94	1.609	1217
	0.78		
Process	3.84	2.39*	1247
	0.853		
Tangibles	3.16	2.71*	1451
	0.48		

*P<.05; **P<.01

The objective of any service organisation shall be providing the total quality service system to ensure quality perceptions to the customers at every moment they experience in the service production and consumption process. As mentioned already, physical environment contributes significantly to the quality perception of the customers.The opinion of the respondents indicates the gap between desirable and available.The management of the bank needs to focus its attention on those areas where the majority of the respondents rated negatively. It is also essential to strengthen further the areas where the majority gave positive ratings.Creating the feeling of excellence in every service moment is the most challenging task to every service organization and particularly to the banking organization. It demands continuous improvement with the support of research and technology adaptation besides feedback from customers.

The opinion on the documents of the bank is collected from the respondents and the data is presented in Figure 11.5. A little over 88 per cent of the respondents revealed that the documents of the bank are simple. As many as 63.3 per cent of the respondents either agree or strongly agree to the statement that 'the documents are understandable'. 'The majority of the respondents (64.7 per cent) were not convinced to the statement 'documents are user friendly'. Their response was neutral for the statement the 'documents seeking unnecessary details'.

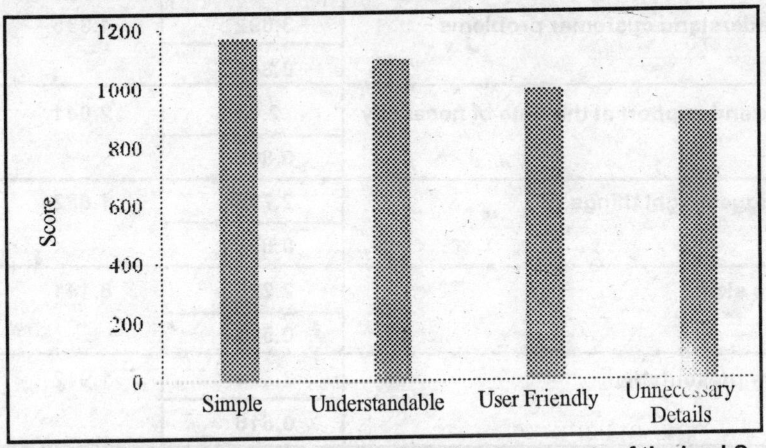

Fig 11.5: What is your opinion on the documents of the bank?

11.3.2 Customer – Employee Interactions

Face to face interaction is considered as the best form of interaction due to several reasons. It provides an opportunity to eliminate communication gaps between the individuals much better than any other interactive system. Frontline employees of the banking organization interact with customers to know their problems and to provide necessary services to the best satisfaction of the customers.Customers will have different sets of needs, wants, ego systems, time pressure, situational pressures, adaptability, temperament, understanding skill, knowledge and participative abilities. Similarly, employees also are human beings with varied needs, wants, ego systems, situational pressures, temperaments, styles, abilities and involvement levels. When employee and customer are interacting, the best result will come out only when they are working positively with high level of understanding and involvement in service process.Service organizations give priority to train the people in order to develop interactive abilities.Many problems in the service organizations will be solved when the employees are good in customer interactions.

Table 11.6: Interactive Behavior of the Employees

(n=300)

PARTICULARS	MEAN / SD	F	SCORE
Employees of the branch are responsive	3.036	7.904	741
	0.958		
Employees are courteous	3.236	2.123	691
	0.697		
Employees are empathetic	3.32	6.231	670
	0.724		
Employees are communicative	3.04	4.429	740
	0.877		
Employees are giving individualized attention	3.312	10.607	672
	0.806		
Employees understand customer problems	3.092	4.335	727
	0.848		
Employees extend support at the time of necessity	2.94	2.041	765
	0.865		
Employees suggest right things	2.736	1.882	816
	0.678		
Employees are skilful	2.228	8.141	943
	0.515		
Employees are presentable	2.524	1.912	869
	0.616		
Employees are service oriented	2.612	4.316	847
	0.715		
Employees are discriminative	2.664	3.811	834
	0.607		
Employees are egoistic	2.98	2.228	755
	0.57		
Employees have gender bias	3.008	1.586	748
	0.646		
Employees have no time sense	2.768	1.897	808
	0.803		

*P<.05; **P<.01

Employee to customer interaction is the key issue in interactive marketing.The respondents were asked to give their opinion on the interactive behavior of the employees of State Bank of India. The respondents were asked to give their rating on the following statements. The ratings of the respondents are collected on five point 'agreement scale' which varied from strongly agree to strongly disagree. Table 11.6 reveals that the majority of the respondents gave positive rating to the statements 'employees of the branch are skillful', 'employees are presentable' and 'employees are service oriented'. The majority of the respondents preferred neutral position for the statements 'employees are courteous', 'employees are empathetic', 'employees are communicative, 'employees understand customer problems', 'employees extend support at time of necessity', 'employees suggest right things', 'employees are discriminative', 'employees are egoistic' and 'employees have gender bias'.The opinion is divided almost equally between neutral and agreement in the case of the statement 'employees have no time sense'. As many as 43 per cent of the respondents either disagree or strongly disagree to the statement 'employees of the branch are responsive'. About 50.40 per cent ventilated their disagreement to the statement 'employees are giving individualized attention'.The opinion is highly divided among agreement, neutral and disagreement for the statement 'employees understand customer problems'. The large number of respondents (41.20 per cent) preferred 'neutral' to the statement 'employees are communicative', while 33.2 per cent of the respondents either disagree or strongly disagree to the statement.

A further insight in to the table reveals that there is a highly significance difference between the zones on interactive behavior of employees.The statements such as 'employees of the branch are responsive' (mean 3.04, F=7.90), 'employees are empathetic' (mean 3.32, F=6.23), 'employees are giving individualized attention' (mean 3.31, F=1.61) and 'employees are skillful' (mean 2.23, F=8.14) attracted different opinions among zones.The following are the other statements attract different opinion among the zones 'employees are communicative' (mean 3.04, F=4.43), 'employees understand customer problems' (mean 3.09, F=4.33), 'employees are service oriented' (mean 2.61, F=4.32) and 'employees are discriminative' (mean 2.66, F=3.81). It can be inferred from the above, that the opinion of the respondents on interactive behavior of the employees in almost all the factors is not significantly positive and in some factors it is either neutral or negative.

The respondents were asked to reveal whether they faced any problems in communicating their problem, getting specific attention to the problem, employee arrogance and non accessibility of concerned employee in interacting with contact employees. The data presented in the Figure 11.6 reveals as many as 66.7 per cent have faced problems some times in communicating their problems to the contact employees.Similarly, 65 per cent of the respondents faced some time the problem of getting specific attention of the contact employees. With regards to employee arrogance, 60 per cent of the respondents never experienced, where as 37 per cent of the respondents revealed that they had such experience sometimes. Non accessibility is never a problem to 82.3 per cent of the respondents, where as 16.3 per cent had such experience sometimes.

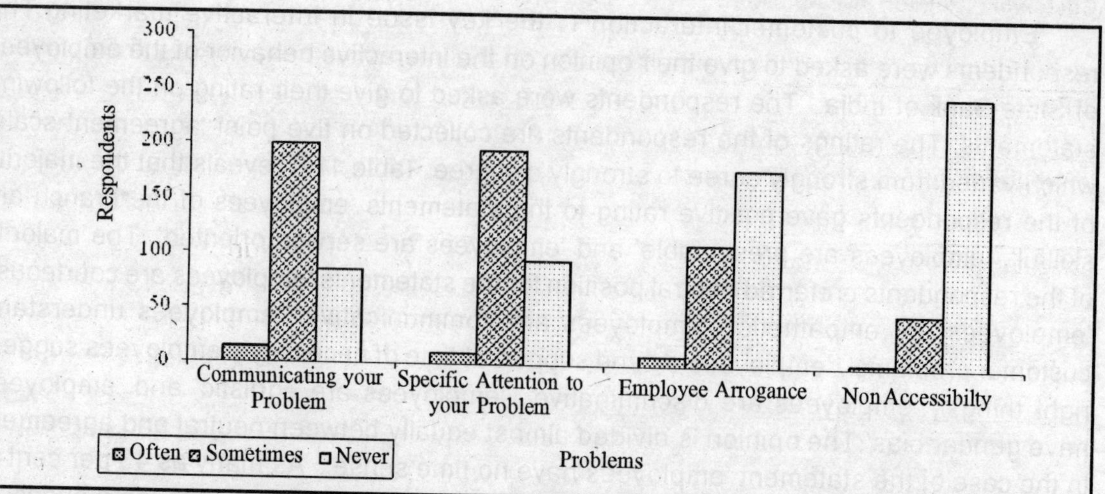

Fig 11.6: Have you faced the problems in interacting with contact employees?

Physical environment is one of the major influencer of the employee as well as consumer behavior in the interactive process.The moods and emotions of the interactive people are greatly influenced by physical environment as well as physical facilities.Customers shall be provided with adequate comforts and support facilities to facilitate their effective participation in service production and consumption process. An attempt is made in the study to know the consumer opinion on the adequacy of physical facilities provided by the bank. The data presented in Table 11.7 shows that the ventilation at the bank service outlet is moderate as 76.3 per cent of the respondents expressed the same.The moving space in the branch is rated moderate by about 70 per cent of the respondents. The 'facilities for sitting' was rated adequate by 20.3 per cent of the respondents, while about 69 per cent rated as moderate. The adequacy of 'writing pads' were rated moderate by 53 per cent of the respondents, while 29.3 per cent of the respondents rated less. As many as 41.3 per cent revealed that the 'toilet facility' is less in the bank outlets, while 28 per cent of respondents rated very less. The adequacy of drinking water, Air conditioning/fans, lighting, counters layout and security were rated moderate by the majority of the respondents. With regard to adequacy of pins and parking place, the majority are of the opinion that the facilities are either moderate or less. Further insight in to the table reveals that all most all the statements were getting a significance difference between the zones. It can be inferred from the above that the respondents expressed their concern over the inadequacy of many physical facilities in the branch.

The quality of physical facilities is another important dimension that influences interactive behavior. The mean value of the opinion of the respondents on quality of toilets was 3.27, while it was 2.28 for drinking water, 2.28 for gum, 2.11 for pins, 2.23 for writing pads and 2 for facilities for sitting.The other variables secure a mean value of less than 2. It indicates from the above that the respondents are unhappy with the quality of toilets, gum, parking place, drinking water and facilities for sitting. However, in the case of other facilities also the opinion of the majority is not favourable in terms of quality.

Table 11.7: How do you rate the physical facilities provided by the bank? (n=300)

PARTICULARS	ADEQUACY			QUALITY		
	MEAN/SD	F	SCORE	MEAN/SD	F	SCORE
Ventilation	1.84	5.55**	1249	1.93	2.79*	1220
	0.459			0.341		
Moving Space	1.93	9.23**	1222	1.97	7.06**	1210
	0.591			0.49		
Facilities for Sitting	1.93	13.93**	1221	2	9.81**	1200
	0.616			0.524		
Writing pads	2.29	15.25**	1114	2.23	32.14**	1130
	0.748			0.683		
Toilets	3.11	3.42**	866	3.27	5.06**	819
	0.892			0.824		
Drinking Water	2.28	9.47**	1115	2.28	5.92**	1115
	0.803			0.756		
Air Conditioning / Fans	1.86	8.10**	1243	1.98	4.09**	1206
	0.586			0.53		
Lighting	1.78	11.96**	1265	1.87	2.42*	1240
	0.487			0.443		
Counters Layout	1.92	7.92**	1224	1.92	3.99**	1225
	0.543			0.459		
Pins	2.25	14.16**	1124	2.11	16.24**	1167
	0.751			0.658		
Gum	2.42	30.20**	1075	2.28	25.08**	1115
	0.89			0.786		
Parking Place	2.58	17.19**	1026	2.4	13.62**	1081
	0.84			0.817		
Security	1.92	6.83**	1225	1.99	6.20**	1202
	0.604			0.567		

*P<.05; **P<.01

The data presented in Figure 11.7 reveals that the opinion of the respondents on the extent to which they were informed about 'all services offered by the bank, interest rates of all types of deposits, interest rates of all types of loans, service charges collected by the bank, credit facilities and bank consumer rights was ascertained. It can be seen from the figure that 73.3 per cent of the respondents revealed they were informed to some extent, 'all the services offered by the bank', where as 20 per cent of the respondents revealed that they were not informed of 'all the services offered by the bank'. As many as 67.2 per cent of respondents revealed that they were informed to some extent about 'interest rates of all type of deposits', while 31.3 per cent of respondents revealed that they were not inform about the same. Out of the total, 50 per cent of the respondents revealed that they were informed to some extent about the interest rates of term loans, where as 43.3 per cent of respondents revealed that they were not informed. Only 12 per cent of the respondents were fully aware of the service charges collected by the bank. Out of the total, 44.3 per cent revealed that they were informed about the service charges collected by the bank to some extent, while 43.7 per cent revealed that they were not informed. The majority of the respondents (53 per cent) were not informed about the credit facilities offered by the bank. Only 12 per cent are well informed and 35 of the respondents informed to some extent. The bank customer rights were not informed to 43.7 per cent of the respondents. Out of the total, 22 per cent revealed they were informed and 34.3 per cent revealed they were informed to some extent about the bank customer rights.

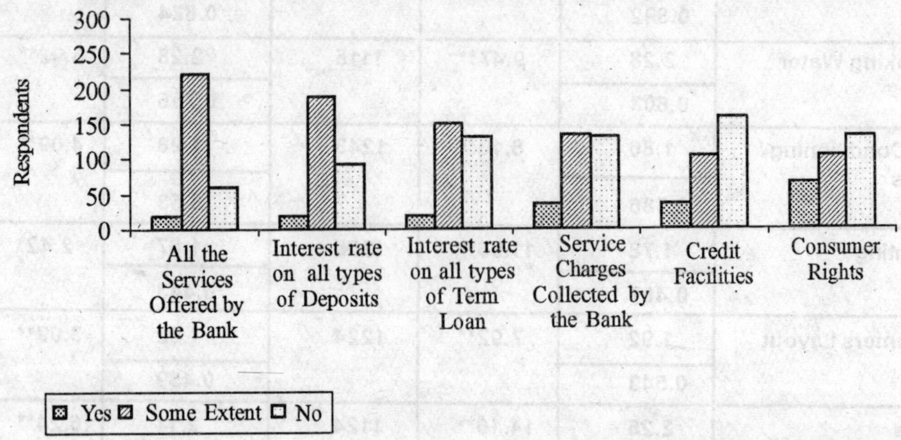

Fig 11.7: To what extent are you informed about the services of the bank?

Table 11.8: How do you get the information relating to the services of the bank?

PARTICULARS	MEAN/SD	F	SCORE
Bank Manager	3	16.18**	815
	1.179		
Bank Employee	1.77	16.86**	1205
	0.99		
Bank Advertisements	3.25	11.21**	695
	1.545		
Print Media	2.33	12.05**	991
	1.097		
Friends and Relatives	3.81	4.92**	591
	1.083		

*P<.05; **P<.01

The respondents rated bank employee as the major source to know the details of bank services.The data presented in Table 11.8, the bank employees secure a score of 1205 and a mean value of 1.77. Print media is the next rated source of information which secured a score of 991 and a mean value of 2.33. Bank manager (score 815, mean 3), bank advertisements (score 695, mean 3.25) and friends and relatives (score 591, mean 3.81) are the other sources of information.

Documentation is the important phase in the interactive process of the bank. Consumers are often required to fill and submit various documents specific to different services of the bank. The opinion of the respondents on their interaction with documents was collected and data is presented in Table 11.9.The vast majority of the respondents opined that the documents required for opening bank account are too many (92 per cent), too much of information required (89.7 per cent) and also time consuming (90.3 per cent). In the case of account operations, excepting a few, the respondents are not having any problem. As many as 44 per cent of the respondents revealed that the documents are creating unnecessary complexity for taking loans. In the case of term deposits and other services, a few respondents expressed some interactive problems.

Table 11.9: Have you faced the following problems in interacting with documents? (n=300)

PARTICULARS	OPENING BANK ACCOUNTS	ACCOUNT OPERATION	TAKING LOANS	TERM DEPOSITS	OTHER SERVICES
Too many	276 (92.00)	34 (11.33)	269 (89.67)	45 (15.00)	39 (13.00)
Too much of information required	269 (89.67)	31 (10.33)	264 (88.00)	49 (16.33)	41 (13.67)
Unnecessary complexity	70 (23.03)	29 (9.67)	132 (44.00)	14 (4.67)	8 (2.67)
Language complexity	33 (11.00)	11 (3.67)	54 (18.00)	10 (3.33)	8 (2.67)
Non availability	20 (6.67)	6 (2.00)	16 (5.33)	4 (1.33)	-
Time consuming	271 (90.33)	109 (36.33)	255 (85.00)	60 (20.00)	51 (17.00)

Figures in parenthesis indicate percentage to the total.

11.4 SERVICE INTERACTION PROCESS

The service interaction process can be divided into three phases.[1] They are joining phase, service process and consumption phase, and detachment phase.The quality of the moments at all three phases will contribute for the customer perceived quality.

The Joining Phase: The joining phase is the first phase of the service consumption process. Some studies identified a pre-joining phase also wherein marketing personnel interact with the customers and persuade or sometimes sell the service. Anyhow, when services are provided at the service outlet, the customer begins with the joining phase. The two important activities in this phase are entry and registration.

The Intensive Consumption Phase: This is a critical phase wherein the service process aims at solving consumer problems.The first step in the process is the perfect diagnosis of the problem. Contact employees will discuss with the consumers and try to define the consumer's problem accurately by getting confirmation from the service consumer.The contact employee proposes the service process and also the cost involved in the service process.There are many factors that influence the effectiveness of the process at this stage. Documentation, queue system, time consumed, accuracy, transparency, customer approval, easy flow, equipment used, performance of the equipment, exclusivity (privacy), flexibility and exceptions are some of the factors that influence the quality.

Detachment Phase: There are two activities that generally take place during this phase. They are payment and registration for next visit. The payment system that is designed, whether cash, credit, installment, office billing, credit card and so on, is the factor that influences the customers. The registration system for the next visit, exit facilities and collection of feedback are the other aspects that need to be managed properly.

The experience of the respondents on the joining phase of the service outlet of State Bank of India is presented in Figure 11.8. The vast majority of the respondents representing 70.7 per cent revealed that some employees of the bank responded immediately when they approached. As many as 22.3 per cent of the respondents revealed that there was delayed response after approach at the joining phase. In the case of 5 per cent of the respondents, some persons of the bank attended immediately after they enter into the bank.Only 4 respondents were greeted by bank employees when they entered the office. The experience of two respondents at the joining phase was that there was response only after repeated approaches.

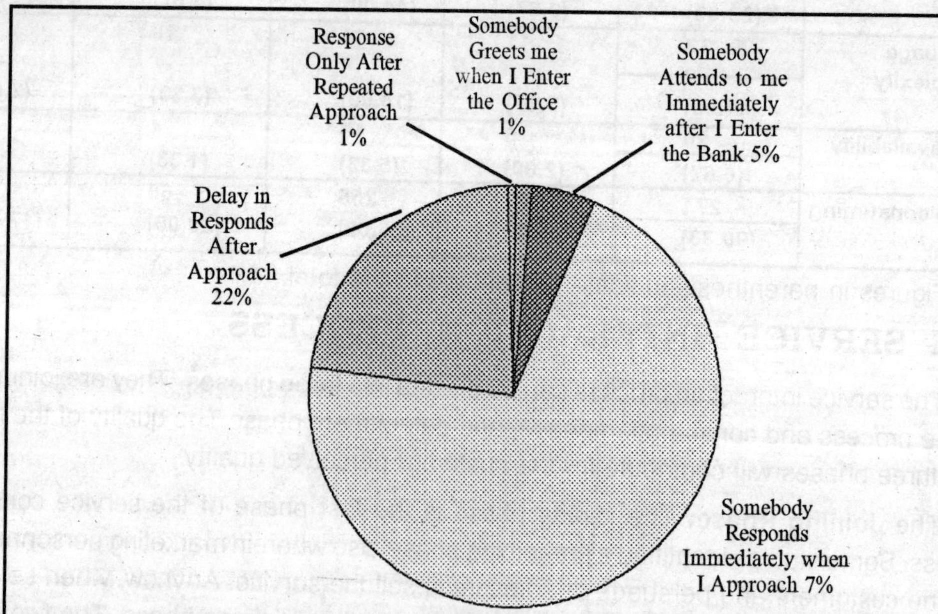

Fig 11.8: What are your experiences at the joining phase of service at the branch?

Time is an important aspect for every customer. When the service is delayed, certainly it will result in frustration to the customers. The reason for the delay sometimes may be due to the customer's fault or some problem in organization. Table 11.10 depicts the problems faced by the respondents in interacting with service processes at the bank.Too many levels for opening bank account and too much time taken by the bank to open an account was the problem expressed by more than 90 per cent of the respondents. Inadequate communication was the problem expressed by 43.3 per cent of the respondents. As far as account operation is concerned, only a few respondents face some problems. The vast majority have not reported any problems. In the case of taking loans too many levels and too much time taken by the bank were the major problems followed by improper and inadequate communication. The vast majority of the respondents have not reported any problems in the case of the process relating to term deposits and other services.

Table 11.10: Have you faced the following problems in interacting with process? (n=300)

PARTICULARS	OPENING BANK ACCOUNTS	ACCOUNT OPERATION	TAKING LOANS	TERM DEPOSITS	OTHER SERVICES
Too many levels	297	25	272	24	47
	(99.00)	(8.33)	(90.67)	(8.00)	(15.67)
Too much time	278	83	266	46	56
	(92.67)	(27.67)	(88.67)	(15.33)	(18.67)
Away from consumers	14	9	21	4	4
	(4.67)	(3.00)	(7.00)	(1.33)	(1.33)
Communication	130	37	154	31	14
	(43.33)	(12.33)	(51.33)	(10.33)	(4.67)
Non visibility	71	11	71	11	6
	(23. 67)	(3.67)	(23.67)	(3.67)	(2.00)

Figures in parenthesis indicate percentage to the total.

The service deficiencies identified by the respondents at the detachment phase were identified and presented in Figure 11.9. The majority of the respondents, representing 57.3 per cent, revealed that there was no response from the contact employee at the detachment phase. As many as 30 per cent of the respondents revealed that there were no attempt from the bank employees to recover the service deficiencies. They said that, the employees are insensitive to suffering of the customer due to service deficiencies.The problems such as 'Responsibility of process accuracy transferred to customer' and 'no follow up' are revealed by only a few respondents.

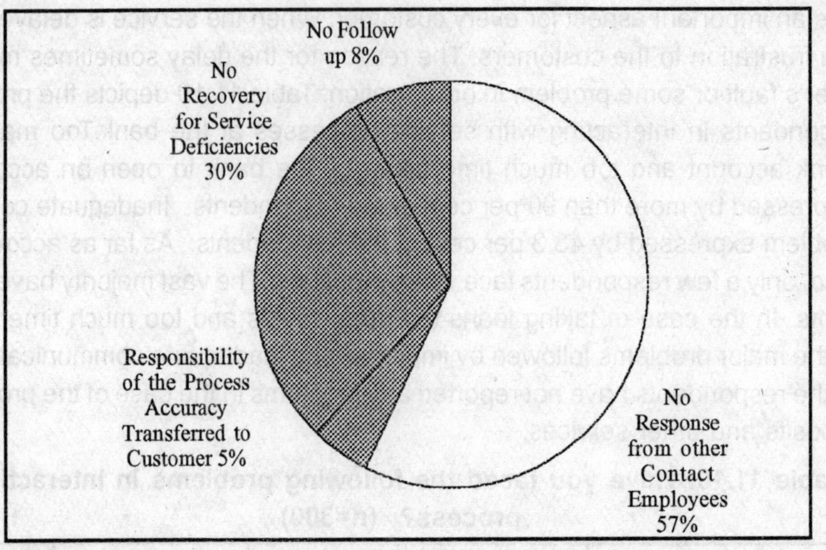

Fig 11.9: What are the service deficiencies you have experienced at the detachment phase of the interaction?

The overall rating of the respondents on the service processes relating to deposits, loans, lockers, withdrawal, pass book entries, payment of bills and collection of cheques, is presented in Table 11.11.The table reveals the majority of the respondents gave 'good' or 'very good' rating to all the processes. However, in the case of loans a significant number of respondents gave 'average' rating.

Table 11.11: How do you rate process in the State Bank of India with regard to the following?

PARTICULARS	SCORE
Deposits	**1222**
Loans	**1097**
Lockers	**1148**
Withdrawal	**1203**
Passbook entries	**1248**
Payment of bills	**1146**
Collection of cheques	**1068**

An attempt is made to know the reaction of the respondents when the service is delayed because of the fault of the respondent. The data presented in Figure 11.10 reveals that more than 76 per cent of the respondents said that they will correct themselves and will not blame anybody for the delay. A few respondents revealed that they 'find fault with employee', or 'don't feel sorry' or 'expect the employee also say sorry.'

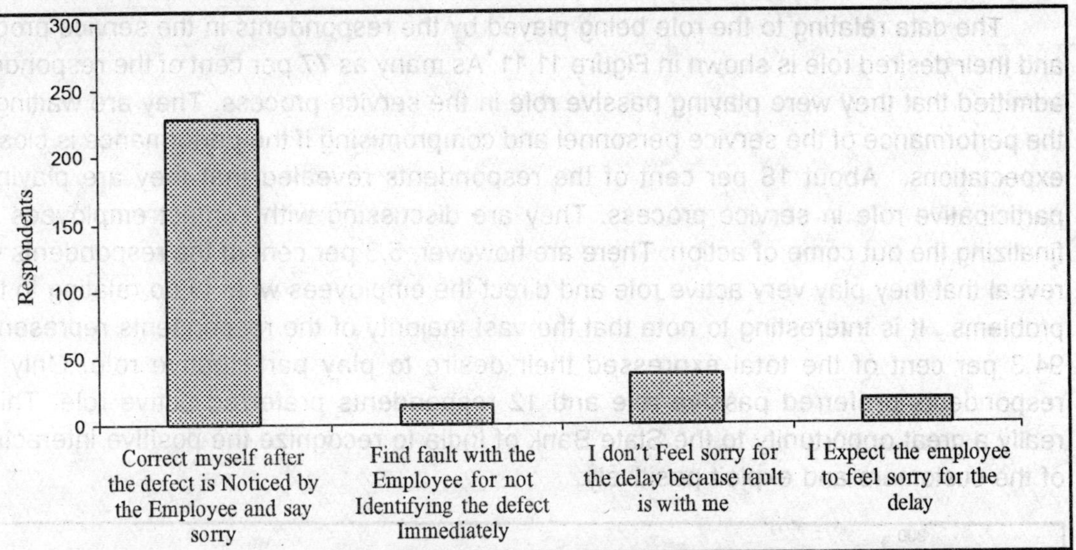

Fig 11.10: When service is delayed because of your fault, how do you react?

Further it was asked to reveal the reactions of the respondents when the service is delayed because of some problems within the service organization.The data presented in Table 11.12 reveals that the respondents' first preference was to 'request the employee for the speedy disposal' (score 1943 and mean 1.01). The second rated reaction was 'complaining to the concern officer' (score 1483, mean 2.83) and the third rated reaction was 'join the voice of resentment with co-customer' (score 676, mean 2.22). The other reactions of the respondents were 'encourage the co-customers to raise the voice against delay' (score 606, mean 2.54), 'complain in the consumer court' (score 518, mean 3.46), 'raise the voice against the delay with contact employees' (score 363, mean 2.05), and 'share the grievance with co-customer' (score 167, mean 2.04).

Table 11.12: If service is delayed because of some problems within service organization, how do you react?

PARTICULARS	N	MEAN RANK	SCORE
Request the employees for the speedy disposal	278	1.01	1943
Share the grievance with co-customer	28	2.04	167
Raise the voice against the delay with contact employees	61	2.05	363
Join the voice of resentment with co-customer	117	2.22	676
Encourage the co-customers to raise voice against delay	111	2.54	606
Complain to the concerned officer	287	2.83	1483
Complain in the consumer court	114	3.46	518

The data relating to the role being played by the respondents in the service process and their desired role is shown in Figure 11.11. As many as 77 per cent of the respondents admitted that they were playing passive role in the service process. They are waiting for the performance of the service personnel and compromising if the performance is close to expectations. About 18 per cent of the respondents revealed that they are playing a participative role in service process. They are discussing with contact employees and finalizing the out come of action. There are however, 5.3 per cent of the respondents who reveal that they play very active role and direct the employees what to do relating to their problems. It is interesting to note that the vast majority of the respondents representing 94.3 per cent of the total expressed their desire to play participative role. Only five respondents preferred passive role and 12 respondents preferred active role. This is really a great opportunity to the State Bank of India to recognize the positive interactions of the customers and exploit positively.

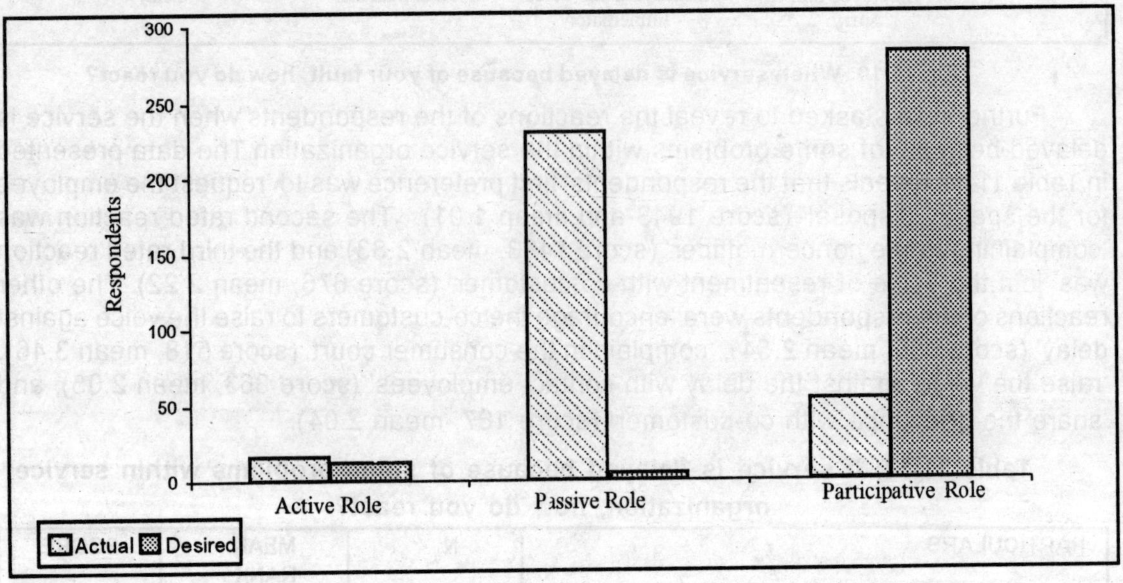

Fig 11.11: What kind of role you want to play in interactions?

A little over 89 per cent of the respondents revealed that the bank employees need to be given special training on customer interactions (Figure 11.12). This opinion of the respondents reflects their accumulated dissatisfaction over the interactions with the employees of the bank. Therefore, the State Bank of India should address this need and design the training program with a special focus on customer interaction.

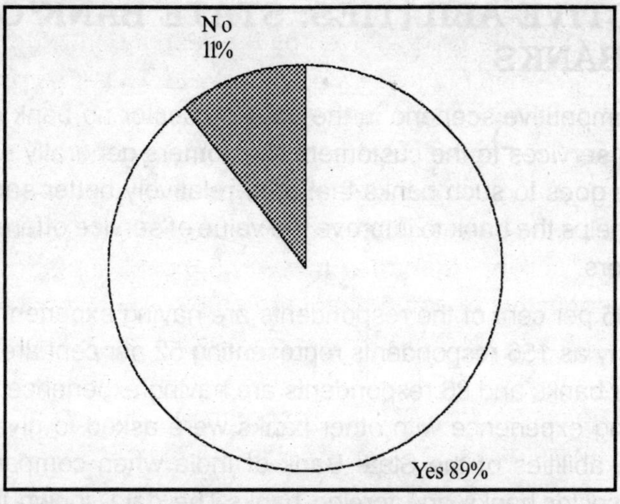

Fig 11.12: Do you think that employees need to be given special training on customer interaction?

Table 11.13 presents the factors that consumer value in interactions. The factors revealed by the respondents include Courtesy, empathy, accuracy, transparency, responsiveness, communication, speed and recognition. It can be seen from the table that the factor which secured highest score was 'accuracy' (score 1791, mean 2.78). The second factor rated by the respondents was 'courtesy' (score 1627, mean 3.37) and the third factor rated was 'transparency' (score 1437, mean 3.72). The factors such as empathy, speed, communication secured 1396, 1392, 1334 scores respectively. Responsiveness secured 973 score and the lowest score was given to recognition by the respondents.

Table 11.13: What are the best things you value in interactions?

PARTICULARS	N	MEAN RANK	SCORE
Courtesy	289	3.37	1627
Empathy	280	4.01	1396
Accuracy	288	2.78	1791
Transparency	272	3.72	1437
Responsiveness	281	5.54	937
Communication	283	4.29	1334
Speed	285	4.12	1392
Recognition	267	7.31	450

11.5 INTERACTIVE ABILITIES: STATE BANK OF INDIA VS. OTHER BANKS

In the growing competitive scenario in the banking sector no bank can isolate itself in designing and offering services to the customers. Customers generally exercise the right of choice and preference goes to such banks that offer relatively better services.Therefore, a comparative analysis helps the bank to improve the value of service offered to the customers greater than competitors.

Out of the total, 65 per cent of the respondents are having experience with other banks (Figure 11.13). As many as 156 respondents representing 52 per cent are having experience with other public sector banks and 86 respondents are having experience with foreign banks. The respondents having experience with other banks were asked to give the rating on SBI employees' interactive abilities of the State Bank of India when compared to other public sector banks, private sector banks and foreign banks.The data shown in the Figure 11.14 reveals that SBI employees' interactive abilities compared to the other public sector banks.The State Bank of India was rated 'good' by about 41 per cent of the respondents.When compared to the private sector banks, the majority of the respondents rated the performance of State Bank of India as 'average'. When compared to the foreign banks, the rating was divided between 'average' and 'poor'.

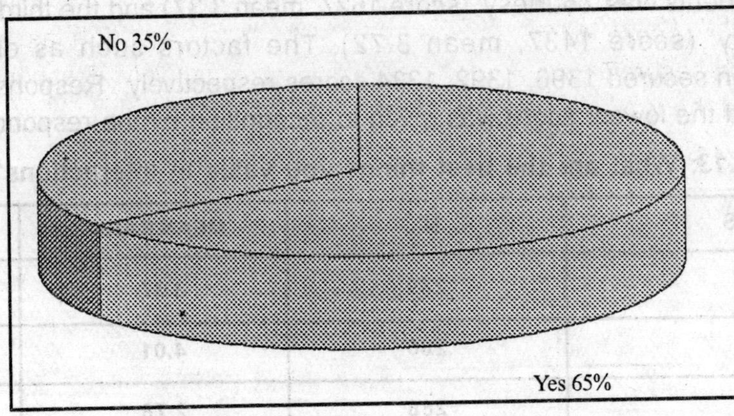

Fig 11.13: Do you have experience with other banks?

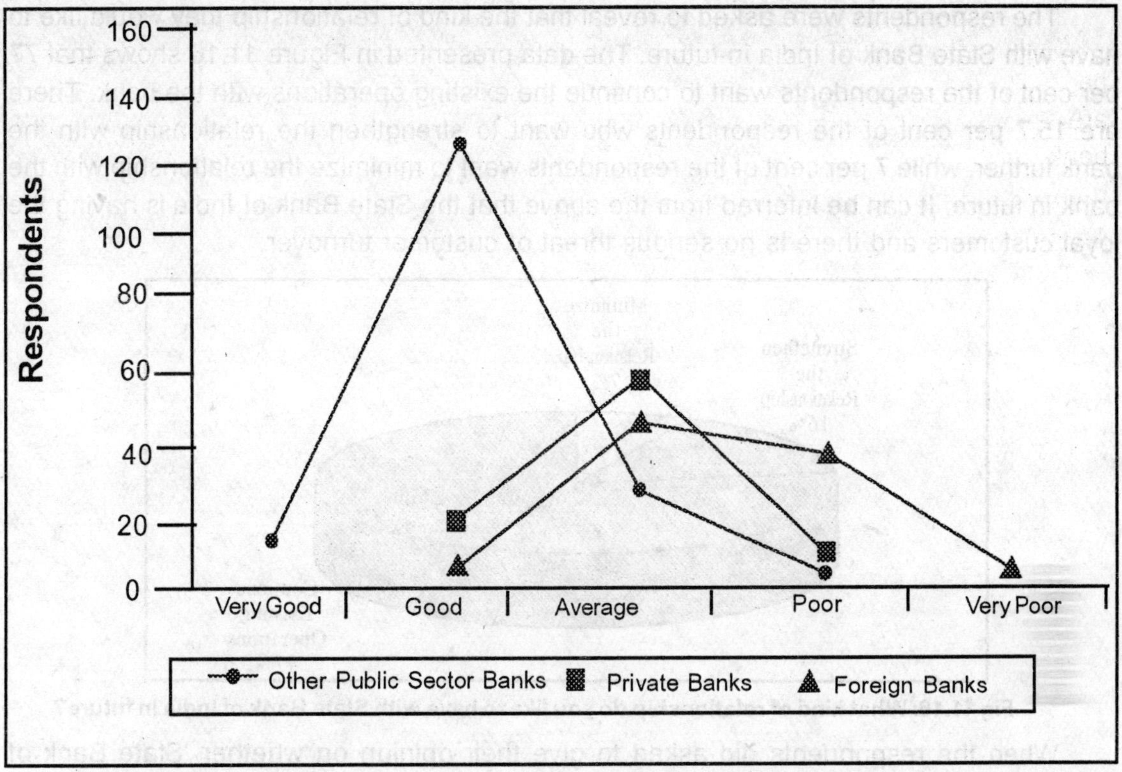

Fig 11.14: Rating on interactive abilities of the employees of SBI compared to other banks in India.

The data presented in Figure 11.15 reveals that 91 per cent of the respondents observed change in the quality of interactions by the State bank of India. However, 88.7 per cent of the respondents consider the change as moderate and 9 per cent of the respondents find the interactions either no change or negative.

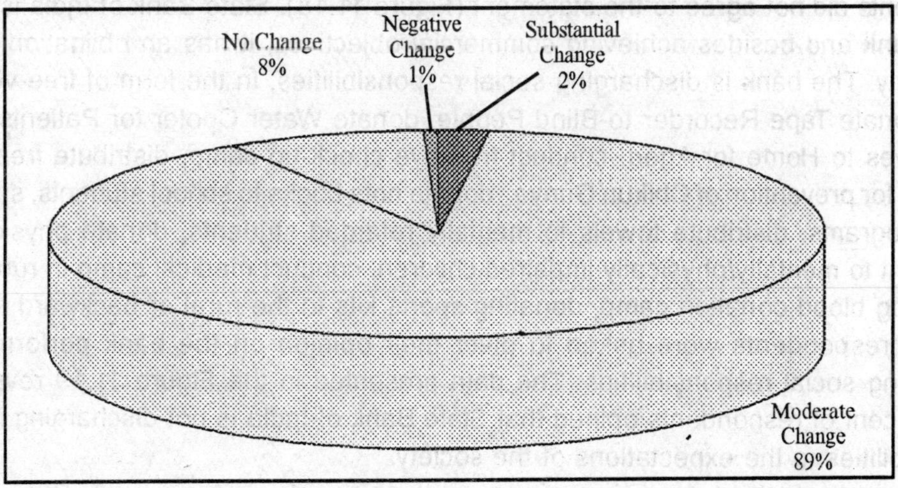

Fig 11.15: Do you find any change in the quality of interactions during the last three years?

The respondents were asked to reveal that the kind of relationship they would like to have with State Bank of India in future. The data presented in Figure 11.16 shows that 77 per cent of the respondents want to continue the existing operations with the bank. There are 15.7 per cent of the respondents who want to strengthen the relationship with the bank further, while 7 per cent of the respondents want to minimize the relationship with the bank in future. It can be inferred from the above that the State Bank of India is having the loyal customers and there is no serious threat of customer turnover.

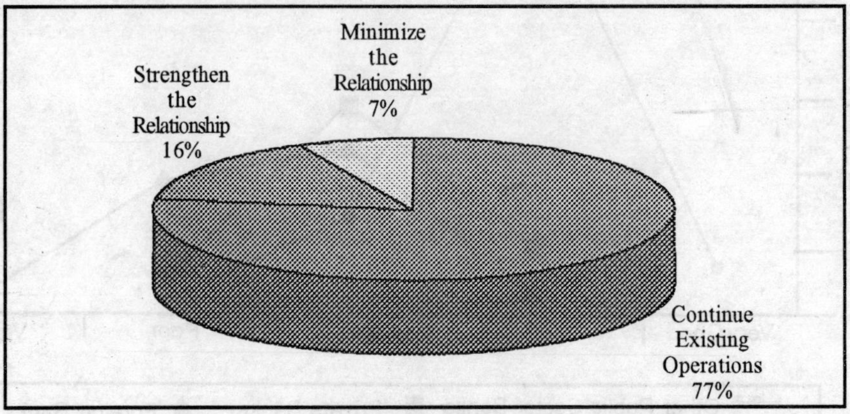

Fig 11.16: What kind of relationship do you like to have with State Bank of India in future?

When the respondents did asked to give their opinion on whether 'State Bank of India continues to be the leader in the country in the changing competitive scenario', 79.7 per cent of the respondents said 'yes' and only 20.3 per cent of the respondents said 'no' (Figure 11.17). The statement 'do you support the policy of the Government to use public sector banks for Government sponsored social welfare measures', out of the total, 73.7 per cent of the respondents agreed to the statement and only 26.3 per cent of the respondents did not agree to the statement (Figure 11.18). State Bank of India is a public sector bank and besides achieving commercial objectives, it has an obligation to serve the society. The bank is discharging social responsibilities, in the form of free veterinary camp, donate Tape Recorder to Blind People, donate Water Cooler for Patients, donate Gas Stoves to Home for Aged, conduct free eye check-up camp, distribute free Homeo medicine for prevention of Chikun Gunya, donate note books to school students, sponsored music programs, distribute towels to mentally retarded students, donate physiotherapy equipment to mentally/physically impaired children, conduct medical camp in rural areas, conducting blood donation camp, donating sports kits to the rural or backward students, etc. The respondents were asked to giver their opinion on the bank performance in discharging social responsibilities. The data presented in the Figure 11.19 reveals that 63.2 per cent of respondents opined that State Bank of India is not discharging its social responsibilities to the expectations of the society.

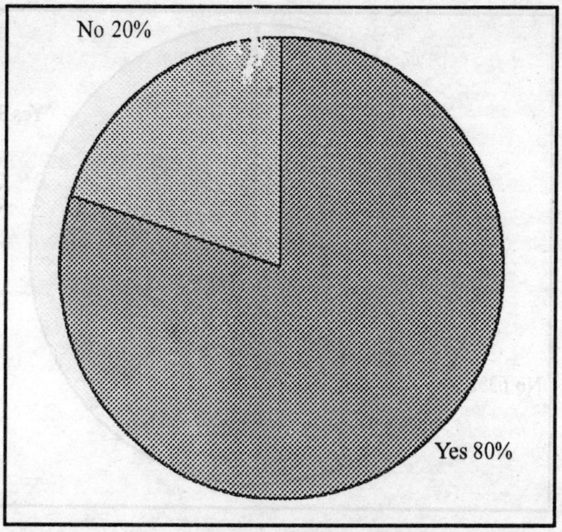

Fig 11.17: Do you think State Bank of India continues to be the leader in the light of changing competitive scenario?

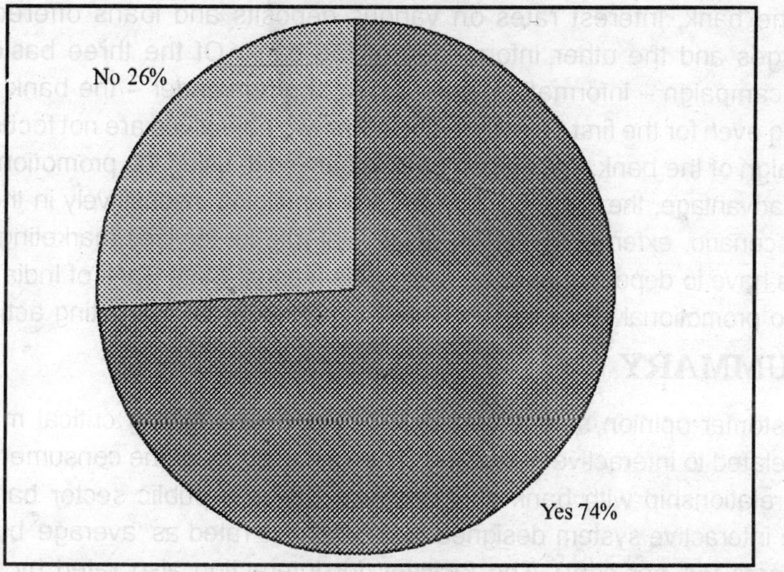

Fig 11.18: Do you support the policy of the Government to use public sector banks for Government sponsored social welfare measures?

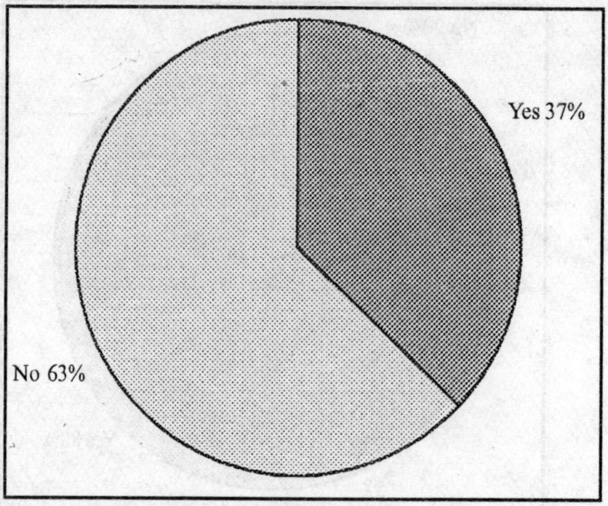

Fig 11.19: Do you believe that the State Bank of India is discharging its social responsibilities?

The study reveals that majority of the consumers are not aware of the variety of products offered by the bank, interest rates on various deposits and loans offered by the bank, service charges and the other information of the bank. Of the three basic objectives of promotional campaign – information, persuasion and remainder – the bank is not securing positive rating even for the first objective. The other two objectives are not focused adequately in the campaign of the bank. While competitive banks are using the promotional media to the best of their advantage, the State Bank of India is remaining insensitively in the fast changing competitive scenario, external marketing plays vital role in services marketing as the service organizations have to depend mostly on pulling the market. State Bank of India should allocate more funds to promotional campaign and intensify the external marketing activities.

11.6 SUMMARY

The customer opinion survey conducted helps in identifying critical marketing issues particularly related to interactive marketing. The vast majority of the consumers are motivated to continue relationship with bank only because SBI is a public sector bank and it offers security. The interactive system designed by the bank is rated as 'average' by the majority of the respondents (54 per cent). The facilities for interaction also rated by the majority as average and more than 20 per cent rated the facilities for interaction as 'poor'. The majority of the respondents (64.7 per cent) are not convinced to the statement 'documents are user friendly'. As many as 43 per cent of the respondents either disagree or strongly disagree to the statement 'employees of the branch are responsive'. About 50.4 per cent of the respondents ventilated their disagreement to the statement 'employees are giving individualised attention'. The large number of respondents (41.20 per cent) are 'neutral' to the statement 'employees are communicative', while 33.2 per cent of the respondents either disagree or strongly disagree to the statement. The majority of the respondents preferred 'neutral' position for the statements 'employees are courteous', 'employees are empathetic', 'employees are understanding customer problems', 'employees extend support at time of necessity', 'employees suggest right things', 'employees are discriminative', 'employees are egoistic' and 'employees have gender bias'. As many as 66.7 per cent have faced problems sometimes in communicating their problems to the contact employees. A little over 43 per cent of the respondents revealed that they were not informed about 'interest rates of term loans'. About 44 per cent revealed that they were not informed of 'service charges collected by the bank'.The bank customer rights were not informed to 43.7 per cent of the respondents. The respondents opined that the documents required for opening bank account are too many (92 per cent), too much of information required (89.7 per cent) and also time consuming (90.3 per cent). Inadequate communication was the problem expressed by 43.3 per cent of the respondents in interacting with processes.The majority of the respondents, representing 57.3 per cent, revealed that there was no response from the contact employee at the detachment phase. As many as 77 per cent of the respondents admitted the fact that they played passive role in the service process. As many as 94.3 per cent of the respondents expressed their desire to play participative role in service processes. Out of the total, 89 per cent of the respondents revealed that the bank employees need to be given special training on customer interactions. Accuracy, Courtesy and Transparency are the expected qualities by the respondents in employee interactions. When compared to the private sector banks, the performance of State Bank of India was rated 'average' by majority of the respondents and when compared to the foreign banks, the rating was divided between 'average' and 'poor'. Out of the total, 91 per cent of the respondents observed change in the quality of interactions by the employees of State Bank of India. However, 88.7 per cent of the respondents consider the change as moderate. As many as 63.2 per cent of the respondents opined that State Bank of India is not discharging its social responsibilities effectively.

❑❑❑

BIBLIOGRAPHY

Abdullah Aldlaigan Saudi Arabia, and Francis Buttle, 'Beyond satisfaction: customer attachment to retail banks', *International Journal of Bank Marketing,* Vol.23, No.4, 2005.

Abhiman Das and Saibal Ghosh, 'Financial deregulation and efficiency: An empirical analysis of Indian Banks during the post reform period', *Review of Financial Economics,* Vol.15, 2006.

Adrian Payne, *'The Essence of Services Marketing',* Prentice Hall of India Pvt. Ltd., New Delhi, 1998.

Albert Caruana and Peter Calleya, 'The effect of internal marketing on organizational commitment among retail bank mangers', *International Journal of Bank Marketing,* Vol.16, No.3, 1998.

All India Rural Credit Survey Committee, appointed by RBI in 1951.

India's Best Banks – The Business Today – KPMG Survey, *Business Today,* 25th February, 2007.

India's Best Banks – The Business Today – KPMG Survey, *Business Today,* 13th December, 2009.

Avadhani, V.A., *'Marketing of Financial Services',* Himalaya Publishing House, Mumbai, 1999.

Avinandan Mukherjee and Prithwiraj Nath, 'A model of trust in online relationship banking', *International Journal of Bank Marketing,* Vol.21, No.1, 2003.

Avinandan Mukherjee, Prithwiraj Nath, and Manabendra Nath Pal, 'Performance Benchmarking and Strategic Homogeneity of Indian Banks', *International Journal of Bank Marketing,* Vol.20, No.3, Jun 2002.

Babu P. George, and Purva G. Hegde, 'Employee Attitude towards Customers and Customer Care Challenges in Banks', *International Journal of Bank Marketing,* Vol.22, No.6, 2004.

Bansal G.L. Banks since Nationalisation, *Birla Insurance of Scientific Research,* New Delhi, 1991.

Barbara R. Lewis, and Sotiris Spyrakopoulos, 'Service Failures and Recovery in Retail Banking: The Customers' Perspective', *International Journal of Bank Marketing;* Vol.19, No.1, 2001.

Benjamin Schneider, John J. Parkington and Virginia M. Buxton, 'Employee and Customer Perceptions of Service in Banks', *Administrative Science Quarterly,* Vol.25, No.2, 1980.

Beth G. Chung-Harrera, Nadav Goldschmidt and K. Doug Hoffman, 'Customer and employee views of critical service incidents', *Journal of Services Marketing,* Vol.18, No.4, 2004.

Bettencourt, Lance A.; and Brown, Stephen W., 'Contact Employees: Relationships among Workplace Fairness, Job Satisfaction and Prosocial service Behaviors', *Journal of Retailing,* 73(1), Sep.1997.

Bezjian-Avery and Alexandra Miranda, 'Cognitive Processing of Interactive Marketing', Dissertation Abstracts International Section A: *Humanities & Social Sciences,* 58(4-A), Oct.1997.

Bhatt-Atual, *'Bank Marketing', Market Research and Indian Banks,* Prajnan, 1991.

Bhole, L.M., *'Financial Institutions and Markets',* Tata McGraw-Hill, New Delhi, 1999.

Bilgrami S.A.R., 'Growth of Public Sector Banks', Deep and Deep Publications, New Delhi, 1996.

Bloch-Ernest, 'Research in Investment Banking: Some Prerequisites for Developing a Marketing Strategy', New York University, 1987.

Cathy Parker and Philippa Ward, 'An analysis of role adoptions and scripts during customer-to-customer encounters', *European Journal of Marketing,* Vol.34, No.3/4, 2000.

Chalam, G.V and Srinivas, L., 'Genderwise Perceptions and Attitudes on HRD Climate in Indian Banking Sector', *The Indian Journal of Commerce,* Vol.58, No.4, Oct. – Dec. 2005.

Chandra Sekhar, A.R., 'Market share of Public Sector Banks in post reform period', *Indian Journal of Commerce,* New Delhi, 1999.

Charalambos Spathis, Eugenia Petridou and Niki Glaveli, 'Managing service quality in banks: customers' gender effects', *Managing Service Quality,* Vol.14, No.1, 2004.

Christian Gronroos, *'Services Management and Marketing',* Maxwell MacIlan publishing, Singapore Pet. Ltd., Singapore, 1990.

Christian Gronroos, 'The Internal Marketing Function – Strategic Management and Marketing in the Service Sector Report', *Marketing Science Institute,* Cambridge, 1983.

Christian Gronroos, 'The perceived service quality concept – a mistake?' *Managing Service Quality,* Vol.11, No.3, 2001.

Christine Sanes, 'Employee impact on service delivery', *Management Development Review,* Vol.9, No.2, 1996.

Christo Boshoff and Janine Allen, 'The influence of selected antecedents on frontline staff's perceptions of service recovery performance', *International Journal of Service Industry Management,* Vol.11, No.1, 2000.

Christopher Lovelock, *'Service Marketing',* Addition Wesley Longman (Singapore) Pvt. Ltd., Delhi, 2001.

Craig C. Julian and B. Ramaseshan, 'The Role of Customer-contact Personnel in the Marketing of a Retail Bank's Service', *International Journal of Retail & Distribution Management,* Vol.22, No.5, 1994.

D.K, Das, Business Processing Reengineering – Achieving excellence through transformation, State Bank Staff College, Hyderabad: 31st March, 2007.

Dawn Iacobucci, "Interactive Marketing and the Meganet: Networks of Networks', http://www3.interscience.wiley.com/cgi-bin, dt. 9-10-2009.

Ding Hooi Ting, 'Service quality and satisfaction perceptions: *curvilinear* and interaction effect', *International Journal of Bank Marketing,* Vol.22, No.6, 2004.

Dwayne D. Gremler, Mary Jo Bitner, and Kenneth R. Evans, 'The Internal Service Encounter', *International Journal of Service Industry Management,* Vol.5, No.2, 1994.

Edward C. Malthouse, and Robert C. Blattberg, 'Relationship Marketing', *Journal of Interactive Marketing,* Vol.19, No.1, 2005.

Edward W. Candif, Richard R. Still and Norman A.P. Eovani, *'Fundamentals of Modern Marketing',* Prentice Hall of India, New Delhi, 1980.

Evans, Martin; Wedande, Gamini; Ralston, Lisa; and Van T Hul, Selma, 'Consumer Interaction in the Virtual Era: Some Qualitative Insights', *Qualitative Market Research: An International Journal,* 4(3), 2001.

Feremy F. Sierra and Shaun McQuitty, 'Service providers and customers: social exchange theory and service loyalty', *Journal of Services Marketing,* Vol.19, No.6, 2005.

Frank Jefkins, *'Advertising',* McMillan, New Delhi, 1999.

G.S. Sureshchandra, Chandrasekharan Rajendran, R.N. Anantharaman and T.J. Kamalanabhan, 'Management's perception of total quality service in the banking sector of developing economy – a critical analysis', *International Journal of Bank Marketing,* Vol.20, No.4, 2002.

G.S. Sureshchandar, Chandrasekharan Rajendran and R.N. Anantharaman, 'The relationship between service quality and customer satisfaction – a factor specific approach', *Journal of Services Marketing,* Vol.16, No.4, 2002.

G.S. Sureshchandar, Chandrasekharan Rajendran, and R.N. Anantharaman, 'Customer Perceptions of Service Quality in the Banking Sector of a Developing Economy: A Critical Analysis', *International Journal of Bank Marketing,* Vol.21, No.5, Oct. 2003.

Ganesan G., 'Commercial Banking beyond 2000', *Kisan World,* 2000.

Golan – Amos, 'A multivariate stochastic theory of size Distribution of firms with empirical evidence', London, 1994.

Haldipur. Rajesh, 'The new face of retail banking', *Indian Management,* 1998.

Harsha, V. Varma, *'Marketing of Services',* Global Business Press, New Delhi, 1993.

http://tobeinformed.com/marketing/interactive-marketing. dt. 15-6-2009.

http://www.h&m.com, and Eric Sylvers, 'Cut-Rate Swedish Retailer Enters the Italian Market', New York Times, August 27, 2003, p.W1.

India's Best Banks, *Business Today,* 2-1-2005.

Jain – Alok-Kumar, 'Marketing Challenges for Commercial Banks in India', 1997.

Jamal, Ahmad, 'Retail Banking and Customer Behaviour: A Study of Self Concept, Satisfaction and Technology Usage', *The International Review of Retail, Distribution and Consumer Research,* Vol.14, No.3, July 2004.

Jap, Sandy D., Manolis, Chris., and Weitz, Barton A., 'Relationship quality and buyer-seller interactions in channels of distribution', *Journal of Business Research,* 46(3), Nov.1999.

Jo Ann M. Duffy, John M. Miller, and James B. Bexley, 'Banking Customers' Varied Reactions to Service Recovery Strategies', *Journal of Bank Marketing,* Vol.24, No.2, 2006.

Joa˜o F. Proenc¸a and Luý´s M. de Castro, '"Stress" in business relationships: a study on corporate bank services', *International Journal of Bank Marketing,* Vol.23, No.7, 2005.

John, Jeannie Denise, 'The Effects of Employee Service Quality Provision and Customer Personality Traits on Customer Participation, Satisfaction, and Repurchase Intentions', Dissertation Abstracts International Section A: *Humanities & Social Sciences.* 65(7-A), No Month Specified, 2005.

Jonathon R.B. Halbesleben, and M. Ronald Buckley, 'Managing Customers as Employees of the Firm: New Challenges for Human Resources Management', *Personnel Review,* Vol.33, No.3, 2004.

Josée Bloemer, and Gaby Odekerken-Schröder, 'The role of Employee Relationship Proneness in Creating Employee Loyalty', *International Journal of Bank Marketing,* Vol.24, No.4, 2006.

Juan Carlos Fandos Roig, Javier Sanchez Garcia, Miguel Angel Moliner Tena and Jaume Llorens Monzonis, 'Customer Perceived Value in Banking Services', *Journal of Bank Marketing*, Vol.24, No.5, 2006.

K. Rama Mohana Rao, *'Services Marketing'*, Pearson Education, New Delhi, 2005.

Kaisa Snellman and Tiina Vihtkari, 'Customer complaining behavior in technology-based service encounters', *International Journal of Service Industry Management*, Vol.14, No.2, 2003.

Karen Maru File, Ben B. Judd, and Russ Alan Prince, 'Interactive Marketing: The Influence of Participation on Positive Word-of-Mouth and Referrals', *Journal of Services Marketing*, Vol.6, No.4, 1992.

Karen Maru File, Judith L.Mack, and Russ Alan Prince, 'The Effect of Interactive Marketing on Commercial Customer Satisfaction in International Financial Markets', *Journal of Business & Industrial Marketing*, Vol.10, No.2, May 1995.

Keith H. Hammonds, *'Michael Porter's Big Ideas'*, Fast Company, March 2001.

Kulshreshtha K., *'Emerging Scenario in Banking and Finance'*, R.B.S.A. publishers, Jaipur, 1995.

Kulwant Singh Pathania., 'HRD Programme and Practice in Cooperative Banks', *The Indian Journal and Commerce*, Vol.L, No.192, Part III, September 1997.

Lance A. Bettencourt and Kevin Gwinner, 'Customization of the service experience: The role of the frontline employee', *International Journal of Service Industry Management*, Vol.7, No.2, 1996.

Madhukar G. Angur, Rajan Nataraajan and John S. Jahera Jr., 'Service quality in the banking industry: an assessment in a developing economy', *International Journal of Bank Marketing*, Vol.17, No.3, 1999.

Mahn Hee Yoon, Jai Hyun Seo and Tae Seog Yoon, 'Effects of Contact Employee Supports on Critical Employee Responses and Customer Service Evaluation', *Journal of Services Marketing;* Vol.18, No.5, 2004.

Mahn Hee Yoon, Sharon E. Beatty and Jaebeom Suh, 'The effect of work climate on critical employee and customer outcomes: An employee-level analysis', *International Journal of Service Industry Management*, Vol.12, No.5, 2001.

Mali Ram, Currency and Banking, Agarwal Press, Agra, 1958.

Mamoria C.B. and Joshi, R.I., *'Principles and Practice of Marketing in India'*, Kitab Manal, Allahabad, 1984.

Mark Durkin, Barry Howcroft, Aodheen O'Donnell and Danielle McCartan-Quinn, 'Retail bank customer preferences: personal and remote interactions', *International Journal of Retail & Distribution Management*, Vol.31, No.4, 2003.

Mary Jo Bitner, 'Servicescapes: The Impact of Physical Surroundings on Customers and Employees', *Journal of Marketing*, Vol.56, 1992.

Mary Jo Bitner, Bernard H. Booms, & Lois A. Mohr, 'Critical Service encounters: The Employee's Viewpoint', *Journal of Marketing,* Vol.58, 1994.

Mary Jo Bitner, Bernard H. Booms, and Mary Stanfield Tetreault, 'The Service Encounter: Diagnosing Favorable and Unfavorable Incidents', *Journal of Marketing,* Vol.54, 1990.

McColl-Kennedy, Janet R., Daus, Catherine S., Sparks, Beverley A., 'The Role of Gender in Reactions to Service Failure and Recovery', *Journal of Service Research,* 6(1), Aug 2003.

Meir Kohn, *'Financial Institutes of Markets',* Tata McGraw-Hill, New Delhi, 1996.

Merchant, R.Y., 'HRD Plan for State Bank of India', *National Institute of Bank Management,* Pune, 1980.

Michael D. Hartline and O.C. Ferrell, 'The Management of Customer-Contact Service Employees: An Empirical Investigation', *Journal of Marketing,* Vol.60, 1996.

Mohapatra, 'Training and Human Resource Development', *Journal of Management Development,* Vol.17, No.45,46,47 & 48, Jan-Dec 1987.

Neelu Rohmetra., 'Human Resource Development in Commercial Banks in India', *IJIR,* Vol.34, No.3, Jan. 1999.

Neeru Malhotra and Avinandan Mukherjee, 'The relative influence of organizational commitment and job satisfaction on service quality of customer-contact employees in banking call centres', *Journal of Services Marketing,* Vol.18, No.3, 2004.

Panadikar S.G., Banking in India, Orient Longmans Ltd., Calcutta, 1951.

Paolo Guenzi and Ottavia Pelloni, 'The impact of interpersonal relationships on customer satisfaction and loyalty to the service provider', *International Journal of Service Industry Management,* Vol.15, No.4, 2004.

Pathak. R.D., 'Job involvement and need satisfaction of bank officers in India', *Vikalpa,* Vol.8, No.4, 1983.

Patrick Barwise and John U. Farley, 'The State of Interactive Marketing in Seven Countries: Interactive Marketing Comes of Age', www3.interscience.wiley.com, *Dt.*10-10-2009.

Peltier, James W., Schibrowsky, John A., Schultz, Don E. and Davis, John, 'Interactive Psychographics: Cross-Selling in the Banking Industry', *Journal of Advertising Research,* Vol.42, No.2, Mar-Apr. 2002.

Peperrmans –Ronals, Verleye – Gino, Vaw Cappellen – Sarah Wall, 'Banking Innovativeness and Computer Attitudes – 25-40 year old ATM – Users on the spot', *Journal of Economic – Psychology,* 1996.

Peter Jones, 'The Changing Use of Old Bank Premises', *Property Management,* Vol.14, No.3, Sep. 1996.

Peter Kangis and Vassilis Voukelatos, 'Private and public banks: a comparison of customer expectations and perceptions', *International Journal of Bank Marketing,* Vol.15, No.7, 1997.

Philip Kotler, *'Marketing Management - Analysis, Planning, Implementation and Control'*, Prentice Hall of India Pvt. Ltd., New Delhi, 1987.

Philip Kotler, *A Framework for Marketing Management,* Pearson Education, (Singapore) Pvt. Ltd., Indian Branch, New Delhi, 2002.

Philip Kotler, and Kevin Lane Keller, *'Marketing Management'*, 12e, Pearson Education, New Delhi, 2006.

Philip Megicks, Atul Mishra, and Jonathan Lean, 'Enhancing Microfinance Outreach through Market-Oriented New Service Development in Indian Regional Rural Banks', *Journal of Bank Marketing,* Vol.23, No.1, Jan 2005.

Rajendran, N., 'HRD Practices in Banking Industry', *Co-operative Perspectives,* Vol.38, Oct-Dec, 2003.

Ramphal M.K. and Gupta S.I., *Services Marketing,* Galgotia Publishing Company, New Delhi, 2000.

Raphaël K. Akamavi, 'Re-engineering Service Quality Process Mapping: e-Banking Process', *International Journal of Bank Marketing,* Vol.23, No.1, 2005.

Rashmi Arya, *'Women in Public Sector Special Reference to Banking Industry'*, Manak Publications Pvt. Ltd., Delhi, 1990.

Report on Currency and Finance, *RBI Publications,* Mumbai, 1998-99.

Report on Currency and Finance, *RBI Publications,* Mumbai, 1999-00.

Report on Trend and Progress of Banking in India, 2006-07, *RBI.*

Reserve Bank of India, Report on Current and Finance, The Author, *Reserve Bank of India Publications,* Mumbai, 1998-99.

Ronald J. Burke, Jim Graham and Frank Smith, 'Effects of reengineering on the employee satisfaction-customer satisfaction relationship', *The TQM Magazine,* Vol.17, No.4, 2005.

Ronald T. Rust, Antony J. Zoharik and Timothy I. Keming Ham, *'Services Marketing',* Addition Wesley Longman, New Delhi, 1999.

Ronalt T. Markes. B., *'Personal Selling an Interactive Approach'*, Allyn and Bacon Inc. Boston, 1981.

Ross D. Petty, 'Interactive Marketing and the Law: The Future Rise of Unfairness', *Journal of Interactive Marketing,* Vol.12, No.3, 1998.

S. Ramachander, 'Interactive Marketing: Boon or Nightmare?', http://www.thehindubusinessline.com/catalyst/2004/04/08/stories/2004040800140400.htm, dt. 15-11-2009.

Sally Kernbach and Nicola S. Schutte, 'Impact of service provider emotional intelligence on customer satisfaction', *Journal of Services Marketing,* Vol.19, No.7, 2005.

Sambre Neena., 'A Sociological Study of Alienation among Bank Employees', *SNDT University,* Mumbai, 1980.

Satyabhusan Dash, Ed Bruning and Kalyan Ku Guin, 'The Moderating Effect of Power Distance on Perceived Interdependence and Relationship Quality in Commercial Banking: A Cross-Cultural Comparison', *International Journal of Bank Marketing,* Vol.24, No.5, 2006.

Shajahan. S, *Services Marketing,* Himalaya Publishing House, Mumbai, 2001.

Sharma, K. Ramakrishna, *'Financial Sector reforms in India',* Abhigyan, 1996.

Sharma, R.D., 'Evaluation of Inbuilt Marketing Orientation in Indian Rural Banking', 2000.

Shivaji, K., 'Human Resource Development in Co-operative Banks', *Indian Co-operative Review,* Apr 1994.

Shollapur, M.R., 'Performance Appraisal of Banks under service area approach – A Comparative Study', *Maharastra Co-operative Quarterly,* 1997.

Singh Rajender Kumar, 'Costing in a Designated Banking Environment', *The Management Accountant,* Kolkata, 2001.

Skaggs, Bruce C. and Huffman, Tammy Ross, 'A Customer Interaction Approach to Strategy and Production Complexity Alignment in Service Firms', *Academy of Management Journal,* Vol.46, No.6, Dec. 2003.

Stephan H. Haeckel, 'About the Nature and Future of Interactive Marketing', *Journal of Interactive Marketing,* Vol.12, No.1, 1998.

Steve Sizoo, Richard Plank, Wilfried Iskat and Hendrick Serrie, 'The effect of intercultural sensitivity on employee performance in cross-cultural service encounters', *Journal of Services Marketing,* Vol.19, No.4, 2005.

Subba Rao, B., Madhusudhana Rao, M. and Suryapraksh Rao, V., *Currency & Banking,* Tata McGraw-Hill Publishing Co., New Delhi, 1992.

Sudarsana Rao, G., 'Marketing of Services - A Study of Marketing Operations of Andhra Pradesh State Electricity Board', Unpublished Thesis, Andhra University, Visakhapatnam, 1991.

Sunil Gupta, Donald R. Lehmann, 'Consumers as assets', *Journal of Interactive Marketing,* Vol.17, No.1, 2003.

Swain. Srinivas, 'A study on work motivation of branch managers in State Bank of India', Pune, *National Institute of Bank Management,* 1993.

Terrence Levesque and Gordon H.G. McDougall, 'Determinants of customer satisfaction in retail banking', *International Journal of Bank Marketing,* Vol.14, No.7, 1996.

Tleonard A. Schiesinger and James I. Heskeltt, 'The Service Driven Service Company', *Harvard Business Review,* Sep – Oct 1991.

Upah, Gregory, Mass Marketing in Service Retailing, A Review and Synthesis of Major Methods, *Journal of Retailing,* Pal 1980.

Vaish M.C., *Monetary Theory,* Vikas Publishing House, New Delhi, 1973.

Van Dolen, Willemijn; de Ruyter, Ko and Lemmink, Jos, "An Empirical Assessment of the Influence of Customer Emotions and Contact Employee Performance on Encounter and Relationship Satisfaction", *Journal of Business Research,* Vol.57, No.4, Apr. 2004.

Verma, M.L., *'Rural Banking in India'*, Kuber Associates and Publishers, Jaipur, 1983.

Varshney and Sundaram , *Banking Theory and Practice,* S. Chand & Sons, New Delhi, 1987.

Vijayakumar, V.S.R., 'Perceived management styles and job satisfaction of executives of private sectors banks', *Indian Journal of Applied Psychology,* Vol.33, No.2, July, 1996.

William J. Stanton, Michael J. Ezel and Brace J. Walker, *Fundamentals of Marketing,* Tata Mc-GrawHill Publishing Co. Ltd., New Delhi, 1994.

www.statebank.com/pdf/SWIFT.pdf, dated 18-08-2007.

Yahya Melhem and Irbid, Jordan, 'The antecedents of customer-contact employees' empowerment' *Employee Relations,* Vol.26, No.1, 2004.

□□□

ANNEXURE

Annexure–I

INTERACTIVE MARKETING

A Case Study Of State Bank Of India

Questionnaire For Employees

1 DEMOGRAPHIC PROFILE

1.1 Name	:		
1.2 Age	:	21-30 ( )	31-40 ( )
		41-50 ( )	51 & above ( )
1.3 Sex	:	Male ( )	Female ( )
1.4 Education	:		
1.5 Designation	:		
1.6 Annual Salary (Rs.)	:	50,001 – 1,00,000 ( )	1,00,001 – 1,50,000 ( )
		1,50,001 – 2,00,000 ( )	2,00,001 – 2,50,000 ( )
		2,50,001 – 3,00,000 ( )	3,00,001 and above ( )

2 RELATIONSHIP WITH BANK

2.1 If you have previous work experience, please give details:

BANK EXPERIENCE	*NON-BANK EXPERIENCE*

2.2 What motivated you to join in banking service? (Rank in the order)

Prestigious job		Suitable to my abilities	
Convenient job		The first job I got	
Career growth opportunities		The best among available	
I have special interest in banking services		Any other (specify):	

2.3 How many times you got transferred in your service in SBI? Give details:

TRANSFER	NO. OF YEARS	TRANSFER	NO. OF YEARS
Joining		Third	
First		Fourth	
Second		Fifth	

3 RECRUITMENT, SELECTION AND TRAINING

3.1 What is your opinion on the recruitment policy of the bank?

a.	
b.	
c.	

3.2 What is your opinion on the selection criteria adopted by bank?

POSITION	OPINION
Officers	
Clerks	

3.3 Are you given training for performing your task effectively? Yes ( ) No ( )

3.4 What are the areas in which you're trained?

AREA OF TRAINING	REMARKS

3.5 Do you think that bank employees be given training periodically? If so, what type of training system do you suggest?

Type of Programme: ______________________________.

3.6 In the changing competitive scenario, do you think the employees need to be given training on special skills, if so what are the skills you are interested be trained?

	TYPE OF SKILL		TYPE OF SKILL
1		4	
2		5	
3		6	

3.7 What is your opinion on the emoluments being received by you for the service?

	VERY GOOD	GOOD	AVERAGE	POOR	VERY POOR
Pay Scale					
Other benefits					

3.8 Do you think that the employee merit is recognized in the bank?

Yes ( ) No ( )

3.9 What is your opinion on upward communication system in your bank?

VERY GOOD	GOOD	AVERAGE	POOR	VERY POOR

4 EMPLOYEE – MANAGEMENT INTERACTIONS'

4.1 How frequently do you meet higher officials of the bank?

POSITION	FREQUENCY OF INTERACTIONS	MODE OF INTERACTIONS
Branch Manager		
Assistant General Manager		
Deputy General Manager		
General Manager		
Chief General Manager		
Deputy Managing Director		
Managing Director		
Chairman		

4.2 What is your rating of the interaction?

PARTICULARS	STRONGLY AGREE	AGREE	NEUTRAL	DISAGRE	STRONGLY DISAGREE
Courteous					
Empathetic					
Responsive					
Objective					
Active					
Friendliness					

5 INTERACTION WITH PHYSICAL ENVIRONMENT, SYSTEMS AND PROCEDURES

5.1 Please give opinion on the following:

PARTICULARS	VERY GOOD	GOOD	AVERAGE	POOR	VERY POOR
Exterior of the bank					
Interior of the bank					
Ambiance					
Layout					
Design of the documents					

Procedures					
Signage					
Equipment					
Furniture					
Support services					
Security					
Ventilation					
Physical Amenities					
Toilets					
Drinking Water					
Canteen					
Bank timings					
Promotion system					
Punishment system					
Quality assurance system					

5.2 What kind of changes do you suggest for the improvement of the physical environment, systems and procedures?

Particulars	Suggestions
Physical Environment	
Systems	
Procedures	

6 INTERACTION WITH CO-EMPLOYEES

6.1 How do you rate your interaction with your colleagues in the bank?

VERY GOOD	GOOD	AVERAGE	POOR	VERY POOR

6.2 What kind of problems do you encounter in interacting with your colleagues?

PROBLEMS	RANK
Language	
Status	
Gender	
Lack of Self-confidence	
Any other (Specify):	

6.3 Please give your rating in the interaction of your colleagues?

PARTICULARS	STRONGLY AGREE	AGREE	NEUTRAL	DISAGREE	STRONGLY DISAGREE
Cooperative					
Helpful					
Understanding					
Courteous					
Righteous					

7 EMPLOYEE – CUSTOMER INTERACTIONS'

7.1 How do you establish first contact with your customer, whenever happens to interact? (choose any one of the following)

I greet every customer all the time	
I greet the customer, when I was not busy	
I greet the customer whom I like	
I greet a few customers, who are highly profitable to the bank	
I greet the customer of opposite gender	
I don't believe greeting the customer has any value	
I greet the customer who visits to my counter	

7.2 Do you agree the concept called "Customer is always right"?

STRONGLY AGREE	AGREE	NEUTRAL	DISAGREE	STRONGLY DISAGREE

7.3 What type of customers do you prefer to interact? (Rank in the order)

Only a few customers	
Regular customers	
Privileged customers	
New customers	
Old customers	
Young customers	
Others (specify):	

7.4 When a customer pickup an argument with you, how do you react? (Rank in the order)

Try to convince the customer	
Seek the help of the colleagues	
Seek the help of co-customers	
Direct the customer to the superior	
Neck out the customer	
Direct the security to handle the customer	
Any other (specify):	

7.5 What is your experience so far with the interaction of the customers?

VERY GOOD	GOOD	AVERAGE	POOR	VERY POOR

7.6 Have you experienced any problems in interacting with customers?

Yes ( )No ( )

7.7 Please give your opinion on the following:

PARTICULARS	STRONGLY AGREE	AGREE	NEUTRAL	DISAGREE	STRONGLY DISAGREE
There is a visible change in the attitude of customers					
Customers are quality conscious					
Customers are time conscious					
Customers are demanding					
Customers are experienced with the services of other banks					
Customers are well informed					
Customers show respect to system designed					
Customers are less tolerant of the system deviations					

Customers are less tolerant on indiscipline					
Customers are less tolerant on system failures					
Customers like to share pleasantries in interactions					

7.8 Do you evaluate yourself the way your interactions taken place

PARTICULARS	EVERY DAY	OCCASIONALLY	ONLY WHEN SOMETHING GOES WRONG	ONLY WHEN PLEASANT THINGS HAPPEN
With superiors				
With co-employees				
With subordinates				
With customers				

7.9 Do you observe the reactions of the opposite party when interactions?

Yes ( )No ( )

7.10 Do you think that you had learning experience in interaction with people?

Yes ( )No ( )

7.11 Do you believe that transfers to various places helped you to better yourself in interactions? **Yes ( )No ( )**

7.12 In your opinion what are the qualities required to interact with bank customers effectively?

	Employee qualities
1	
2	
3	

7.13 What kind of support from management is required to be effective in interactions?

PARTICULARS	SUPPORT REQUIRED
Superiors	
Colleagues	
Subordinates	
Customers	

8 MISCELLANEOUS

Please give your opinion on the following:

PARTICULARS	STRONGLY AGREE	AGREE	NEUTRAL	DISAGREE	STRONGLY DISAGREE
State Bank of India continues to be the leader in the Indian banking system.					
SBI is the best bank to serve.					
The bank is pursuing customer centric policies.					
The bank offer better quality of service to the customers compared to:					
Other public sector banks					
Private sector banks					
Foreign banks					
Customer loyalty is very high in SBI.					

The employees of the bank are respected, because of their:					
Expertise in banking operations					
Interactive skills					
Quality consciousness					
SBI is highly adaptable to the changing market requirements.					
Competitors could not attack the SBI from any quarter.					
The employees of SBI feel proud of the performance of the bank.					
The employees of the SBI are highly motivated.					
The employee morale is high.					
Very strong service culture has been established throughout the organization.					
All the employees are involved in the process of development of the bank.					
Internal disturbances are almost absent in the bank.					
The employees are well compensated.					
The interests of the employees are taken care of by management.					
SBI should be given total autonomy.					

Annexure–II

INTERACTIVE MARKETING

A Case Study Of State Bank Of India

Questionnaire For Customers

1. DEMOGRAPHIC PROFILE

1.1 Name :

1.2 Age : 21-30 ( ) 31-40 ( )
41-50 ( ) 51 & above ( )

1.3 Sex : Male ( ) Female ( )

1.4 Education :

1.5 Occupation :

1.6 Annual Income Rs. : 50,001 – 1,00,000 ( ) 1,00,001 – 1,50,000 ( )

1,50,001 – 2,00,000 ( ) 2,00,001 – 2,50,000 ( )

2,50,001 – 3,00,000 ( ) 3,00,001 and above ( )

2. RELATIONSHIP WITH BANK

2.1 Since how long you are a customer of this bank. No. of years____________

2.2 Please give the types of accounts you are maintaining in the Bank

TYPE OF ACCOUNT	YES	NO
Savings Account		
Current Account		
Deposits		
Loan Account		
Others (specify):		

2.3 How many times do you visit the bank in a Month? No. of times__________.

2.4 What motivated to you establish relationship with the bank? (rank in the order)

Public sector bank		Customer care	
Largest bank		Accessibility	
Qualitative operations		Network	
Others (specify):			

2.5 In your opinion what are the criteria for choosing a bank to open an account? (rank in the order)

Security		Customer service	
Credibility		Package of services	
Accessibility		Others (specify):	

3. INTERACTIONS'

3.1 How do you interact with the bank?

PARTICULARS	PERCENTAGE	PREFERENCE
Personal visit to the branch		
ATM		
Telephone		
Internet		

3.2 Whom do you interact in the bank?

PARTICULARS	MOSTLY	OCCASIONALLY
Grahak Mitra		
Front line Officers		
Back office employees on the line of visibility		
Branch Manager		
Co-Customers		

3.3 Please give your opinion on following:

PARTICULARS	EXCELLENT	VERY GOOD	GOOD	AVERAGE	POOR	VERY POOR	TERRIBLE
Exterior of the bank							
Ambience							
Layout							
Signage							
Interactive System							
Facilities for interaction							
Process							
Tangibles							

3.4 What is your opinion on the documents of the bank?

PARTICULARS	STRONGLY AGREE	AGREE	NEUTRAL	DISAGREE	STRONGLY DISAGREE
Simple					
Understandable					
User friendly					
Unnecessary details					
Others(Specify):					

3.5 Please give your response to the following statements.

PARTICULARS	STRONGLY AGREE	AGREE	NEUTRAL	DISAGREE	STRONGLY DISAGREE
Employees of the branch are responsive					
Employees are courteous					
Employees are empathetic					
Employees are communicative					
Employees are giving individualized attention					

Employees understand customer problems					
Employees extend support at the time of necessity					
Employees suggest right things					
Employees are skilful					
Employees are presentable					
Employees are service oriented					
Employees are discriminative					
Employees are egoistic					
Employees have gender bias					
Employees have no time sense					

3.6 Have you faced the following problems in interacting with contact employees?

PARTICULARS	OFTEN	SOMETIMES	NEVER
Communicating your problem			
Specific attention your problem			
Employee arrogance			
Non accessibility			
Others (specify):			

3.7 How do you rate the physical facilities provided by the bank?

PARTICULARS	ADEQUACY					QUALITY				
	1	2	3	4	5	1	2	3	4	5
Ventilation										
Moving space										
Facilities for sitting										
Writing pads										
Toilets										

Drinking water								
Air conditioning / Fans								
Lighting								
Counters layout								
Pins								
Gum								
Parking place								
Security								
Sign boards								
Others (specify)								

1: Adequate; 2: Moderate; 3: Less; 4: Very less; 5: Nil.

3.8 To what extent you are informed about the following:

PARTICULARS	YES	TO SOME EXTENT	NO	DO YOU WANT TO KNOW	BY WHAT MEANS
All the services offered by the bank					
Interest rate on all types of deposits					
Interest rate on all types of term loans					
Service charges collected by the bank					
Credit facilities					
Consumer rights					

3.9 Generally how do you get the information relating to the services of the bank? (rank in order)

Bank Manager	
Bank Employees	
Friends and relatives	
Print media	
Bank advertisements	
Others (specify):	

3.10 Have you faced the following problems in interacting with documents?

PARTICULARS	OPENING BANK ACCOUNTS	ACCOUNT OPERATION	TAKING LOANS	TERM DEPOSITS	OTHER SERVICES
Too many					
Too much of information required					
Unnecessary complexity					
Language complexity					
Non availability					
Time consuming					
Others (Specify):					

3.11 How do you rate the joining phase of service at the branch?

PARTICULARS	YES	NO
Somebody greets me when I enter the office		
Somebody attends to me immediately after I enter to bank		
Somebody respond immediately when I approach		
Delayed response after approach		
Response only after repeated approaches		

3.12 Have you faced the following problems in interacting with process?

PARTICULARS	OPENING BANK ACCOUNTS	ACCOUNT OPERATION	TAKING LOANS	TERM DEPOSITS	OTHER SERVICES
Too many levels					
Too much time					
Away from consumers					
Communication					
Non visibility					
Others (specify):					

3.13 What are the service deficiencies you have experienced at the detachment phase of the interaction?

No response from the contact employee	
Responsibility of the process accuracy is transferred to customer	
No recovery for service deficiencies	
No follow up	

3.14 How do you rate process in this bank with regard to the following?

PARTICULARS	SBI	COMPARED TO		
		OTHER PUBLIC SECTOR BANKS	PRIVATE SECTOR BANKS	FOREIGN BANKS
Deposits				
Loans				
Lockers				
Withdrawal				
Pass Book entries				
Payment of bills				
Collection of cheque				

5: Very Good 4: Good 3: Average 2: Poor 1: Very Poor

3.15 When service is delayed because of your fault, how do you react? (Choose any one of the following)

PARTICULARS	
Correct my self after the defect is noticed by the employee and say sorry	
Find fault with the employee for not identifying the defect immediately	
I don't feel sorry for the delay because fault is with me	
I expect the employee also to feel sorry for the delay	
Others (specify):	

3.16 If the service is delayed because of some problems within service organization, how do you react? (rank in the order)

PARTICULARS	RANK
Request the employees for the speedy disposal	
Share the grievance with co-customer	

Raise the voice against the delay with contact employees	
Join the voice of resentment with co-customers	
Encourage the co-customers to raise voice against delay	
Complain to the concerned officer	
Complain in the consumer court	
Others (specify):	

3.17 What kind of role you want to play in Interactions?

PARTICULARS	ACTUAL	DESIRED
Active role (Directing the employees what to do)		
Passive role (Waiting for the performance of service and compromise if the performance is close to your expectation)		
Participative role (Discussing with contact employees and finalizing the best course of action)		

3.18 Do you think that employees need to be given special training on customer interactions? **Yes( ) No ( )**

3.19 What are the best things you value in interactions? (rank in the order)

Courtesy		Responsiveness	
Empathy		Communication	
Accuracy		Speed	
Transparency		Recognition	
Other (Specify):			

3.20 Do you have experience with other banks?Yes ( ) No ( )

3.21 How do you rate interactive abilities of the employees of State Bank of India compared to other bank employees?

PARTICULARS	EXCELLENT	VERY GOOD	GOOD	AVERAGE	POOR	VERY POOR	TERRIBLE
Public Sector Banks							
Private Sector Banks							
Foreign Banks							

3.22 Do you find any change in the quality of Interactions during the last three years? (choose any one of the following)

Substantial Change	
Moderate Change	
No Change	
Negative Change	

3.23 In a bank branch with whom do you feel comfortable to interact?

PARTICULARS	PUBLIC SECTOR BANKS		PRIVATE SECTOR BANKS	FOREIGN BANKS
	SBI	OTHER BANKS		
Branch manager				
Officers				
Clerks				
Attenders				

4. MISCELLANEOUS

4.1 What kind of relationship do you like to have with SBI in future?

Continuing existing operations	
Strengthen the relationship further	
Minimize the relationship	
Cutoff relationship	

4.2 Do you think State Bank of India continuous to be the leader in the light of changing competitive scenario? Yes ( ) No ( )

4.3 Do you support the policy of the Government to use public sector banks for Government sponsored social welfare measures? Yes ( ) No ( )

4.4 Do you believe that the State Bank of India is discharging its social responsibilities? Yes ( ) No ( )

❑❑❑